ARE WE TOGETHER?

A Roman Catholic Analyzes Evangelical Protestants

EDUARDO J. ECHEVERRIA

lectio

Lectio Publishing, LLC
Hobe Sound, Florida, USA

www.lectiopublishing.com

Cover art: *Luther Before the Diet of Worms* by Anton von Werner (1843–1915). Public domain.

Design by Linda Wolf

Paperback ISBN 978-1-943901-24-1
Library of Congress Control Number: 2022940206
e-Book ISBN 978-1-943901-25-8

Published by Lectio Publishing, LLC
Hobe Sound, Florida 33455
www.lectiopublishing.com

ENDORSEMENTS

Eduardo Echeverria is one of the most important Catholic voices in ecumenical dialogue with Evangelicals. Although there has been, since the early 1990s, greater cooperation and understanding between Catholics and Evangelicals resulting in a better appreciation of our common theological heritage, some have resisted this movement. They argue that Catholicism and Evangelicalism are not communities in schism whose adherents worship the same Christ, but two incommensurable traditions that merely use the same language. In this timely volume, Professor Echeverria answers this charge with careful scholarship and gracious engagement. As someone who has lived on both sides of the Tiber, I am appreciative of the author's remarkable conversance with both Catholic and Evangelical thought.

—*Francis J. Beckwith*, Professor of Philosophy & Church-State Studies, Baylor University;
former president of the Evangelical Theological Society (2006–07)
and the American Catholic Philosophical Association (2017–18)

Eduardo Echeverria has written a beautiful Christian, ecumenical, Roman Catholic book. He does so as a scholar, rooted both in the Reformed Evangelical and in the Roman Catholic traditions. Where some evangelicals emphasize that Protestants and Roman Catholics only share words but live in different worlds, Echeverria stresses that we have common ground in the christological and trinitarian statements of faith. Baptized in one baptism and believing in one Lord, we might have differences concerning Scripture and tradition, nature and grace, ecclesiology, and sacramental economy. But what Echeverria does is important: cherish what we share, explain where we differ. With a strong ecumenical intention and from a committed Roman Catholic perspective, Echeverria gives a good example of how to keep Evangelicals and Catholics together. I hope that this book will contribute to a better understanding and a growing unity of Evangelicals and Catholics!

—*J.M. Burger*, Associate Professor of Systematic Theology,
Theological University Kampen

A closely argued book revealing both areas of agreement and continuing challenges—and perhaps misunderstandings—between evangelical and Roman Catholic ecclesiologists. An important contribution to ecumenical theology.

—*Timothy George*, Distinguished Professor,
Beeson Divinity School of Samford University;
Co-chair of Evangelicals and Catholics Together

It takes fortitude to face the question posed by the title of this book. It takes heroism to answer the question, as Eduardo Echeverria has done. He frankly acknowledges the reasons for Evangelical-Catholic divisions, and still he finds greater strength in what unites us. This is not ecumenism lite. Nor is it a manifesto for mere co-belligerency against secularism. This book genuinely advances an important and difficult conversation. Echeverria seeks a reconciliation that's true, that does not require compromise on essentials—which is the only possible fulfillment of Jesus' prayers (John 17:11, 21-22).

—*Scott Hahn*, Fr. Michael Scanlan Professor of Biblical Theology
and the New Evangelization,
Franciscan University of Steubenville

Eduardo Echeverria, by his combination of philosophical and theological gifts, and acquaintance with the best of Dutch Reformed dogmatics, is uniquely placed to critique the recent revival of an intelligent but misguided anti-Catholicism among (some) Evangelicals in Europe and America. His careful dissection of their body of work, and charitable reconstruction of the Christian doctrines concerned, exemplify Catholic ecumenism at its best.

—*Aidan Nichols, OP*
St. Michael's Theological College and Seminary,
Kingston, Jamaica

This is an insightful and intricate work of theological rigor, ecumenical sensitivity, and apologetic precision, all at the service of authentic understanding and unity. Both Catholics and Evangelicals will benefit from this deeply learned and erudite book."

—*Carl E. Olson*, Editor of Catholic World Report

This is the sort of book I like, not because it is ecumenical in spirit or because I may or may not agree with the author, but mostly because it is written by a person I know personally (professor Eduardo Echeverria) about a person I also know personally (Leonardo de Chirico). Why would I—or anyone else for that matter—read this book? A Roman-Catholic professor with roots in the Reformed and Evangelical tradition investigates the claims of an Evangelical theologian regarding whether the two Christian traditions (Roman Catholicism and Evangelicalism) worship the same God. Knowing both the author and the person he writes about, having had the chance to see their personal dedication to the cause of Christianity, I am eager to recommend this work to anyone whose interest in furthering the Gospel is not only genuine, but also a matter of deep conviction.

—*Corneliu C. Simu*, PhD, Professor of Theology,
Aurel Vlaicu University, Romania

"Holy Father, keep them in your name, which you have given me, that they may be one, even as we are one.... so that the world may believe that you have sent me."

—John 17:11, 21

"I appeal to you, brethren, by the name of our Lord Jesus Christ, that all of you agree, and that there be no divisions among you, but that you be united in the same mind and the same judgment."

— 1 Corinthians 1:10

CONTENTS

ACKNOWLEDGMENTS

I would like to express my gratitude to the many people that have supported me in the publication of this work. As always, I continue to be grateful for the support of the administrators and staff, of my many friends and colleagues, of Sacred Heart Major Seminary. I also want to thank Msgr. Thomas Guarino, of Seton Hall University, for his friendship and for his ongoing spiritual and intellectual support throughout the years. I am grateful for my membership in the ecumenical initiative of Evangelical and Catholics Together, particularly for its practice of receptive ecumenism.

I wish to thank Erika Zabinski, copy editor and indexer of this book. In addition, I extend my gratitude to the endorsers of my book: Francis Beckwith, Hans Burger, Timothy George, Scott Hahn, Aidan Nichols, OP, Carl Olson, and Corneliu C. Simut. Also, my gratitude to Eric and Linda Wolf of Lectio Publishing for their continued support of my work.

Last but not least, to my wife DonnaRose, the *sine qua non* of my life and work—always and forever.

> *May God grant that I speak with judgment and have thoughts worthy of what I have received, for he is the guide even of wisdom and the corrector of the wise. For both we and our words are in his hand, with all our understanding, too.*
>
> — Wis 7:15-16

LIST OF ABBREVIATIONS

References to these works are cited parenthetically in the text. Full publication information is found in the Bibliography.

40 Questions	Gregg Allison, *40 Questions About Roman Catholicism.*
CCC	*Catechism of the Catholic Church* (2003).
DV	Vatican II, *Dei Verbum*, Dogmatic Constitution on Divine Revelation (18 November 1965).
ETP	Leonardo De Chirico, *Evangelical Theological Perspectives on Post-Vatican II Roman Catholicism.*
FR	John Paul II, *Fides et Ratio*, Encyclical Letter (14 September 1998).
GS	Vatican II, *Gaudium et Spes*, Pastoral Constitution on the Church in the Modern World (7 December, 1965).
LG	Vatican II, *Lumen Gentium*, Dogmatic Constitution on the Church (21 November 1964).
MH	Henry Jackman, "Meaning Holism," The Stanford Encyclopedia of Philosophy.
RCTP	Gregg Allison, *Roman Catholic Theology & Practice: An Evangelical Assessment.*
SAC	G. C. Berkouwer, *De Sacramenten*. English translation: *The Sacraments*; trans. Hugo Bekker.
SWDW	Leonardo De Chirico, *Same Words, Different Worlds: Do Roman Catholics and Evangelicals Believe the Same Gospel?*
UR	Vatican II, *Unitatis Redintegratio*, Decree on Ecumenism (21 November 1964).
UUS	John Paul II, *Ut Unum Sint*, Encyclical Letter (25 May 1995).
VCNT	G. C. Berkouwer, *Vatikaans Concilie en Nieuwe Theologie*. English translation: *The Second Vatican Council and the New Catholicism*; trans. Lewis Smedes.

Note on Sources

Quotations of Vatican II documents are from *The Documents of Vatican II*, ed. Walter M. Abbott (London: Chapman, 1966). Papal and other magisterial documents, unless otherwise noted, are from www. vatican.va. Scripture quotations are from the Revised Standard Version, Catholic Edition.

Throughout the book, if an English translation of a source is cited in addition to the original, the original page number is given first, followed by the English pagination in square brackets [ ].

James A. De Jong translated into English the untranslated Dutch citations of Berkouwer's writings.

INTRODUCTION

Our thoughts about the future of the Church must come out of tensions in the present, tensions that must creatively produce watchfulness, prayer, faith, and commitment, love for truth and unity, love for unity and truth.
—G. C. Berkouwer[1]

Are Roman Catholics and Evangelical Protestants really together, united in a common faith in Jesus Christ? Yes, according to the teachings of the Second Vatican Council (1962–1965). No, according to some Evangelical Protestants, such as Francis A. Schaeffer (1912–1984) and R. C. Sproul (1939–2017), and more recently Gregg Allison and Leonardo De Chirico.[2] Schaeffer and Sproul claim that Roman Catholics and Evangelical Protestants do not share a common cause in the Gospel and hence have no "alliance" in carrying out the missionary mandate of the Church. These evangelicals introduce the term "co-belligerency" to suggest that Roman Catholics and Evangelical Protestants can be united on matters of cultural importance, for example, promoting a culture of life. The antithesis between alliance and co-belligerency, and hence the incommensurability between Roman Catholics and Evangelical Protestants, is presupposed by Allison and De Chirico in their writings, as I make clear in this study.

Although I am a committed Roman Catholic theologian doing theology within the normative tradition of confessional Catholicism, and thus in the light of Catholic teaching, this critical study is an ecumenical work.[3] I have roots in the Evangelical and Reformed traditions and hence I listen attentively to the writings of fellow Christian theologians from these traditions of reflection and argument. In this ecumenical light, I engage the Evangelical Protestant writings of Gregg Allison and Leonardo De Chirico; the former is professor

3

of Christian theology at the Southern Baptist Theological Seminary, Louisville, Kentucky; the latter is lecturer in Historical Theology at the Instituto di Formazione Evangelica e Documentazione in Padua, Italy, and a Pastor in the Evangelical Reformed Baptist churches of Italy.[4] Furthermore, this study is a work in receptive ecumenism.[5] Receptive ecumenism means, according to John Paul II: "Dialogue is not simply an exchange of ideas. In some way it is always an 'exchange of gifts'. ... Dialogue does not extend exclusively to matters of doctrine but engages the whole person; it is also a dialogue of love" (*UUS* §§28, 47, respectively). My commitment to ecumenical dialogue with both the Evangelical and Reformed traditions is evident from many of my writings.[6] Furthermore, I am also a member of the more than twenty-year-old American ecumenical initiative, Evangelicals and Catholics Together.

My study does not purport to be a comprehensive examination of Allison's and De Chirico's writings on Catholicism.[7] Within limits, then, it is organized as follows. In Chapters 1–2, I begin by analyzing their approach to the interpretation of Roman Catholicism and hence its implication for ecumenism. Essentially, they defend an incommensurability between Roman Catholicism and Evangelical Protestantism such that these two systems represent a basic clash between two different worlds, to put it in relativistic terms. "Formally the Roman Catholic words are the same. Substantially they are not" (*SWDW*, 121). On their view, we can no longer talk of "the world" but only "worlds." I follow up in Chapter 3 with the issues of Scripture, tradition, and the Church. In Chapter 4, I examine what they call the "Evangelical Hermeneutics of Roman Catholicism," that is, their criticism of the hermeneutical framework of Roman Catholicism (*ETP*, 163–85). They call this hermeneutics the "two axes of Roman Catholicism," namely, "the nature-grace interdependence," and the "Christ-church interconnection." Says De Chirico, "[T]he two axes ... form the backbone of the Roman Catholic system. It is around the nature-grace interdependence and the Christ-church interconnection that one can find the theological frame of reference that shapes Roman Catholic *words*" (*SWDW*, 2; emphasis added). In Chapter 5, in light of their criticism of the Christ-Church interconnection, I examine the sacramentology informing Roman Catholicism and the Reformed tradition, and the Evangelical sacramentology—which tilts in the direction of Zwinglianism—informing the theology of

Allison and De Chirico. Lastly, I examine their interpretation of the "law of Incarnation" and the corresponding idea that the Church is a prolongation of the Incarnation, meaning thereby that the Church mediates the grace of God to the world. In this connection, I examine their critique that Catholic ecclesiology has the tendency to assimilate Christology into ecclesiology. I conclude my book with a brief reflection on how to get beyond anti-Catholicism.

It is important to note that as used by them, the term "Evangelical" varies, given its reference to several Protestant traditions who do not share the same theological views as Allison and De Chirico. For example, Baptists such as Allison differ with the Reformed tradition—Herman Bavinck and G. C. Berkouwer—on sacramentology. Both De Chirico and Allison differ with others, such as William Lane Craig and Bavinck, over the legitimacy of theistic arguments, and hence the understanding of faith and reason. Yes, Allison, for one, does "not claim to speak for all Evangelicals or to represent the many versions of Evangelical theology; given the expansive nature of Evangelicalism, no one person and no one particular theological swath can accomplish that task" (*RCTP*, 18). Yet, despite his disclaimer, Allison inconsistently persists in speaking for "evangelical theology" throughout his book. De Chirico does, however, address the question of theological diversity within Evangelical theology in his early book on post-Vatican II Roman Catholic theology (*ETP*, 42–47). I will consider this question of diversity in Chapter 2 in the context of Vatican II's teaching concerning the "hierarchy of truths."

Honest questions deserve honest answers. Allison and De Chirico's writings raise such questions—which is not the same as saying that the interpretation raised by their Evangelical hermeneutics of Roman Catholicism is correct. Still, in this work I follow the guidelines stipulated by *Unitatis Redintegratio* in order to promote mutual and improved understanding between Roman Catholicism and Evangelical Protestantism, namely, "We must come to understand the outlook of our separated brethren. Study is absolutely required for this, and should be pursued with fidelity to truth and in a spirit of good will" (*UR*, §9). Hence, to elaborate:

> The manner and order in which Catholic belief is expressed should in no way become an obstacle to dialogue with our brethren. It is, of course, essential that the doctrine should be clearly presented in its entirety. Nothing is so foreign to the spirit of ecumenism as

> a false irenicism, in which the purity of Catholic doc-
> trine suffers loss and its genuine and certain meaning
> is clouded. At the same time, the Catholic faith must
> be explained more profoundly and precisely, in such
> a way and in such terms as our separated brethren
> can also really understand. Moreover, in ecumenical
> dialogue, Catholic theologians standing fast by the
> teaching of the Church and investigating the divine
> mysteries with the separated brethren must proceed
> with love for the truth, with charity, and with humil-
> ity. (*UR*, §11)

Still, ecumenical dialogue is not just about having a discussion regarding questions where there exists a common basis of discussion.
We must pursue discussion on issues for which the common basis
is lacking. Furthermore, although exposing differences between Roman Catholicism and Evangelical Protestantism is important, that
is not "for the sole purpose of 'listening' to each other," as Charles
Cardinal Journet rightly states.[8] In this connection, I shall distinguish three dimensions in the work of ecumenism following the
Congregation for the Doctrine of the Faith in its "Doctrinal Note
on Some Aspects of Evangelization." This Doctrinal Note states:
"Above all, there is [1] *listening*, as a fundamental condition for any
dialogue, then, [2] *theological discussion*, in which, by seeking to understand the beliefs, traditions and convictions of others, agreement
can be found, at times hidden under disagreement." This second dimension includes ecumenical apologetics. Such apologetics and receptive ecumenism are not at odds. It is best illustrated in a book
such as Matthew Levering's *Mary's Bodily Assumption*. "Inseparably
united with this second dimension is another essential dimension
of the ecumenical commitment: [3] *witness and proclamation* of elements which are not particular traditions or theological subtleties,
but which belong rather to the Tradition of the faith itself" ("Doctrinal
Note," §12). I illustrate these dimensions throughout this work. Moreover, this CDF document elaborates:

> Ecumenism does not have only an institutional di-
> mension aimed at "making the partial communion
> existing between Christians grow towards full com-
> munion in truth and charity." It is also the task of
> every member of the faithful, above all by means of
> prayer, penance, study and cooperation. Everywhere
> and always, each Catholic has the right and the duty
> to give the witness and the full proclamation of his

faith. With non-Catholic Christians, Catholics must enter into a respectful dialogue of charity and truth, a dialogue which is not only an exchange of ideas, but also of gifts, in order that the fullness of the means of salvation can be offered to one's partners in dialogue. In this way, they are led to an ever deeper conversion to Christ. (ibid.)

Regarding the question of evangelizing non-Catholic Christians—separated brethren—to come into full communion with the Catholic Church and hence to an ever-deeper conversion to Christ, the document explains:

> In this connection, it needs also to be recalled that if a non-Catholic Christian, for reasons of conscience and having been convinced of Catholic truth, asks to enter into the full communion of the Catholic Church, this is to be respected as the work of the Holy Spirit and as an expression of freedom of conscience and of religion. In such a case, it would not be a question of proselytism in the negative sense that has been attributed to this term. (ibid.)

It helps to turn to a document produced by a working group organized by the Catholic Church and the World Council of Churches: "The Challenge of Proselytism and the Calling to Common Witness." The group formulated some basic points about what would constitute improper "proselytizing" in an ecumenical context:

1. Unfair criticism or caricaturing of the doctrines, beliefs, and practices of another church without attempting to understand or enter into dialogue on those issues.

2. Presenting one's church or confession as "the true church" and its teachings as "the right faith" and the only way to salvation.

3. Portraying one's own church as having high moral and spiritual status over against the perceived weaknesses and problems of other churches.

4. Offering humanitarian aid or educational opportunities as an inducement to join another church.

5. Using political, economic, cultural, and ethnic pressure or historical arguments to win others to one's own church.

6. Taking advantage of lack of education or Christian instruction, which makes people vulnerable to changing their church allegiance.

7. Using physical violence or moral and psychological pressure to induce people to change their church affiliation.

8. Exploiting people's loneliness, illness, distress or even disillusionment with their own church in order to "convert" them.[9]

Only point 2 raises fundamental ecclesiological questions (the rest may be accepted as unethical means, without any theological difficulty). The ecclesiological question has to do with ecclesial unity and diversity of the one Church.[10] I have addressed this question elsewhere, and hence will not consider it in this small book. For now, I conclude this Introduction with the aim of Catholic ecumenism.

> As explicitly recognized in the Decree on Ecumenism [*Unitatis Redintegratio*] of the Second Vatican Council, "it is evident that the work of preparing and reconciling those individuals who desire full Catholic communion is of its nature distinct from ecumenical action, but there is no opposition between the two, since both proceed from the marvelous ways of God." Therefore, the work of ecumenism does not remove the right or take away the responsibility of proclaiming in fullness the Catholic faith to other Christians, who freely wish to receive it. ("Doctrinal Note," §12)

NOTES

1. *Vatikaans Concilie en Nieuwe Theologie*. English translation: *The Second Vatican Council and the New Catholicism*, trans. Lewis Smedes, 250. The phrase "nieuwe theologie" (literally "new theology") in the Dutch title of the book is a clear reference to the *nouvelle théologie* of Henri de Lubac, Yves Congar, et al. That reference is lost in the English translation, which speaks of "New Catholicism." The Dutch historian of the Reformation and Reformed theologian Heiko Oberman (1930–2001) describes Berkouwer's book on Vatican II as "breathtakingly important" (*Evangelische Theologie* 28 [1968]: 388). See my work, *Berkouwer and Catholicism: Disputed Questions*, Studies in Reformed Theology 24.

2. Francis A. Schaeffer, *The Church at the End of the Twentieth Century*; R. C. Sproul, *Are We Together? A Protestant Analyzes Roman Catholicism*; Gregg Allison and Chris Castaldo, *The Unfinished Reformation*; Leonardo De Chirico, "Cooperating with the Catholic Church? A Lesson from Francis A. Schaeffer (1912–1984)," *Vatican Files*, April 1, 2016.

3. This study is a revised and expanded version of a review article of Gregg Allison's *Roman Catholic Theology & Practice: An Evangelical Assessment*: "A Catholic Assessment of Gregg Allison's Critique of the 'Hermeneutics of Catholicism,'" *Called to Communion*, August 17, 2015.

4. Allison, *Roman Catholic Theology & Practice*, 42–67; idem, *40 Questions About Roman Catholicism*, 47–68. Further references to these works will be cited par-

enthetically in the text. Leonardo De Chirico, *Evangelical Theological Perspectives on Post-Vatican II Roman Catholicism*, Religions and Discourse 19); idem, *Same Words, Different Worlds: Do Roman Catholics and Evangelicals Believe the Same Gospel?* Here, too, references to these works will be cited parenthetically in the text.

5. The phrase "receptive ecumenism" was coined by Paul Murray, Dean and Director of the Centre for Catholic Studies, University of Durham, UK. It means: "The essential principle behind Receptive Ecumenism is that the primary ecumenical responsibility is to ask not 'What do the other traditions first need to learn from us?' but 'What do we need to learn from them?' The assumption is that if all were asking this question seriously and acting upon it then all would be moving in ways that would both deepen our authentic respective identities and draw us into more intimate relationship."

6. Eduardo Echeverria, *Dialogue of Love: Confessions of an Evangelical Catholic Ecumenist*; *Berkouwer and Catholicism: Disputed Questions*, Studies in Reformed Theology 24; *Divine Election: A Catholic Orientation in Dogmatic and Ecumenical Perspective*; and *Revelation, History, and Truth: A Hermeneutics of Dogma*.

7. I have written extensively elsewhere on Catholic ecclesiology, Vatican II and doctrinal development, and on Christ, world religions, and the salvation of non-Christians. The first topic is addressed by Allison and De Chirico, but the second, albeit briefly, by De Chirico, and the third by Allison. For the former topic, see Eduardo Echeverria; "The One Church, the Many Churches: A Catholic Approach to Ecclesial Unity and Diversity—with Special Attention to Abraham Kuyper's Ecclesiastical Epistemology," *Journal of Biblical and Theological Studies* 5, no. 2 (2020): 239–64; idem, "Vincent of Lérins and the Development of Christian Doctrine," in *"Faith Once for All Delivered": Tradition and Doctrinal Authority in the Catholic Church*; idem, "The Salvation of Non-Christians? Reflections on Vatican II's *Gaudium et Spes* 22, *Lumen Gentium* 16, Gerald O'Collins, SJ, and St. John Paul II," *Angelicum* 94 (2017): 93–142.

8. *The Primacy of Peter from the Protestant and Catholic Point of View*, trans. John Chapin, xi.

9. "The Challenge of Proselytism and the Calling to Common Witness," *The Ecumenical Review* 48 (1996): 212–21.

10. I address this question at length here: Eduardo Echeverria; "The One Church, the Many Churches: A Catholic Approach to Ecclesial Unity and Diversity—with Special Attention to Abraham Kuyper's Ecclesiastical Epistemology."

Chapter 1

INCOMMENSURABILITY?

[T]he "problem of Catholicism" is not merely one doctrine or in some superficial differences on secondary issues. Its problem lies at the very heart of its system and is pervasively present in all its expressions: from the Trinity to Mariology, from the sacraments to soteriology, from ecclesiology to the manifold devotions. Everything is infected by it. (SWDW, 114)

Allison and De Chirico consider not only beliefs that Catholics and Protestants share in common, but also where there are areas of doctrinal differences (see 40 Questions, 69–80; SWDW, 32–69). But their treatment of Roman Catholicism is unique because they treat it as a comprehensive world and life view. Says De Chirico, "Given the impossibility of hermeneutic neutrality, the attempt to construct an appropriate, adequate theological hermeneutic. … In order to give help in understanding the basics of Roman Catholicism, an interpretative model would need to single out the fundamental aspects of Roman Catholicism as a unified whole" (ETP, 166; 98–100). In an earlier work (ETP, 166–89), De Chirico explicitly traces the origin of this approach—treating Roman Catholicism as a system—to the 1898 Stone Lectures of Abraham Kuyper (1837–1920), *Lectures on Calvinism*.[1] Following Kuyper, De Chirico explains, "Roman Catholicism has to be assessed using macro-categories able to hold together the largest possible number of elements. Failing to do this will lead to a collection of fragments, just pieces of Catholicism, which will not allow for a real understanding of its dimensions, depth, connections and projects" (SWDW, 10; 100). As such, I support the project of treating Roman Catholicism and Evangelical Protestantism as examples of comprehensive worldviews. Indeed, in response to De Chirico, I would state that Catholic intellectuals do share the aim of an Evangelical hermeneutics of Roman Catholicism, having a focus on Catholicism as an interconnected whole, as a structured and coherent whole (cf. *ETP*, 186; 98–100).

Representatives of Catholic treatments of Roman Catholicism as an interconnected whole are, according to De Chirico, found in John Henry Newman, Romano Guardini, Hans Urs von Balthasar, and, I would add, Karl Adam[2] and John Paul II. For instance, consider the latter's reflections in his 1998 encyclical *Fides et Ratio* on the "sapiential dimension" of philosophical inquiry. "To be consonant with the Word of God, philosophy needs first of all to recover its *sapiential dimension* as a search for the ultimate and overarching meaning of life," that is, "the ultimate framework of the unity of human knowledge and action." In sum, adds John Paul, "the Word of God reveals the final destiny of men and women and provides a unifying explanation of all that they do in the world" (§81).

Nevertheless, the problem with Allison and De Chirico's treatment of doctrinal commonality and difference in light of a comprehensive worldview, and its corresponding theological system, is that they subscribe to a philosophical view of meaning called "meaning holism" (Jackman). (As I shall show below, John Paul II does not share that view of meaning.) De Chirico states:

> Words do not live in isolation. They have their own specific connotation, but part of their meaning comes from the way they are connected with one another. When linked together they are part of a bigger whole that influences the way people and institutions understand them. The same is true for words related to faith. A theological word is not a self-contained unit. Though it carries its own semantic weight, it is also defined by when and where it is found, the web of references which are associated with it. . . . If these theological words are approached superficially and atomistically, one may get the impression that they belong to the same deposit of Christian faith shared by all who claim some kind of allegiance to it. A closer look will reveal that, beyond some commonality, they also carry significant differences which, taken as a whole, form another "world"—one that is different from the world of the biblical faith (*SWDW*, 32).

Of course, De Chirico is right that it is surely simplistic to ignore the context in understanding, as Berkouwer puts it, "the various terms, concepts, images, and propositions that the Church has used to confess its faith." He is also surely right that the meaning of dogmas is not always immediately transparent. For example, there exists unclear terms "in the christological and trinitarian controversies, such words as consubstantial, hypostasis, person, nature, and many others. The terms often evoked misunderstandings, and different interpretations of them created conflict of opinion" (VCNT, 85 [74]).[3] Yet, that is something different than meaning holism. De Chirico treats the meaning of all of the words and concepts in a language system, and hence in a theological system, as interdependent, such that we can no longer talk of "reality," of the "world," but only "realities," and "worlds." He merges the world view approach to Roman Catholicism and by implication to Evangelical Protestantism with meaning holism. This was not the case in his earlier 2003 study on post-Vatican II Catholicism. But he now says that Roman Catholicism "is a complex yet coherent system that gives meaning to the words that are used" (SWDW, 4). Notice that it is the coherent system that gives meaning to the words and concepts used rather than the world, reality. On De Chirico's view—as we shall see below—what the world is like is relative to a system; hence, since Roman Catholicism and Protestantism think of "the world" differently, then there must be different worlds, indeed, different realities. The "world" or "reality" recedes behind different theological systems, with the implication that it is no longer independent of the way individuals think of it, and hence, as Roger Trigg correctly concludes about this view, "we can no longer talk of 'reality' but only 'realities'" (Reason and Commitment, 9).

Following De Chirico, Allison stresses, "Roman Catholic theology and practice and Protestant theology and practice are very different systems operating on different principles. This diversity should caution us that, even when the two traditions use similar words, they may mean significantly different things by those similar terms. ... [T]he two different systems of theology and practice often have different concepts at work when they use ... terms. Thus, both traditions need to be cautious about embracing commonalities that have only a thin veneer of agreement" (40 Questions, 74).

Similarly, but even more emphatically than Allison, De Chirico stresses the *incommensurability* between Catholicism and Protestantism because the meaning of all of the words in a theological system are interdependent (SWDW, 7–31). "So, these faiths [Catholicism and Protestantism] look somewhat similar, yet they are radically different. The question is: how can we meaningfully speak of the 'same' gospel if the two have core commitments that do not match. The problem lies with the way in which the same words are understood differently" (*SWDW*, 1). This view is such that what is meant by a word and concept is relative to all of the beliefs or inferences made within a respective system, namely, Catholicism or Protestantism. Therefore, two individuals would only mean the same thing by any of these words and concepts if all their beliefs or inferences were *identical* (*MH*).

I said above that the question raised by De Chirico is: "how can we meaningfully speak of the 'same' gospel if the two have core commitments that do not match. The problem lies with the way in which the same words are understood differently" (*SWDW*, 1). De Chirico's answer to this question reflects his commitment to meaning holism. The words that Catholicism and Protestantism share in common cannot be thought of as different attempts to describe the same reality or world. "Reality" is made relative to the different theological systems, and if different systems describe "the world" differently, then, according to De Chirico, there must be different worlds. This is what the title of De Chirico's book claims about the incommensurability between Roman Catholicism and Evangelical Protestantism: *Same Words, Different Worlds*. His answer to the question posed in the subtitle of the book is "no." *Do Roman Catholics and Evangelicals Believe the Same Gospel?* "In many respects Roman Catholicism is really alien to the evangelical faith" (*SWDW*, 1). For example, "Calling the Nicene faith the common basis can be an emotional appeal, but it is not a responsible action because, while the impression is given that we say the same things, the reality is that we are saying *different* things" (SWDW, 18). Thus, "We are talking about different things, using the same words to describe radically different worlds" (*SWDW*, 19). In other words, given that there must be different worlds because "reality" is relative to different conceptual systems, this view entails an anti-realist view of truth because "the world" seems totally irrelevant to questions of meaning and truth.

Briefly, meaning holism confuses the distinction "between change/ differences of meaning and change/differences of belief" (*MH*). Consequently, it follows that it cannot account for change of mind, disagreement, and, accordingly, criticism and refutation of each other's systems, and informative communication. Given meaning holism, the latter is impossible because "[n]o one would mean the same thing by any of their [words and concepts] unless they shared all the same beliefs" (*MH*). In this case, informative communication pertains particularly to cognitive meaning—sometimes called "assertive, informational, descriptive, factual, or declarative meaning [which refers] to statements that give information and claim that information as true (or false)."[4] For a realist about truth such information pertains to factual meaning—"cognitive assertions that purport to be true about the world independently of our statements about them."[5]

Take any proposition *p*—God doesn't exist—that I no longer hold to be true but now consider false. According to meaning holism, changing my belief entails not that I simply now assign a different truth value to proposition *p* but rather that the meaning of my belief changes. "As a result," according to Jackman, "there is no proposition that I previously thought to be true that I now treat as false." For example, consider the creedal definition of God in the 1561 *Belgic Confession of Faith*. The atheist once held this proposition to be false but now as a theist regards it to be true:

> We all believe with the heart, and confess with the mouth, that there is one only simple and spiritual Being which we call God; and that He is eternal, incomprehensible, invisible, immutable, infinite, almighty, perfectly wise, just, good, and the overflowing fountain of all good.[6]

For the atheist and the theist these are now two different propositions because their respective meaning has changed. Meaning holism erases the distinction between changing my mind about the truth-status of a belief and changing the meaning of that belief. "However, since the most natural way to make sense of changing one's mind about something is in terms of changing the truth-value one assigns to a single proposition, the intuitive notion of change of mind seems lost" (*MH*).

Consequently, meaning holism also imperils the matter of disagreement between two people, and hence the "one [system] cannot criticize or refute the other."[7] We no longer think of disagreement between, say, the atheist and the theist as those who assign different truth values to the same proposition—God exists. Hence, these propositions cannot stand in a contradictory relation to each other. Rather, they must differ in what they mean by that proposition, and hence meaning holism cannot make sense of disagreement about that proposition since they both do not accept the meaning of that proposition.

For example, De Chirico argues that Roman Catholics and Evangelical Protestants do not share the same Christology precisely because they differ in their ecclesiology. Again, given his meaning holism, it follows, "the meaning of all their terms and content of all of their beliefs must differ" (*MH*). He illustrates this point about incommensurability in regard to the Christ-Church interconnection: "the *Catechism* [*of the Catholic Church*] speaks of Christ [but] *interweaves him with the church to the point of making them one*, which is unacceptable for evangelicals who consider the exaltation of a created reality an instance of idolatry" (*SWDW*, 8; emphasis added). In other words, De Chirico criticizes the Catholic Church's ecclesiology for its alleged tendency, in the words of Kevin Vanhoozer, "to assimilate Christology into ecclesiology," or make "the church … constitutive of the Son's identity as are the Father and the Spirit" (*Biblical Authority after Babel,* 152). Allison, too, raises a similar objection. He is deeply distressed by the tendency in Catholic theology of substituting "'the church in the place of its absent Lord.'"[8]

De Chirico refers us to the words of Pius XII in his 1943 encyclical *Mystici Corporis Christi* to make his point: "the church subsists 'almost like a second person in Christ'" ["*quasi altera Christi persona*"] (*SWDW*, 107). In his first book on Roman Catholicism, De Chirico correctly states that "the 'quasi' of the encyclical moderates the terms of the identification [of Christ and the Church] and paves the way for the subsequent specification by Vatican II that it is an analogical identification" (*ETP*, 261). In his most recent book, his assessment has changed. He now argues that Pius XII is saying that Christ becomes one with the church in the sense that the church becomes another Christ.

This, too, is Allison's view. "The Roman Catholic Church acts as another (or second) person of Christ, mediating between the two realms [of nature and grace]" (*40 Questions,* 59). Consequently, De Chirico asks, "Is the Christ of the Catechism the Jesus Christ of the Bible [and the early creeds of Nicaea and Chalcedon] or the Christ of the Roman Church?" (*SWDW*, 8–9).

There is much to be said here in criticism of De Chirico's views of the Christ-Church interconnection and meaning holism. First, these few words from Pius XII must be examined in context of the entire passage from *Mystici Corporis Christi* (§§ 52–53) which reads:

[T]he social Body of the Church should be honored by the name of Christ—namely, that our Savior Himself sustains in a divine manner the society which He founded. [T]his appellation of the Body of Christ is not to be explained solely by the fact that Christ must be called the Head of His Mystical Body, but also by the fact that He so sustains the Church, and so in a certain sense lives in the Church, that she is, as it were, another Christ [emphasis added].

In what sense is the Church another Christ? The Catholic tradition does not assimilate or reduce Christology to ecclesiology; nor does it understand the Church's relationship to Christ as substantially constitutive of Christ's identity, as if to suggest that the Church was now the "subject" rather than Christ. De Chirico is wrong in charging the Church with idolatry. In his earlier work on Roman Catholicism, he states that "Catholic theology, in its Twentieth century outlook, has been well aware of the potential dangers that an unqualified and vague identification between the Incarnation of the Son of the God [sic] and the ecclesial continuation could lead to" (*ETP*, 257). He explains the dilemma:

If Protestant ecclesiology is always in danger of falling into Nestorian traps by dissolving the visible, institutional profile of the Church, the incarnational ecclesiology of the Roman Catholic Church may run the risk of not upholding the Christological paradox applied to ecclesiology by deifying the Church and therefore lapsing into a kind of ecclesiological Monophysitism (*ETP*, 257).

In this earlier book, De Chirico is appreciative of recent developments in Roman Catholic ecclesiology because of the Christological grounding of the Church and a renewed pneumatological perspective. He adds,

In fact, recent developments in Roman Catholic ecclesiology have seen a significant theological reappreciation of the essential role of the Holy Spirit in determining the nature and mission of the Church. The result of this on-going process is that the dangers of ecclesiological reductionism [monophysitism] which may have affected the tradition … [has] been faced with the early Twentieth century emphasis on the Church as the mystical body and, even more efficaciously, with the present-day reflection on the fundamental relationship between Christology, pneumatology and ecclesiology. (*ETP*, 262–63)

In his recent book on Catholicism, however, De Chirico is far less careful in his interpretation of post-Vatican II Catholic ecclesiology and charges Catholicism with "elevating the church into a quasi-divine body" (*SWDW*, 107). With this charge he is mistaken and a careless interpreter.

In Catholic ecclesiology, Christ precedes the Church as its Head; the Church mediates the light of the nations that is Christ. De Chirico, et al., does not take seriously the *Catechism of the Catholic Church*'s understanding of the Church's Christological consciousness, in other words, her awareness that the Catholic Church is the Church "of Christ": "*Lumen gentium cum sit Christus*" (*LG*, §1). As Marc Cardinal Ouellet explains the teaching of *Lumen Gentium* 1 and hence of the *Catechism of the Catholic Church* (*CCC*):

> The light of nations [*lumen gentium*] is Christ and not the Church, but this light shines on the Church's countenance. This Christological consciousness is expressed in the first paragraph of the Dogmatic Constitution on the Church [*Lumen Gentium*], when it uses the term 'sacramentum' to express the relationship between the visible reality of the Church and the invisible mystery—'mysterion'—of God in Christ: "the Church is in Christ like a sacrament or as a sign and instrument both of a very closely knit union with God and of the unity of the whole human race" (*Mystery and Sacrament*, 24).

In particular, precisely with respect to the claim that the Church's relationship to Christ is such that the Church is substantially constitutive of Christ's identity, Swiss Catholic theologian Charles Cardinal Journet refutes this claim. He correctly asserts that there is an *insurmountable difference* in level between Head and Body because Christ belongs to the hypostatic order and the Church does not so belong. He says, "The sanctity of Christ is unique and belongs to the hypostatic order; the sanctity of the Church belongs to the order of created grace and the indwelling of the Holy Spirit" (*Primacy of Peter*, 17).

In other words, "Christ, who is the Head, is God; the Church, which is the Body, is a creature. The life of the Head flows into the Body, but with a radical difference in level. Christ, on the one hand, is situated at the level of the hypostatic union; his divine personality is incommunicable, but in addition it calls down into his soul the fullness of communicable grace: charity, the indwelling of the Holy Spirit and all the created gifts" (*Theology of the Church*, 384–85).

Of course, if De Chirico and Allison are mistaken regarding their claim that Catholicism reduces Christology to ecclesiology, then there is no reason why Catholicism and Evangelical Protestantism do not substantially share the Nicene Creed or the Creed of Chalcedon. The Christ of the *Catechism of the Catholic Church* is, indeed, the Jesus Christ of the Bible and the early creeds of Nicaea and Chalcedon. *Pace* Chirico, there is no antithesis between Rome and the Bible. I will return to the Christ-Church interconnection below. For now, in preparation for the next chapter on ecumenism, let's turn to the anti-realist implications of De Chirico's meaning holism and hence its inability to account for the relation between meaning, justification, and truth.

Although De Chirico and Allison do not tease out the implications of their meaning holism for the question of justification and truth, I shall now argue that given that there must be different worlds because "reality" is relative to different conceptual systems, their view entails an anti-realist view of truth. Therefore, on De Chirico's view, "the world," indeed, "reality" seems totally irrelevant to questions of meaning and truth. Therefore, since everything is relative to our conceptual system, then the justification of our beliefs is relative to our system—to the relation between beliefs and beliefs within a system rather than between beliefs and the world. On this view, not only justification of beliefs but also truth itself is made to depend on systems, given that the meaning holism of De Chirico and Allison rules out the possibility of there being any reality independent of the respective systems.

The question then arises as to how an Evangelical Protestant justifies his views to a Roman Catholic given that their respective views cannot stand in a contradictory relation to each other, and, accordingly, making impossible criticism and refutation of each other's systems. The implication of this approach is made clear by Ernest Sosa:

> If all I say when I say that our system is justified (etc.) is that it is justified (etc.) relative to itself, and, if all this amounts to is that it approves of itself, either explicitly or implicitly, and, if many clashing systems do the same, how then can my commitment to our system be anything more than arbitrary willfulness? And, if that is its status, how can justification of any-

> thing relative to such a system rise above that level of
> arbitrary willfulness? Where would the extra incre-
> ment of justification come from? And how could it
> possibly make up the lack in its fundamental prin-
> ciples, the principles relative to which one must attain
> whatever justification one ever does attain? ("Serious
> Philosophy and Freedom of Spirit," 715)

The only way a commitment to our system can rise above "arbitrary willfulness," making up a lack in its fundamental principles, John Paul II rightly argues, is by embracing a realist notion of truth and a corresponding epistemic realism such that we can justifiably know the truth about reality.[9] John Paul II holds that "philosophy [should] verify the human capacity to *know the truth*, to come to a knowledge which can reach objective truth by means of that *adaequatio rei et intellectus*" (*FR*, §82). The Catholic philosophical tradition presupposes a realist account of truth and hence, says John Paul, "the capacity of man to arrive at the knowledge of truth" (ibid.). The standard realist definition of truth is as follows: a proposition is true, if, and only if, what it asserts is in fact the case about objective reality; otherwise, it is false.

Furthermore, the Catholic tradition also stipulates the need for "a philosophy of genuinely metaphysical range... in order to attain something absolute, ultimate and foundational in its search for truth." Explains John Paul II, "Here I do not mean to speak of metaphysics in the sense of a specific school or a particular historical current of thought. I want only to state that reality and truth do transcend the factual and empirical, and to vindicate the human being's capacity to know this transcendent and metaphysical dimension in a way that is true and certain, albeit [our knowledge is] imperfect and analogical" (*FR*, §83; see also 84).

Given the commitment of De Chirico and Allison to the truth and knowledge of the Christian faith, as well as the confidence that they exhibit in distinguishing truth and falsity, I cannot imagine that they would reject the Catholic tradition of realism in truth and knowl-edge and the necessity of a metaphysics. As John Paul states, "A the-ology without a metaphysical horizon could not move beyond an analysis of religious experience, nor would it allow the *intellectus fidei* to give a coherent account of the universal and transcendent value of revealed truth" (*FR*, §83). Yet, to embrace that tradition and to do genuine Christian theology, De Chirico and Allison must abandon their commitment to radical meaning holism and its implications.

Otherwise, given meaning holism and its implications, then Catholics and Evangelicals cannot disagree about the truth or falsity of any proposition. They cannot disagree over a single proposition in their respective theological systems since they must differ in what they mean by it. Furthermore, then, substantive communication—as I described it above—as is demanded by genuine ecumenism, would be impossible in light of their meaning holism. Both De Chirico and Allison ignore the obvious conclusion that their writings on Catholicism and Evangelical Protestantism are self-referentially inconsistent, given their meaning holism and its implications, in particular, incommensurability, and their claim that the systems of Roman Catholicism and Evangelical Protestantism are not semantically comparable (Devitt, 169).

NOTES

1. *Lectures on Calvinism*, Chapter 1, "Calvinism as Life-System," 9–40.

2. See Karl Adam, *The Spirit of Catholicism*, trans. Dom Justin McCann, OSB, 210.

3. Franz Dünzl states that the terminology of the Church's doctrine of the Trinity at the ecumenical councils of Nicaea and Constantinople "is not immediately comprehensible today [but that] is no obstacle to its making important statements which can still be explained" (*A Brief History of the Doctrine of the Trinity in the Early Church*, trans. John Bowden, 136).

4. Peter A. Angeles, "Cognitive Meaning," in *The Harper Collins Dictionary of Philosophy*, 2nd ed. (New York: HarperPerennial, 1992), 179.

5. Ibid., "Factual Meaning," 180.

6. *Reformed Confessions Harmonized, With an Annotated Bibliography of Reformed Doctrinal Works*, ed. Joel R. Beeke and Sinclair B. Ferguson, Article 1, 6.

7. Michael Devitt, *Realism and Truth*, 2nd ed., 168.

8. Michael Horton cited by Allison, *RCTP*, 65. See also, Benjamin B. Warfield, *The Plan of Salvation*, "But in the present dispensation, the Church, in large measure, has taken over the work of Christ. It is in a real sense, a reincarnation of Christ to the end of the continuation and completion of his redemptive mission. . . . In one word, the Church in this [Romish] system is conceived to be Jesus Christ himself in his earthly form, and it is therefore substituted for him as the proximate object of the faith of Christians" (50–51). Karl Barth voices a similar objection that Roman Catholicism reduces or assimilates Christology to ecclesiology: "Their presupposition is that the being of the Church, Jesus

Christ, is no longer the free Lord of its existence, but that He is incorporated into the existence of the Church, and is thus ultimately restricted and conditioned by certain concrete forms of the human understanding of His revelation and of the faith which grasps it" (*Church Dogmatics* I/I, 2nd ed., trans. G. W. Bromiley, 40. See Donald W. Norwood, *Reforming Rome: Karl Barth and Vatican II.*

9. See Eduardo Echeverria, "The Splendor of Truth in *Fides et Ratio*," *Quaestiones Disputatae* 9, no. 1 (Fall 2018): 49–78; idem, "Realism, Truth, and Justification: The Contribution of Michael Polanyi," *Josephinum Journal of Theology* 26, nos. 1 & 2 (2019): 199–227.

CHAPTER 2

ECUMENISM

The very mystery of the Church invites, rather compels us, to ask about the perspective ahead for the difficult way of estrangement and rapprochement, of dialogue, contact, controversy, and for the ecumenical striving to overcome the divisions of the Church. (Berkouwer, VCNT, 316 [249])

Taking up an idea expressed by Pope John XXIII at the opening of the Council, the Decree on Ecumenism mentions the way of formulating doctrine as one of the elements of a continuing reform. Here it is not a question of altering the deposit of faith, changing the meaning of dogmas, eliminating essential words from them, accommodating truth to the preferences of a particular age, or suppressing certain articles of the Creed under the false pretext that they are no longer understood today. The unity willed by God can be attained only by the adherence of all to the content of revealed faith in its entirety. In matters of faith, compromise is in contradiction with God who is Truth. In the Body of Christ, "the way, and the truth, and the life" (Jn 14:6), who could consider legitimate a reconciliation brought about at the expense of the truth? (UUS, §18)[1]

Receptive Ecumenism

In the new book by Richard J. Mouw on the neo-Calvinist doctrine of common grace, he asks the question that I pose in the title of a recent essay, "Do you have to be a Calvinist in order to be a Kuyperian?"[2] This question is raised in a section entitled "An Ecumenical Spirit," where Mouw gives us a sense of the ecumenical spirit of neo-Calvinism, for example, Abraham Kuyper (1837–1921), and other neo-Calvinists, such as Herman Bavinck (1854–1921)[3] and Canadian scholar Albert Wolters (*God Cares*, 133; see also, 129). Kuyper himself wrote in his famous 1898 Princeton Stone Lectures, *Lectures on Calvinism*, about his alliance with Roman Catholics. There is no false irenicism on Kuyper's part. He gives a very articulate statement, not only of the common creedal heritage of faith shared by Reformed Christians with the tradition of Catholic Christianity but also of the common spiritual enemies of both, such as atheism and pantheism. Kuyper wrote,

> Now, in this conflict [with theological liberalism and secularism] Rome is not an antagonist, but stands on our side, inasmuch as she also recognizes and maintains the Trinity, the Deity of Christ, the Cross as an atoning sacrifice, the Scriptures as the Word of God, and the Ten Commandments as a divinely-imposed rule of life. Therefore, let me ask if Romish theologians take up the sword to do valiant and skillful battle against the same tendency that we ourselves mean to fight to the death, is it not the part of wisdom to accept the valuable help of their elucidation? . . . I for my part am not ashamed to confess that on many points my views have been clarified through my study of the Romish theologians. (*Lectures on Calvinism*, 183–84)

But there are also Wesleyan neo-Kuyperians, such as Richard Middleton. Mouw cites an introductory remark that Middleton made when Mouw was a guest speaker at Roberts Wesleyan College: "Like Rich Mouw I am a Kuyperian. But while he is a Calvinist Kuyperian I'm a *Wesleyan* Kuyperian" (*God Cares*, 129). Mouw alludes to "folks many of us know who wed key neo-Calvinist themes to Lutheran and Catholic theological allegiances." What themes? "[T]he supreme kingship of Christ, the antithesis, common grace, sphere sovereignty" (ibid., 128).[4] Furthermore, Mouw cites Al Wolters, who captures what is philosophically essential to the Kuyperian tradition (ibid., 123), namely, "the philosophical commitment to the constancy of creation, and to creation as delivered by the creator, prior to the Fall, as the normative standard to which creation is being redeemed and restored."[5] Now, I am a "*Roman Catholic* Kuyperian" who is not only deeply committed to the truth of Catholic doctrines but also affirms Kuyperian themes as listed above by Mouw. Mouw rightly explains that Kuyperians with Catholic theological allegiances have "likely done some serious theological work in exploring ways in which neo-Calvinist ideas can be grounded in non-Calvinist confessional commitments" (*God Cares*, 131). I agree with Mouw. In my article, I sketch briefly some "meta-Catholic" considerations in which I justify how Kuyperian ideas could be grounded in Catholic confessional commitments. For now, I justify the ecumenical engagement between Catholics and Evangelical Protestants.

The Roman Catholic Church, according to John Paul II, holds that "full [visible] communion of course [would] have to come about through the acceptance of the whole truth into which the Holy Spirit guides Christ's disciples." Thus the Church's vision of visible unity "takes account of all the demands of revealed truth." Therefore, she seeks to avoid all forms of reductionism or facile agreement, false irenicism, indifference to the Church's teaching, and common-denominator ecumenicity. John Paul II correctly writes, "Love for the truth is the deepest dimension of any authentic quest for full communion between Christians." In other words, he adds, "The unity willed by God can be attained only by the adherence of all to the content of revealed faith in its entirety. In matters of faith, compromise is in contradiction with God who is Truth. In the Body of Christ, 'the way, and the truth, and the life' (Jn 14:6), who would consider legitimate a reconciliation brought about at the expense of the truth? ... A 'being together' which betrayed the truth would thus be opposed both to the nature of God who offers his communion and to the need for truth found in the depths of every human heart." In short, "Authentic ecumenism is a gift at the service of truth" (*UUS*, §§36, 79, 18, and 38). These are some of the presuppositions of an ecumenism of conviction.

Most important, an interior conversion of the heart, indeed, repentance, is required as a precondition for engaging in ecumenical dialogue. Why this summons to conversion? "*Christian unity is possible,*" says John Paul, "provided that we are humbly conscious of having sinned against unity and are convinced of our need for conversion" (*UUS*, §34; see also §82). In this light, we can understand why an examination of conscience is required for authentic dialogue; confessing our sins, repentance, putting ourselves, by God's grace, in that "interior space where Christ, the source of the Church's unity, can effectively act, with all the power of his Spirit, the Paraclete" (*UUS*, §35). The journey of ecumenical dialogue is thus an ongoing "dialogue of conversion," *on both sides*, trusting in the reconciling power of the truth that is Christ, to overcome the obstacles to unity. Furthermore, "Prayer is the 'soul' of the ecumenical renewal and of the yearning for unity," adds John Paul II. In short, "it is the basis and support for *every-thing the [Second Vatican Ecumenical] Council defines as 'dialogue'"* (*UUS*, §28). Indeed, prayer is the heart of spiritual ecumenism. Moreover, dialogue must be deepened in order to engage the other person in a relationship of mutual trust and acceptance as a fellow Christian, responsive to him in Christian love.

Sometimes dialogue is made more difficult, indeed, impossible, when our words, judgments, and actions manifest a failure to deal with each other with understanding, truthfully and fairly. "When undertaking dialogue, *each side must presuppose in the other a desire for reconciliation, for unity in truth*" (*UUS*, §29). Therefore, a necessary sign of this encounter is that we have passed from "antagonism and conflict to a situation where each party recognizes the other as a partner." (*UUS*, §41). "You shall love your neighbor as yourself" (Gal 5:14), and in St. Paul's words, "especially those who are of the household of faith" (Gal 6:10).

Clearly, the Church regards non-Catholic Christians as belonging, however imperfectly, to the household of faith, and hence she speaks of them as "separated brethren." Notwithstanding their separation, they are still brethren, brothers and sisters in the Lord Jesus Christ. Thus: we must speak the truth in love (Eph 4:15). "With non-Catholic Christians," the Congregation for the Doctrine of the Faith adds, "Catholics must enter into a respectful dialogue of charity and truth, a dialogue which is not only an exchange of ideas, but also of gifts [see *UUS*, §§28, 47, respectively], in order that the fullness of the means of salvation can be offered to one's partners in dialogue. In this way, they are led to an ever deeper conversion in Christ" ("Doctrinal Note," §12). In short, the ecumenism of conversion embodies the conviction that "dialogue is not simply an exchange of ideas. In some way it is always an 'exchange of gifts'," indeed, a "dialogue of love" (*UUS*, §§28, 47, respectively). This is receptive ecumenism at its best, and it is sorely missing in both Allison's and De Chirico's writings on Catholicism.

In the report of the second phase of the ecumenical conversations between the World Alliance of Reformed Churches and the Pontifical Council for Promoting Christian Unity (1984–1990), three contemporary Reformed and Evangelical attitudes toward the Roman Catholic Church are distinguished: "There are within the Reformed [and Evangelical] family those whose attitude to the Roman Catholic Church remains essentially negative: [1] some because they remain to be convinced that the modern development of the Roman Catholic Church has really addressed the issues of the Reformation, and [2] others because they have been largely untouched by the ecumenical exchanges of recent times and have therefore not been challenged or encouraged to reconsider their traditional stance. But this is only one part of the picture. [3] Others in the Reformed [and Evangelical] tradition have sought to engage in a fresh constructive and critical evaluation both of the contemporary teaching and practice of the Roman Catholic Church and of the classical controverted issues."[6] How do those who belong to positions [1] and [2] make the transition to position [3]?

The last chapter of Allison's *RCTP* is not entitled "ecumenical ministry with Catholics," but rather "evangelical ministry with Catholics." This says a great deal about Allison's stance towards the question of Christian unity between Evangelicals and Catholics. Apparently, Catholics as such need to be evangelized, given their rejection of "Protestant principles of *sola Scriptura* and justification by grace alone through faith alone" (*RCTP*, 172). Furthermore, Evangelical Protestant theology cannot agree with the hermeneutics of Catholicism, meaning thereby "the axioms of the nature-grace interdependence and the Christ-Church interconnection" of Catholicism. Hence Allison does not call Evangelical Protestants to engage in ecumenical dialogue with fellow-believing Christians, that is, Catholics, with the aim of restoring visible communion between these divided brethren. This move "should [not] even be pursued," he says, indeed, stronger, it is "not permissible" (172).[7]

In light of Vatican II's approach to ecumenism, the Church now engages in receptive ecumenism. In the Introduction to this book, I stated that the practice of receptive ecumenism means: "Dialogue is not simply an exchange of ideas. In some way it is always an 'exchange of gifts'…. Dialogue does not extend exclusively to matters of doctrine but engages the whole person; it is also a dialogue of love" (*UUS*, §§28, 47, respectively). More exactly, this practice presupposes the distinction between propositional truths of faith and their formulations in reflecting on the sense in which a doctrine, already confirmed and defined, is more fully known and deeply understood by another Christian tradition. John XXIII drew this distinction in his opening address at the Second Vatican Council:

> For the deposit of faith, the truths contained in our

venerable doctrine, are one thing; the fashion in which they are expressed, but with the same meaning and the same judgment [*eodem sensu eademque sententia*], is another thing. (*Gaudet Mater Ecclesia*, §14)

The subordinate clause, which I have cited in its Latin original, is part of a larger passage from the First Vatican Council's Dogmatic Constitution on Faith and Reason, *Dei Filius* (1869–1870). The phrase is earlier invoked by Pope Pius IX in the bull of 1854, *Ineffabilis Deus*, and also cited by Pope Leo XIII in his 1899 encyclical letter, *Testem benevolentiae Nostrae*. And this formula in *Dei Filius* is itself taken from the *Commonitorium* of St. Vincent of Lérins (445 AD), a Gallic monk, and the chief theologian of the Abbey of Lérins:

Therefore, let there be growth and abundant progress in understanding, knowledge, and wisdom, in each and all, in individuals and in the whole Church, at all times and in the progress of ages, but only within the proper limits, i.e., within the same dogma, the same meaning, the same judgment" [*in eodem scilicet dogmate, eodem sensu eademque sententia*]. (Denzinger, §3020)

This italicized phrase means to say that the truth of a proposition is inextricably connected with its meaning. As to meaning, the way things are is what makes "meaning" true or false. Therefore, a proposition is true if what it says corresponds to the way objective reality is; otherwise, it is false. In the words of Bernard Lonergan, "Meaning of its nature is related to a 'meant,' and what is meant may or may not correspond to what is so. If it corresponds, the meaning is true. If it does not correspond, the meaning is false" ("Dehellenization of Dogma," 14 [scare quotes added]). Thus, a dogma's meaning is unchangeable because that meaning is true. The truths of faith are, if true, always and everywhere true; the different way of expressing these truths may vary in our attempts to communicate revealed truths more clearly and accurately, but these various linguistic expressions do not affect the truth of the propositions.

John XXIII intuitively understood that propositions—contents of thought that are true or false, expressible in various languages, but more than mere words, expressing possible, and if true, actual states of affairs—do not vary as the language in which they are expressed varies. He speaks of immutable or unalterable truths, suggesting that truths of faith are more than their linguistic expression. What, then, is the ecumenical import of this distinction for understanding the continuity and material identity of dogma between Roman Catholicism and Evangelical Protestantism?

In this Vincentian light, Vatican II's Decree on Ecumenism, *Unitatis Redintegratio* (§17; see also 4, 6) provides a justification for legitimate differences in the elaboration of revealed truth, and hence for receptive ecumenism.

> It is hardly surprising, then, if from time to time one tradition has come nearer to a full appreciation of some aspects of a mystery of revelation than the other, or has expressed it to better advantage. In such cases, these various theological expressions are to be considered often as mutually complementary rather than conflicting.... Thus they promote the right ordering of Christian life and, indeed, pave the way to a full vision of Christian truth.[8]

The ecumenical import of the distinction between truth and its formulations is also recognized by Pope John Paul II in his 1995 encyclical on ecumenism, *Ut Unum Sint*, §§ 57 and 81. Both these documents speak to the issue of legitimate, inter-confessional diversity in theological expressions of doctrine. John Paul states, quoting the Decree on Ecumenism: "'It is hardly surprising if sometimes one tradition has come nearer than the other to an apt appreciation of certain aspects of the revealed mystery, or has expressed them in a clearer manner. As a result, these various theological formulations are often to be considered as complementary rather than conflicting.' Communion is made fruitful by the exchange of gifts between the Churches insofar as they complement each other." Philosophical issues of meaning and truth are at stake in discussing legitimate diversity in complementary theological, rather than contradictory, expressions of doctrine. In sum, we must face here the question of "commensurable pluralism," as Guarino calls it, meaning, thereby, that different theological systems cannot hold positions that are fundamentally contradictory. In other words, variety in theological expression must not be understood as equivalent to opposition; rather, such variety, Guarino explains, "must be commensurable with the fundamental creedal and doctrinal affirmations of faith. These affirmations are patient of reconceptualization, but always adhering to the '*eodem sensu eademque sententia*.'" This distinction between unchangeable truths and its formulations has ecumenical significance—

"promoting the right ordering of Christian life, paving the way to a full vision of Christian truth." I have in mind here, for example, Kuyper's three-volume work (1911–1912), *Pro Rege: Living under Christ's Kingship*, where he shows that he has a fuller appreciation of that aspect of a mystery of revelation that complements rather than conflicts with Catholic theology. I return below to receptive ecumenism and the ecumenical implications of distinguishing between truth and its formulations in a Vincentian vein.

It is not surprising, then, that the writings of Allison and De Chirico have no basis for engaging in ecumenical dialogue. Given meaning holism, its implications that I discussed above, in particular, incommensurability, and that the respective terms in Roman Catholic and Evangelical Protestant systems are not semantically comparable, Evangelicals and Catholics can never be together.[9] Nevertheless, both Allison in his two books on Catholicism *(RCTP, 40 Questions)* and De Chirico in his two books *(ETP, SWDW)*, write about Roman Catholicism with confidence about what is true and false, and that confidence is inconsistent with their meaning holism.

Still, against the background of meaning holism discussed in Chapter 1, it is not surprising that neither Allison's nor De Chirico's work encourage the reader to participate in the already substantial dialogue between Protestants from varied confessional traditions (Methodist, Lutheran, Reformed, and Anglican) and Catholics, striving for reconciliation in the biblical faith. For one thing, their studies appear more apologetical than ecumenical, and they have not passed from "antagonism and conflict to a situation where each party recognizes the other as a partner" *(UUS §41)*. For instance, De Chirico states in his recent book, *Same Words, Different Worlds*, "The ultimate problem of Roman Catholicism is that it is not committed to the biblical gospel but to a spurious synthesis of Yes and No responses to it. This Yes and No pattern is embedded in all its expressions" *(SWDW, 4; see also, 116)*. In other words, it is a synthesis of biblical and non-biblical ideas. For another, they pay no real attention to ecumenism and an evangelical perspective on John 17:21 in which Christ calls all his disciples to unity.

Absent that perspective in their books, Allison and De Chirico are prevented from substantially advancing the discussion between Catholics and Evangelicals. They are both stuck in an *a priori* stance towards the Catholic Church on the traditional issues that have alienated Evangelicals and Catholics, and consequently are unable "to engage in a fresh constructive and critical evaluation both of the contemporary teaching and practice of the Roman Catholic Church and of the classical controverted issues" (see stance 3 above). Given Allison's "own long-term familiarity with the Church" (RCTP, 18–19), why is his stance toward Catholicism finally one of "intrigue" rather than that of a fellow believer when he speaks of "the book's appreciation of and thanksgiving for many commonalities between Catholic and evangelical theology" (RCTP, 28)? This perspective, although expressing appreciation and thanksgiving, seems hard to reconcile with his acceptance of the incommensurability thesis.

The word "intrigue" makes Allison sound like an outsider rather than one, like G. C. Berkouwer, who holds that all Christians share responsibility, as Berkouwer wrote, for "the Church as it is now, with its tensions and problems, its guilt and dividedness" (VCNT, 316 [249]). Allison is stuck at intrigue, which manifests an external stance, but has not yet developed a stance towards Catholics that I described above as stance 3. This stance is where an authentic inter-confessional dialogue is made possible because each confessional interlocutor recognizes the other as an ecumenical partner, as a fellow believer in Christ, in the common cause of the Gospel, especially regarding the question of the visible unity of the Church. This is receptive ecumenism at its best, and it is sorely missing in Allison's work.

Allison shows no evidence that he is committed to the ecumenical imperative of the Christian faith as it is paradigmatically expressed by Christ in the Gospel According to John 17:20–26. This shared responsibility for realizing "the unity of the Church will have meaning *for our time*," says Berkouwer, "only when the question of unity is both honestly and stubbornly faced as the important issue." Berkouwer continues: "New Testament eschatology—pointing as it does to the Church's final victory—is charged with a sense of urgency as it calls us to do for the Church, here and now, what our hands find to do. It is no accident that Christ's prayer for the unity of the Church in John 17 [20–23] includes a prayer that the Church may be kept from the Evil One [17:15]" (ibid., 321 [254]). Lead us not into the temptation of regarding our disunity as normal, rather than as scandal and wound, but deliver us from the evil of our divisions. Berkouwer makes an ecumenically decisive point here, namely, it is no longer possible to remain divided because in willing the Church, God willed unity as a gift and task, "that they may all be one" (Jn 17:21).

Allison has interacted with Catholics for many years, yet he appears reticent to move to the stance of receptive ecumenism, as I described it above. Although Allison identifies "with fascination and appreciation the commonalities between Catholic and [his own version of] evangelical theology" (*RCTP*, 18), there is no evidence in his book that he thinks Evangelicals who share his theological convictions may learn from Catholics, particularly with respect to the issues that have divided them.

Whenever I read Allison and De Chirico I am reminded of Berkouwer's statement: "Every kind of Protestantism that stands merely in a protest-relationship is stricken with unfruitfulness" (*Recent Developments*, 10). Why? Christ calls all his disciples to unity. Hence, as John Paul II pointedly asks, "How is it possible to remain divided, if we have been 'buried' through Baptism in the Lord's death, in the very act by which God, through the death of his Son, has broken down the walls of division?"

> For this reason he sent his Son, so that by dying and rising for us he might bestow on us the Spirit of love. On the eve of his sacrifice on the Cross, Jesus himself prayed to the Father for his disciples and for all those who believe in him, that they *might be one*, a living communion. This is the basis not only of the duty, but also of the responsibility before God and his plan, which falls to those who through Baptism become members of the Body of Christ, a Body in which the fullness of reconciliation and communion must be made present. Division "openly contradicts the will of Christ, provides a stumbling block to the world, and inflicts damage on the most holy cause of proclaiming the Good News to every creature" (*UUS* §6).[10]

So, although Allison's first book is, indeed, a good first step to understanding the Catholic tradition, his approach does not represent a significant shift in stance toward Roman Catholicism by a well-known Evangelical Protestant theologian who is a confessional Baptist. The same is true of De Chirico's first work on an Evangelical theological perspective of post-Vatican II theology. That work is an instructive study of post-Vatican II Catholicism, considering the variety of Evangelical scholars who attempted to come to terms with what De Chirico calls an "Evangelical Hermeneutics of Roman Catholicism," in particular, the "two axes of Roman Catholicism," namely, "the nature-grace interdependence," and the "Christ-church interconnection."

Allison's book clearly exhibits the second stance in his Evangelical assessment of the *Catechism*, as does De Chirico, in particular, on the classical controverted issues that have divided Protestants and Catholics.[11] For example, his first book on Roman Catholicism appears uninformed by the results of the last half-century of bilateral ecumenical dialogues on the Trinity and Christology, salvation, justification, and sanctification, on ecclesiology, sacramentology, and Mary between the Pontifical Council for the Promotion of Christian Unity and the various confessional traditions of Methodists, Lutherans, Anglicans, and Reformed on precisely the classical controverted issues listed above.[12]

Allison's book is also uninformed by the bilateral dialogues of the Anglican-Roman Catholic International Commission from 1971–2014 (Parts I–III) on authority in the Church, the sacraments, salvation, the moral life in Christ, and Mary. In addition, his work is uninformed by the French-speaking ecumenists, *Le Groupe des Dombes*, comprised of Roman Catholic and Reformed scholars/pastors, who since 1937 until the present have written on the question of Christian unity, the teaching authority of the Church, ordained ministry, Mary's place in the plan of God, and others.

This limitation has somewhat changed in his recent book *40 Questions About Roman Catholicism* as far as sources he considers are concerned. But his assessment of Roman Catholicism has not changed on the "two axes of Roman Catholicism," namely, "the nature-grace interdependence," and the "Christ-church interconnection." Also, on Catholic sacramentology, and biblical authority, Scripture and tradition, his assessment remains the same. I'll return to these matters below.

Yet for Christians from varied confessional traditions interested in pursuing ecumenical dialogue, knowledge of these documents is imperative. Not that Allison needed to discuss all these documents in his study of *CCC*. Rather, his study should at least have shown some familiarity with documents that are the fruits of years of ecumenical dialogue. Thus, his discussion of the classical controverted issues is unable "to engage in a fresh constructive and critical evaluation both of the contemporary teaching and practice of the Roman Catholic Church and of the classical controverted issues" (Rusch and Gros, 187).

For instance, in his earlier discussion on the doctrine of justification, there is not even a reference to the 1999 Joint Declaration on the Doctrine of Justification, by the World Federation of Lutherans and the Catholic Church. Such an influential text on a topic that still alienates some Protestants and Catholics should inform one's theological analysis. Again, this has changed in his book *40 Questions About Roman Catholicism*.

What is the ecclesiological starting point for ecumenical dialogue, according to Vatican II? Consider briefly the ecclesiological question concerning the unity of the Church, namely, the relationship of the Catholic Church to its separated brethren. Allison says, "Catholicism's position that evangelical ecclesial communities are not even churches does nothing to overcome the problem of disunity" (*RCTP*, 172).

Although Allison recognizes (*RCTP*, 162) that *Lumen Gentium, Unitatis Redintegratio*, and, I would add, *Ut Unum Sint*, affirm that there are many elements of truth and sanctification outside the visible boundaries of the Church, he nowhere sees the significant ecumenical implications this affirmation has: separated brethren are in real, albeit imperfect, communion with the Catholic Church. In other words, Christians—Protestants and Catholics alike—are brothers and sisters in Christ. Furthermore, Allison nowhere acknowledges that this affirmation contributes to overcoming the problem of disunity. Those many elements, John Paul II claimed, do not exist in an "ecclesial vacuum" (*UUS* §13), because there is ecclesial reality, however fragmented, and to greater or lesser degrees, outside the visible boundaries of the Church that "participate in the Church of Christ in a qualified but real way" (to quote Thomas Guarino). Catholic ecclesiology rejects the following dilemma:[13]

- *either* correctly affirming that the Church of Christ fully and totally subsists alone in its own right in the Catholic Church, existing uniquely and incommunicably in this concrete Church, because the entire fullness of the means of salvation are present in her, and then implausibly denying that Orthodoxy and the historic churches of the Reformation are churches in any real sense whatsoever, such that there exists an ecclesial wasteland or emptiness outside the Church's visible boundaries. (*LG* §8; *UR* §§3-4; *UUS* §14)
- *or* rightly affirming that they are churches in some sense, in a

lesser or greater degree to the extent that there exist ecclesial elements of truth and sanctification in them, but then wrongly accepting ecclesiological relativism or pluralism—meaning thereby that the one Church of Christ Jesus subsists in many churches, with the Catholic Church being merely one among many churches. (*LG* §8; *UR* §§3-4, 20-21, 23)

Much discussion has been had in the last half-century regarding this dilemma in Catholic ecclesiology. None of the fruits of these dialogues inform Allison's and De Chirico's approach to Roman Catholicism in their writings on ecclesiology. Now, given the limits of this small study, I will not repeat the arguments that I developed elsewhere informing an approach that strives to avoid this dilemma.[14] I only want make one important point of particular ecumenical significance, namely, the difference between *subsistit in* and *est* (is). Ratzinger explains the difference and then its ecumenical significance.

> At this point, it is important to examine the word *subsistit* a bit more closely. With this term, the Council explicated the formula of Pope Pius XII, who had stated in his encyclical letter *Mystici Corporis Christi* that the Church "is" (*est*) the one mystical body of Christ. In this distinction between *subsistit* and *est* is hidden the entire ecumenical problem. ... [15] *Subsistere* is special case of *esse*. It refers to existence in the form of an individual subject. That is exactly what it means here. The Council wanted to say that the Church of Jesus Christ, as a concrete subject in the world, is found in the Catholic Church. This can only occur in a single instance, and thus the notion that *subsistit* could be multiplied precisely misses the meaning of the term. With the word *subsistit*, the Council wanted to express the singularity and non-multiplicability of the Church of Christ, the Catholic Church: the Church exists as a single subject in the reality of history.[16]

But then Ratzinger turns to explain the ecumenical significance of this distinction for understanding ecclesial division. Adds Ratzinger, "[F]or while the Church is only one and really exists, there is *being* which is from the Church's *being*—there is ecclesial reality—outside the Church. Because sin is contradiction, the difference between *subsistit* and *est*, cannot, in the final analysis, be completely resolved logically" (ibid., 28). Therefore, "The lack of unity among Christians is certainly a *wound* for the Church; not in the sense that she is deprived of her unity, but 'in that it hinders the complete fulfillment of her universality in history.'"[17]

The concluding point I do wish to make bears on the theology of Catholic ecumenism, and it follows from the meaning of *subsistit in* as explained above. Regarding the question of ecclesial unity and diversity, unity is a given, a gift, existing already in the Catholic Church, rather than something we strive after from the starting point of non-Catholic diversity of Christian confessions. Yves Congar rightly insists, "For its part, a Catholic ecumenism cannot forget that the church of Christ and the apostles *exists*. Therefore, the point of departure for Catholic ecumenism is this existing church, and its goal is to strengthen within the church the sources of catholicity that it seeks to integrate and to respect all their legitimate differences" (*True and False Reform*, 293). Of course, what has been called the scandal of ecclesiological particularity in this concrete Church, the Catholic Church, "provokes opposition in other churches and church communities."[18] I have dealt with this opposition elsewhere,[19] and thus will not repeat myself here.

Significantly, Allison's *RCTP*, in particular, lacks any reference to the master of dogmatic and ecumenical theology, Reformed theologian G. C. Berkouwer (1903–1996), who discusses the development of Catholic theology in general but also, in particular, the issue of Scripture and tradition in his 1964 work, *Vatikaans Concilie en Nieuwe Theologie*.[20] In this study on Vatican Council II, which Reformed theologian Heiko Oberman (1930–2001) called "breathtakingly important," Berkouwer gives a Reformed theological assessment of the influence of the *nouvelle théologie* on the Council. This work of Berkouwer is necessary reading for anyone, particularly an Evangelical theologian, who is attempting to come to terms with the *Catechism of the Catholic Church*, which is the fruit of the Second Vatican Council. There is also no sign that Allison is informed by the debates leading up to the Council in the writings of, for example, J. R. Geiselmann and Joseph Ratzinger, and after the Council in the writings of, for example, the French Catholic theologian Yves Congar, *Tradition and Traditions*, and *The Meaning of Tradition*.

Moreover, Allison, unlike De Chirico, makes no reference to the work of Evangelicals and Catholics Together on this topic: *Your Word Is Truth*. In this collection, his fellow Evangelicals, such as Timothy

George, J. I. Packer, and John Woodbridge (all of whom belong to Evangelicals and Catholics Together), enter into a discussion of the issue of Scripture and Tradition.[21]

The practice of receptive ecumenism, therefore, seeks to avoid all those assumptions that sometimes plague ecumenical dialogue: forms of reductionism, such as doctrinal minimalism, or facile agreement, false irenicism, indifference to the Church's teaching, and common-denominator ecumenicity (*UUS* §84). Inter-confessional dialogue as such between Evangelical and Reformed Protestants, on the one hand, and Catholics, on the other, is often taken to be a "sign of weakness."

Berkouwer disagrees, and I think he is right. He insists that concern for the visible unity of the Body of Christ does not mean the leveling out of all genuine differences between Catholics and Evangelical/Reformed Christians. That is because an ecumenism based on anything else than truth—an ecumenism of conviction—is empty. Berkouwer correctly understands that "'dialogue' ... does not signify *a priori* a relativizing approach to ecumenism" (*De Kerk*, Vol. I, 91n130 [74n71]). He adds, "Many Protestants suspect that by taking these confrontations seriously, we may water down the differences and lose some of the old convictions of the struggle." On the contrary, argues Berkouwer, "Responsible encounter is not a sign of weakness; it is rather recognition of the seriousness of the division of the Church" (*VCNT*, 28–29 [30]). Hence, he concludes, "the question of the gospel and unity in Christ must be both honestly and stubbornly faced as the important issue" (ibid., 321 [254]).

Hierarchy of Truths

De Chirico mentions Vatican II's notion of the "hierarchy of truths" in passing when briefly considering Evangelical theology's "distinction between primary and secondary doctrines, essential and non-essential ones, foundations and adiaphora [matters of indifference]" (*ETP*, 42–43). He seems to suggest that these distinctions find a place in the notion of the "hierarchy of truths." He is mistaken in this suggestion because it suggests indifferentism; but he also never considers the ecumenical implication of these distinctions. In the following, I argue against his suggestion and, thereafter, go on to show the ecumenical implications of the "hierarchy of truths."[22]

In Pope Francis's 2013 Apostolic Exhortation, *Evangelii Gaudium*,

§246, he remarks on the notion of the "hierarchy of truths." He says, "If we concentrate on the convictions we share, and if we keep in mind the principle of the hierarchy of truths, we will be able to progress decidedly towards common expressions of proclamation, service and witness." Pope Francis joins the chorus of voices which include luminaries like G. C. Berkouwer,[23] Oscar Cullmann, and Karl Rahner,[24] regarding the Roman Catholic Church's bold, new approach to ecumenism in Vatican II's *Unitatis Redintegratio* ("Decree on Ecumenism"), which represents a significant breakthrough, especially in view of one of its key principles, namely, the "hierarchy of truths." This stated principle regarding the hierarchy of truths was not only unexpected but also, says Berkouwer in his second Vatican II book, *Nabetrachting op het Concilie* [*Retrospective of the Council*], "a highly remarkable viewpoint brought in direct connection with the ecumenical problematic" (102).[25] Neither Allison nor De Chirico attend to this point. Here is the well-known paragraph from the Decree on Ecumenism:

> The way and method in which the Catholic faith is expressed should never become an obstacle to dialogue with our brethren. It is, of course, essential that the doctrine should be clearly presented in its entirety. Nothing is so foreign to the spirit of ecumenism as a false irenicism, in which the purity of Catholic doctrine suffers loss and its genuine and certain meaning is clouded. At the same time, the Catholic faith must be explained more profoundly and precisely, in such a way and in such terms as our separated brethren can also really understand. Moreover, in ecumenical dialogue, Catholic theologians standing fast by the teaching of the Church and investigating the divine mysteries with the separated brethren must proceed with love for the truth, with charity, and with humility. When comparing doctrines with one another, they should remember that in Catholic doctrine there exists a "hierarchy" of truths, since they vary in their relation to the fundamental Christian faith. Thus, the way will be opened by which through fraternal rivalry all will be stirred to a deeper understanding and a clearer presentation of the unfathomable riches of Christ. (*UR*, §11)[26]

In this paragraph, two things must be highlighted. One, there is an order of priority or hierarchy among truths resulting from their different relation to the foundation of the Christian faith ("faith in the triune God, One and Three, and in the incarnate Son of God, our Redeemer and Lord" [*UR*, §12]). Two, attending to this hierarchy of revealed truths helps us to understand better what unites and divides Christians in matters of doctrine. Two points need to be emphasized if we are to understand properly what is meant by a "hierarchy of truths," namely, one, the nature of the order of priority and, two, that there is no quantitative reductionism in this hierarchy. Let me briefly explain each of these points.[27]

Regarding point one, Christian truths are seen in relationship not only to each other but chiefly in respect of the central truths of the Christian faith. The nature of this relation is such, Rahner rightly states, that "one can first of all quite properly say that it consists of the fundamental truths of faith, those truths, therefore, on which everything else is based and which themselves are not actually derived from other truths" (*Hierarchy of Truths*, 164).[28]

Following Rahner, let's call this an "'objective' hierarchy of truth" (ibid., 165). Thus, the Immaculate Conception of Mary and papal infallibility derive their justification from foundational truths such as the Trinity and the Incarnation. For example, "the dogma of Mary's Immaculate Conception, which may not be isolated from what the Council of Ephesus declares about Mary, the Mother of God, presupposes before it can be properly grasped in a true life of faith, the dogma of grace to which it is linked and which in its turn necessarily rests upon the redemptive incarnation of the Word."[29] The upshot of the objective hierarchy of truths is that any truth of divine revelation—the entire hierarchy—must be connected to the foundations of the Christian faith.

Regarding point two, exactly how attention to the hierarchy of truths helps us to have a better estimate of what divides Christians is unclear. Berkouwer notes, "It is not enough to merely gauge the meaning and scope of this expression. It is undoubtedly flabbergasting that this 'concentration' (on the fundamentals) that pretty much occupies all churches today is unexpectedly set forth in a conciliar decree and that this did not elicit more opposition despite its 'strangeness'" (*Nabetrachting*, 103).

Indeed, that lack of clarity led to misunderstanding the hierarchy of truths in a "quantitative" fashion as if a reduction of Christianity to its essential content was the point of the hierarchy. In this regard, the "hierarchy of truths" is taken to mean ranking truths in the order of their importance such that there was a reduction of some truths to ultimate importance and others to relative importance.[30]

Consequently, so it was said, we may adopt an attitude of indifference regarding those truths lower in importance in that hierarchy with respect to the foundation of our faith, say, the Assumption of Mary. In other words, the latter could no longer remain a church-dividing issue because of its low rank—nonfundamental truths—in regard to the foundation of faith and hence the fundamental revealed truths at its base. This interpretation of the hierarchy is evident in the following passage: "A hierarchy of truths implies that an ecumenical consensus need not take place in every detail but, rather, on the more basic and fundamental truths of Christianity."[31]

But this interpretation of the hierarchy of truths is mistaken, as Berkouwer himself notes, because it breeds theological indifference. "Hierarchy is the very opposite of indifferentism" (*Nabetrachting*, 108). Thus, the hierarchy of truths is not about separating nonnegotiable teaching from optional teachings of the Church. Rather, it brings an integral perspective to bear upon the whole body of truths by considering the question of their interconnectedness with the central mystery of Christ and the Trinity. Berkouwer explains: "In the first place, embedded in this expression in the decree is the question of the connection that binds together the 'elements' of doctrine, and above all the 'nexus' with Christ as the foundation, and of the variation in the connection with this foundation." Furthermore, adds Berkouwer, "The background of the hierarchy of truths lies in the perception that in the doctrine of the Church one can speak about the *center*, about the fundamental mystery of salvation, and also about the fact that not everything that the Church teaches can be called *central* in the same sense and without nuance" (ibid., 103). In other words, the fundamental issue of the hierarchy is the question regarding the relation of all revealed truths to the foundation of the Christian faith, the Christological concentration, as Berkouwer and others have called it (ibid., 102, 106, respectively).[32]

This conclusion should not lead us to overlook the legitimate sense in which some truths are weightier than others. Most important, the last consideration is a material principle—Christological concentration—that is, a principle of interpretation, not a selective principle (Kasper, *Introduction to Faith*, 103). As Walter Kasper explains: "It may even be—and has indeed often been in the history of the Church—that fundamental principles have been resolved on the basis of relatively peripheral questions. At the Council of Ephesus in 431, for example, the true incarnation of God was discussed on the basis of the title 'Godbearer' (*Theotokos*). The so-called peripheral truths should therefore not be treated with indifference" (ibid., 103–4).

Furthermore, this mistaken interpretation implies an opposition between the hierarchy of truths of Vatican II's Decree on Ecumenism and Pius XI's 1928 encyclical *Mortalium Animos*. "In the encyclical '*Mortalium animos*' the distinction between '*capita fundamentalia*' and '*capita non-fundamentalia*' is rejected. The value of this kind of distinction was opposed with the question of whether God had not revealed all truths, thus without nuancing them" (Berkouwer, Nabetrachting, 101). In his own words, Pius XI wrote:

> In connection with things which must be believed, it is nowise licit to use that distinction which some have seen fit to introduce between those articles of faith which are fundamental and those which are not fundamental, as they say, as if the former are to be accepted by all, while the latter may be left to the free assent of the faithful: for the supernatural virtue of faith has a formal cause, namely the authority of God revealing, and this is patient of no such distinction. For this reason it is that all who are truly Christ's believe, for example, the Conception of the Mother of God without stain of original sin with the same faith as they believe the mystery of the August Trinity, and the Incarnation of our Lord just as they do the infallible teaching authority of the Roman Pontiff, according to the sense in which it was defined by the Ecumenical Council of the Vatican. Are these truths not equally certain, or not equally to be believed, because the Church has solemnly sanctioned and defined them, some in one age and some in another, even in those times immediately before our own? Has not God revealed them all? (*Mortalium Animos*, §9)

Pius's point is, essentially, that all revealed truths must be held with the same divine faith because they are revealed and the Church infallibly declares them to be true. This very point was made by Archbishop Andrea Pangrazio of Gorizia (Italy) to the Council in its discussion of the schema on ecumenism, November 1963, when he introduced the principle of the "hierarchy of truths." Still, Archbishop Pangrazio did not fail to add that some of these truths are more important than others. More important, in what sense?

We can get at that sense by following a distinction first drawn by Herbert Mühlen, and referred to by Thomas Guarino, between a "doctrine's content from the authority with which it is proposed." Alternatively put, in the words of Guarino, "the distinction is between *centrality* to the foundation of the faith as opposed to the *certainty* with which the Church teaches it." In this regard, dogmas, such as the Immaculate Conception (1854) and Mary's Assumption (1950), may be very high in certainty but "relatively low with regard to the central truths of the Christian faith" (*Revelation and Truth,* 142–43). So, some revealed truths may be important because they provide the foundation to nonfoundational teaching; in that regard they are central to the Christian faith. Yes, as *Mysterium Ecclesiae* reiterates, "all dogmas, since they are revealed, must be believed with the same divine faith." But what kind of ecumenical importance does this emphasis leave us with? Are we back to Pius XI, unable to make a distinction "between the act of faith by which a Christian believes in the Incarnation and that of the infallible papal magisterium [?]" (Guarino, *Revelation and Truth,* 147). I don't think that is the case. Congar's respectful criticism of *Mortalium Animos* is apt here:

> While valid on its own level, Pius XI's criticism does not quite accord with reality. It is somewhat one-sided. Faith can be considered from two perspectives, either from that of its content, the objects to which it relates—I would say the *quod*—or from that of the formal motive, that is to say, what motivates us to believe—one might say the *quo*. ... From this point of view it is clear that the mystery of the holy Trinity is more fundamental and more important for the nature of Christianity than that of the Immaculate Conception, and the mystery of the incarnation more fundamental and more important than the infallibility of the papal *magisterium*! (*Diversity and Communion,* 119)[33]

Thus, we can hold on to Pius's point—that all revealed truths must be held with the same divine faith because they are revealed—without forfeiting the distinction between foundational and nonfoundational teachings. We may do so by focusing on the distinction between the *certainty* with which the Church teaches, the *quo* or formal authority infallibly declaring this or that dogma, and the *centrality of content*, the *quod* or material content of a doctrine. In terms of the former, we can now say that all revealed truths are equal; but in terms of the latter we can say that some truths are more fundamental and more important than others. In this sense, then, there is no inconsistency between *Unitatis Redintegratio* and *Mortalium Animos*.

What, then, are the practical implications of the idea of a "hierarchy of truths" in an approach to ecumenical dialogue where significant theological differences remain between Reformed and Catholic Christians in their advancement of unity in truth? (Berkouwer, *Nabetrachting*, 108). The most important implication is that the hierarchy of truths is essential for discerning the extent of agreement between us regarding the foundations of faith as well as the basic differences that remain on particular questions. Properly understood, using the "hierarchy" also illustrates the revealed truths that vary in importance, depending on their closeness to that foundation. These so-called peripheral truths, such as the four Marian dogmas, are not negotiable, and hence we are not indifferent to them. Still, the question arises as to how exactly we deal with these differences in ecumenical conversation when for the Church they remain church-dividing issues. This, too, is Berkouwer's question:

> The question can come up, then, of whether believers, Catholic and non-Catholic, cannot find one another in confessing the *central* doctrines and of whether a marked difference in "weight" and importance does not exist within the circle of the Church's doctrines, for example, between the doctrines of the seven sacraments and the hierarchical structure of the church, and the doctrine of the incarnation as the central, major mystery of the faith. In this way, exclusive attention to the *ranking order* is placed ahead of the *breadth* of doctrine; and ranking order of doctrine is not fixed arbitrarily, but from the perspective of proximity to the center. One could ask the question of whether the idea of a hierarchy of truths in the Roman Catholic system of doctrine is not a huge risk ... now that this 'ranking order' will need to be subjected to the judgment of other churches in connection with their 'proximity' and believing connection to Christ as the foundation. (*Nabetrachting*, 104)

Berkouwer does not say what risk he has in mind. But one can surmise from everything else he says that the risk is that the "hierarchy of truths" is misused in such a way that those truths, the so-called peripheral ones, having less weight in the hierarchy, will somehow be treated with indifference. We may counter this misuse in ecumenical dialogue by keeping our focus on the relation of a stated teaching to the foundation, of proximity to the center, showing the sense in which it derives its justification from that foundation.

In this regard, Berkouwer's student, the late Canadian Reformed ecumenist George Vandervelde, rightly notes, "the discussion of differences must remain open and move toward greater agreement concerning the core of faith." He adds: "Precisely such a notion as the 'hierarchy of truths' can help maintain the ecumenical dynamic in the face of differences. This notion can break through a static fixation of 'basic differences' by constantly forcing dialogue partners to the unity that is to be found in the 'foundation of faith', while at the same time opening up the possibility of articulating the confessional expression of that unity" ("*BEM* and the 'Hierarchy of Truths,'" 83–84). Putting into practice Vandervelde's ecumenical proposal requires that the Catholic ecumenist be clear that the Church rejects ecclesiological relativism ("all churches are basically the same"), false irenicism (a false conciliatory approach), doctrinal indifferentism ("doctrine divides"), a common-denominator ecumenism ("mere Christianity"), and, last but not least, ecumenical dialogue when it is understood as a negotiating or cognitive bargaining of doctrines ("these doctrines are non-negotiable as opposed to more peripheral aspects of Catholic teaching").

Of course, in order to move beyond a static fixation of basic differences, Catholic ecumenical dialogue requires that we "understand the outlook of our separated brethren," as the Decree on Ecumenism states. Maintaining the ecumenical dynamic requires that we understand and practice authentic ecumenism as a gift of God's grace that is at the service of truth (*UUS*, §39). The journey of ecumenical dialogue is thus an ongoing "dialogue of conversion," on *both* sides, trusting in the reconciling power of the truth which is Christ to overcome the obstacles to visible unity.

In the Introduction, I distinguished three dimensions in the work of ecumenism following the Congregation for the Doctrine of the Faith in its "Doctrinal Note on Some Aspects of Evangelization." This Doctrinal Note states: "Above all, there is [1] *listening*, as a fundamental condition for any dialogue, then, [2] *theological discussion*, in which, by seeking to understand the beliefs, traditions and convictions of others, agreement can be found, at times hidden under disagreement. Inseparably united with this is another essential dimension of the ecumenical commitment: [3] *witness and proclamation* of elements which are not particular traditions or theological subtleties, but which belong rather to the Tradition of the faith itself" (§12). In the first place, then, listening means letting your ecumenical interlocutor speak for himself as a partner.

For example, consider Berkouwer's critique of the specious dilemma of symbol or reality in Reformed sacramentology. He defends a Reformed version of "Real Presence," but not substantial presence, in the Eucharist, and affirms the sacramental significance of the signs of bread and wine and the connection between them and that which is signified, namely, the body and blood of Christ, resulting then in the defense of a Reformed understanding of "sacramental realism." This means that a sacrament is not merely a declarative sign, but is an efficacious one, efficacious in communicating the fruits of our redemption. In short, the sacraments are means of grace. This results in Berkouwer's definitive rejection of understanding Christ's true and real presence as merely a spiritual presence. Indeed, there is much that Reformed and Catholic theologies have in common when it comes to the doctrine of the sacraments. For example, consider the Westminster Confession of Faith (1647) and the Second Helvetic Confession (1566). They agree that the sacraments are means of grace, rather than merely outward and empty signs.[34] In short, they agree that God really does impart his grace by sacramental means. God is the principal efficient cause and the sacraments are examples of instrumental efficient causality.[35] They also agree, as Bavinck states, that God alone is the author, initiator, and efficient cause of the sacraments. In particular, Berkouwer takes seriously the fundamental question that informs his dialogue with Catholics: what "grounds the conjunction between the sign and the signified firmly in the acts of God."

Berkouwer's answer to this question advances the discussion between Catholic and Reformed sacramentology. Says Berkouwer, "This is to reject the automatic conjunction which depersonalizes the sacrament, but also to reject the notion of the mere sign in itself, for through the Spirit because of its institution by God the sign is full of efficacy with respect to faith. That is why the *per sacramentum* and the *cum sacramento* can be accepted simultaneously without involving us in contradictions" (*SAC*, 101–2 [87–88]).

Now, on the one hand, the automatic conjunction of sign and the

thing signified, that depersonalizes the sacrament, is rightly rejected by Berkouwer. I will argue later in this chapter, and in greater
detail in Chapter 5, that Catholic sacramentology does not suffer
as such from sacramental automaton,[36] ritualism, juridicism, cheap
grace, a deistic view of *ex opere operato*,[37] such that the sacraments are
divorced from their Christological foundation, that is, "from their
proper and sole source, namely from Christ, the true and only giver
of grace, and gives them an independent status" (Adam, 27). In this
light, we can understand why Edward Schillebeeckx speaks of this
view rejected by Berkouwer as "the headless corpse of sacramentalism,"[38] meaning thereby that the sacraments have been severed from
the "Christological foundation of the *ex opere operato efficacy*" (*Christ the
Sacrament*, 85).[39] On the other hand, the sacraments are not empty and
outward signs, not means of grace, suggesting that faith is the cause
of the grace imparted.

Furthermore, Berkouwer advances the ecumenical dialogue on
sacramentology, particularly, the fundamental matter of Eucharistic
presence because he understands that the crux of the matter between
Catholic and Reformed sacramentology "is not a difference between
praesentia realis or not, but a difference regarding the *mode* of this
presence" (*SAC*, 101–2 [87–88]). Most important, this conclusion permits
us to underscore one of the main claims of Vatican II's Decree on
Ecumenism, namely, that listening opens one up to understanding
that "sometimes one tradition has come nearer than the other to
an apt appreciation of certain aspects of a revealed mystery, or has
expressed them in a clearer manner. As a result, these various theological formulations are often to be considered as complementary
rather than conflicting" (*UR*, §17).[40] I think this is what the doctrinal
note means in saying that sometimes the ecumenical dynamic will
be maintained by finding agreement that at times is hidden under
disagreement.

Furthermore, inseparably united with listening is the necessity of
theological discussion, of comparing and contrasting different theological viewpoints, and furthermore critically examining disagreements that are obstacles to full visible unity with the Church, and
hence dialogue—with the two dimensions of listening and theological discussion—is a means for resolving doctrinal disagreements and
determining whether the beliefs of our ecumenical interlocutor are
true or false in light of the authoritative sources of the faith (*UUS*,

§35). Hence, ecumenical apologetics is also a dimension of theological discussion.

Finally, again following the recent doctrinal note regarding some aspects of evangelization, there is the third dimension of witness and proclamation. In other words, as I understand the doctrinal note it urges us to distinguish *witness and proclamation* of the truths that belong to the Tradition of the faith (e.g., "Real Presence") itself rather than elements which are particular traditions, say Aristotelian Thomism, or theological subtleties (concepts of substance/accidents), which are expressed in various theological formulations. That is, as Aidan Nichols puts it, "the Church should not oblige her theologians to do theology using the technical Aristotelian-Thomist concepts of substance and accidents" (*Holy Eucharist*, 115).[41] "Nevertheless," adds Nichols, the Church seeks "to safeguard her faith in the eucharistic presence" by defending "the non-technical content of those concepts." Consider here, for instance, the concept of substance. This is not a matter of philosophy but of a "common-sense judgment that things exist independently of the thinking subject." Nichols explains, "Revelation confirms this common sense judgment by the doctrine of creation which tells me that the ground of the independence I ascribe to the things I know is the triune God." Thus, "If I say that a thing manifests itself to me as enjoying independent existence as the particular kind of being it is, I implicitly affirm that it is a substance." Nichols concludes:

> In the case of the Eucharist, the Church safeguards her confession of faith in the [real] presence by insisting, *inter alia*, that the independent reality of things be duly recognized. Without such recognition, we cannot speak of the eucharistic change as taking place where it most profoundly does: at the level of the creative activity of God touching this bread and this wine. (Ibid.)

This third dimension is, arguably, based on the distinction between truth and its historically conditioned formulations, between form and content, propositions and sentences, which was invoked by John XXIII in his opening address at Vatican II, *Gaudet Mater Ecclesia*. The pope made this distinction between truth and its formulations in a famous statement at the beginning of Vatican II: "The deposit or the truths of faith, contained in our sacred teaching, are one thing, while the mode in which they are enunciated, keeping the same meaning and the same judgment [*eodem sensu eademque sententia*], is another." I already explained above the roots of this distinction in Vatican I and St. Vincent of Lérins. In sum, elaborates Nichols,

> [I]t is true that, in principle, a Council's formulations of the Church's faith may be transposed into other conceptualities if they can be or need be. It can be argued, though, that the metaphysical analysis found in the concept of transubstantiation derives from questions about the world so fundamental that they are pervasive in every culture, and built into the fabric of human rationality itself. No one is rational who cannot ask, What is it? or see the meaning of that question. (Ibid., 74–75)

Let me be clear that the distinction between truth and its theological formulations is not made because inadequacy and incompleteness of expression leads to inexpressibility of truth, as if to say that truth can never be expressed determinatively, such as the natural truth that things exist independently of the thinking subject. No, theological formulations must bear some relationship to truth because language, and the theological propositions it expresses, has a proper function of referring to reality, some state of affairs.[42] In other words, judgments expressing propositions are true because they correspond to reality; they are as true judgments an *adequatio intellectus et rei*, corresponding to what is, and hence "a claim to the possession in knowledge of what is" (Mansini, "Dogma," 242). But however important the question of truth is and the proper function of propositions referencing reality,[43] it is not merely a question of a "bare *adequatio*" between propositions and reality. Rather, Christians are called to be engaged in effectively communicating the Christian faith. John Paul rightly says, "Because by its nature the content of faith is meant for all humanity, it must be translated into all cultures. Indeed, the element which determines communion in truth is *the meaning of truth*. The expression of truth can take different forms. The renewal of these forms of expression becomes necessary for the sake of transmitting to the people of today the Gospel message in its unchanging meaning" (*UUS*, §19). Notice that John Paul does not hold the truth itself to be variable with time and place, but only the formulations.

Although I cannot argue this point here, I think that making the distinction between truth and its formulations in the sense I have explained above also has ecumenical significance.[44] Both Vatican II's

Unitatis Redintegratio and John Paul II's *Ut Unum Sint* held this position. Thus, it is not surprising that the doctrinal note does so as well.

Furthermore, I have argued elsewhere that Berkouwer, too, was persuaded of the ecumenical import of this distinction.[45] In Berkouwer's 1964 ecumenical study, *Vatikaans Concilie en Nieuwe Theologie* (chapter 3), which was his first book on Vatican II, he is especially concerned to show the influence of the *nouvelle théologie* on the discussions of Vatican II. The crux of the relevance of the *nouvelle théologie*, not just for the Catholic Church, but also for the Reformed tradition is, according to Berkouwer, to be found in its conviction that a distinction could be made between truth and its formulations in dogma, between form and content, content and context, a distinction that made possible internal renewal within the Catholic Church by virtue of rediscovering the riches of the sources of the Christian faith. Berkouwer rejected the relativistic implications that some drew from this distinction. In the last year of the Second Vatican Council (1965), Berkouwer was asked in an interview whether he regarded himself to belong to the Catholic renewal movement of the *nouvelle théologie*. He replied,

> There are very many valuable new elements in the *nouvelle théologie*: the growing conviction that theology can never be finished; that the Word of God is inexhaustible; that we see through a glass, darkly (1 Cor 13:12); and that we must live with the awareness that theology cannot exist by repeating the formulations that were at one time expressed. (Puchinger, *Gesprekken over Rome-Reformatie*, 308)

In sum, these elements helped contribute to a renewal that "can be an authentic enrichment of our understanding of unchangeable truth" in order to meet truly the contemporary challenges faced by the Church. Thus, according to Berkouwer, the distinction between truth and its formulations highlights in the approach of the *nouvelle théologie* "the abundant richness of God's Word." Indeed, he adds, that point "actually strikes both sides of the divide between Rome and the Reformation" (*VCNT*, 76 [66]).

Returning then to the doctrinal note's third dimension of ecumenism, in my judgment, a good example of what this note has in mind here is found in Edward Schillebeeckx's 1967 study on Christ's Eucharistic Presence.[46] Pared down for my purpose here, I want to highlight Schillebeeckx's one point regarding what the Council of Trent taught in its Decree on the Sacrament, especially in the Canons, of the Eucharist about Christ's real presence in the Eucharist (Denzinger, §§1635–61; for the Canons §§1651–61).

Schillebeeckx correctly argues that the genesis of these canons reveals three different levels in Trent's definition. The first canon affirms a specific and distinctive Eucharistic presence: the real presence of Christ's body and blood under the sacramental species of bread and wine. He explains: This is (1) "a presence which is understood in so deep and real a sense that Jesus was able to say, This here, this is my body [cf. Luke 22:19]; I hand it over to you for you to eat, so that you may have communion with me. For this reason, Christ is 'truly, really, and substantially' present." Furthermore, (2) "The Council of Trent was unable to express this Eucharistic real presence in any other way than on the basis of a change of the substance of bread and wine into the substance of Christ's body and blood (canon 2)." The question that immediately arises concerns the relationship between the first and second canon. Briefly, Schillebeeckx argues that because a real ontological change of one substance into another is entailed by the real Eucharistic presence of Christ, therefore "this change of bread and wine was very suitably ['fittingly', 'most appropriately'] called transubstantiation (the concluding sentence of canon 2)" (*Christus Tegenwoordigheid*, 32–35 [44–45]). This is how Trent chooses to describe the conversion taking place truly, really, substantially (*vere, realiter, substantialiter*) (Denzinger, §1636). This conclusion raises the question whether a real ontological change of bread and wine—the basic reality of the thing, what it is in itself—is a dogmatic requisite of faith? In other words, does it belong to the content of faith, being therefore a true datum of faith?

Schillebeeckx says "yes" to this question, but I cannot lay out his reasons now. Still, what I must say is that he makes the crucial point that since we are after all not bound by the Church's faith to the philosophical conceptuality of Aristotelian Thomism for expressing the Catholic dogma of Christ's real presence in the Eucharist, we may express that faith in other conceptualities, as I said above. Consider the circumstance in which a "new interpretation may be necessary because the old interpretations have ceased to speak to us within our contemporary experience of faith," as some have argued about the conceptuality used to give an account of transubstantiation. It may also be that in ecumenical dialogue regarding Christ's presence, the mode of presence, and particularly its relation to the bread and wine (to quote the Decree on Ecumenism again), "one tradition has come nearer than the other to an apt appreciation of certain aspects of a revealed mystery," say, the sacramental realism of the Eucharist's Presence of Christ, "or has expressed them in a clearer manner." The upshot is that "these various theological formulations are often to be considered as complementary rather than conflicting" (*UR*, §17). In either case we must ask whether, as Schillebeeckx rightly notes, "full justice is done to the deepest meaning of the datum of faith." Yes, he adds, it may be true that "No single formulation can exhaust the faith, but this does not make every expression of faith true, meaningful or in accordance with faith" (*Christus Tegenwoordigheid*, 126 [158]).

This important point led Schillebeeckx to reaffirm transubstantiation. The latter concept is irreplaceable because the dogma of Eucharistic presence affirms the substantial change of bread and wine—"This here, this is my body"[47]—and hence this dogma, says Schillebeeckx, "obliges the Catholic to admit the profound realism, or the ontological dimension, of the Eucharistic presence in such a way that after the consecration the *reality* present is no longer ordinary or natural bread and wine, but our Lord himself in the presence of bread and wine which has become sacramental" ("Transubstantiation," 332). What this means is that notions like transignification (change in meaning) and transfinalization (change in purpose) will not capture the ontological dimension, namely, the "metaphysical density," of Eucharistic presence. Alternatively put, Wolfhart Pannenberg emphasizes that we cannot avoid answering "the question of how that which the words of institution state as a promise can become a reality for us, how [Christ's real presence] can be related to an understanding of reality which is at all accessible to us" ("A Protestant View," 141). Still, the claim that transubstantiation is irreplaceable does not mean that these two latter notions are not essential. The only question is in what sense. Schillebeeckx replies, "In the Eucharist, transubstantiation (*conversio entis*—what is the present reality? Christ's body) and transignification (the giving of a new meaning or new sign) are indissolubly connected, but it is impossible simply to identify them. ... Reality is not man's handiwork—in this sense, [metaphysical] realism is essential to the Christian faith" (*Christus Tegenwoordigheid*, 121 [150–51]). Earlier in his address to the bishops at Vatican II he said, "But in its ontological reality, to the question 'What *is* this bread ultimately, what *is* this wine ultimately?' one can no longer answer, 'Bread and wine,' but instead, 'The real presence of Christ offered under the sacramental sign of bread and wine.' Therefore, the *reality* (that is the *substance*, because that is the meaning of 'substance') which is before me, is no longer bread and wine, but the real presence of Christ offered to me under the sign of food and drink" ("Transubstantiation," 337).[48]

Thus, Christ offers his intimate presence to us as the revelation of the mystery of God himself, Trinitarian love, by means of his true, real, and substantial presence in bread and wine. These sacramental signs realize his presence. "The bread and wine have become this real presence offered by Christ, who gave his life for us on the cross; offered by Christ in order that we participate in this sacrifice and in the new covenant which is life for us all" ("Transubstantiation," 337). In other words, according to the Catholic tradition, the foundation and presupposition of Eucharistic faith—an interpersonal relationship between Christ and us, communion with himself—is that Christ is truly, really, and substantially present in the Eucharist, and hence it is only with respect to the latter that the *salvific* purpose of that real presence may be realized in which we receive his free gift of salvation—sharing in a perfect communion of love between Father, Son, and Holy Spirit—through communion in his body and blood. It is that saving *purpose* that belongs to the Tradition of the faith—to use the language of the doctrinal note—such that we may bear witness and proclaim that Christ's real presence when accepted effects "the union of believers with Christ, and their union with each other in the Church" (Nichols, *Holy Eucharist*, 76). As St. Paul states, that purpose is realized in Eucharistic unity: "The bread which we break, is it not a participation in the body of Christ? Because there is one bread, we who are many are one body, for we all partake of the one bread" (1 Cor 10:16–17). Indeed, this Eucharistic union with Christ and his body is what we must bear witness to and proclaim.

Finally, the Church teaches that "each Catholic has the right and duty to give the witness and full proclamation of his [Eucharistic] faith." "With non-Catholic Christians," the document adds, "Catholics must enter into a respectful dialogue of charity and truth, a dialogue which is not only an exchange of ideas, but also of gifts, in order that the fullness of the means of salvation can be offered to one's partners in dialogue. In this way, they are led to an ever deeper conversion to Christ" ("Doctrinal Note," §12).[49] Participating in the real presence of Christ in the Eucharist joins us with the mystery of God himself, Trinitarian love, and hence with the Father, in Christ, through the power of the Holy Spirit. Indeed, the Church's Eucharistic faith is the very mystery of the Church. In this connection, we may conclude with Berkouwer who shares the heart of the ecumenical calling:

> The very mystery of the Church invites, rather compels us, to ask about the perspective ahead for the difficult way of estrangement and rapprochement, of dialogue, contact, controversy, and for the ecumenical striving to overcome the divisions of the Church. (*VCNT*, 316 [249])

In conclusion of this chapter and in preparation for the next, I want to emphasize that in a theology of ecumenical dialogue the notion of the hierarchy of truths plays a fundamental role.[50]

1. Such a theology does not begin with doctrinal differences, but rather with the basis of common ground in the fundamental Christological and Trinitarian statements of faith.

2. It attempts then to understand existing theological differences better in light of, and in connection with those fundamental statements, in order to recognize possible convergences beneath the theological differences. We must keep our focus on the relation of a stated teaching to the foundation, showing the sense in which it derives its justification from the foundation.

3. Accordingly, Vandervelde rightly notes, "the discussion of differences must remain open and move toward greater agreement concerning the core of faith. ... Precisely such a notion as the 'hierarchy of truths' can help maintain the ecumenical dynamic in the face of differences. This notion can break through a static fixation of 'basic differences' by constantly forcing dialogue partners to the unity that is to be found in the 'foundation of faith,' while at the same time opening up the possibility of articulating the confessional expression of that unity" ("*BEM* and the 'Hierarchy of Truths,'" 83–84). In the next three chapters, I follow this ecumenical approach in the discussion of Scripture and tradition, nature and grace, ecclesiology, and sacramental economy.

NOTES

1. The pope in this passage is referring to John XXIII, *Gaudet Mater Ecclesia*, Allocution on the Occasion of the Solemn Inauguration of the Second Ecumenical Council (October 11, 1962), §14. He also refers to Vatican II's Decree on Ecumenism, *Unitatis Redintegratio*, §17.

2. Richard J. Mouw, *All That God Cares About: Common Grace and Divine Delight*, 135. This book is a follow-up to his book, *He Shines in All That's Fair: Culture and Common Grace*, The 2000 Stob Lectures. Eduardo Echeverria, "Do You Have to Be a Calvinist in Order to Be a Kuyperian?", *Pro Rege* 49, no. 3 (March 2021): 1–18. The next three paragraphs are adapted from this article.

3. Herman Bavinck, "The Catholicity of Christianity and the Church," at 245. Bavinck praises "Jesuits [who] are diligently at work reconstructing theology and politics, history, and philosophy. In every field they have taken up the challenge and are doing such impressive work that only the naive Protestant or rabid antipapist can fail to acknowledge or appreciate it."

4. An argument can be made for the complementary nature of "sphere sovereignty" and the Catholic principle of subsidiarity; they are both anti-totalitarian principles seeking to recognize intermediate structures between the state and the individual. See *Compendium of the Social Doctrine of the Church*, Chapter 4, Principles of the Church's Social Doctrine, §§160–96.

5. Albert Wolters, "What Is to Be Done? Toward a Neo-Calvinist Agenda," at 38.

6. "Towards a Common Understanding of the Church," at 187.

7. In a personal email to me of December 4, 2015, Allison states that he doesn't so much as ignore the ecumenical dialogue of the Catholic Church and other Christian traditions (Methodist, Anglican, Reformed, and Lutheran) but rather has a fundamental disagreement with the aim of the dialogue itself, which is clear from the statement quoted in the text. De Chirico also has a fundamental disagreement with the aim of ecumenical dialogue. He has recently written regarding Al Mohler's Presidential Address at the 73rd annual convention of the Evangelical Theological Society, "many evangelicals hold a very 'sentimental' perception of Roman Catholicism." He explains, according to Mohler, "Some mistake it for one of the many Christian denominations (perhaps a little 'stranger' than others); others, frightened by the increasing challenges of secularization, see Rome as a bulwark for defending Christian 'values'; still others, wanting to be legitimized at the ecumenical and interreligious table, overlook the theological differences in order to highlight what appears to unite all." Hence, he urges that Evangelicals exercise spiritual vigilance about the temptation of aligning with Roman Catholicism ("Roman Catholicism as 'Temptation' for Evangelical Theology," *Vatican Files*, January 1, 2022).

8. See Eduardo Echeverria, *Pope Francis: The Legacy of Vatican II*, revised and expanded 2nd ed., 245–97.

9. With this conclusion they share the view of the late R.C. Sproul's 2012 book, *Are We Together? A Protestant Analyzes Roman Catholicism*. The title of my book

derives from Sproul's title but the subtitle is reversed: *Are We Together? A Roman Catholic Analyzes Evangelical Protestants*.

10. The quote within the quote is from *Unitatis Redintegratio*, §1.

11. John Paul II, *Ut Unum Sint*, §79, gives the following as examples of issues that need further ecumenical dialogue: "1) the relationship between Sacred Scripture, as the highest authority in matters of faith, and Sacred Tradition, as indispensable to the interpretation of the Word of God; 2) the Eucharist, as the Sacrament of the Body and Blood of Christ, an offering of praise to the Father, the sacrificial memorial and Real Presence of Christ and the sanctifying outpouring of the Holy Spirit; 3) Ordination, as a Sacrament, to the threefold ministry of the episcopate, presbyterate and diaconate; 4) the Magisterium of the Church, entrusted to the Pope and the Bishops in communion with him, understood as a responsibility and an authority exercised in the name of Christ for teaching and safeguarding the faith; [and] 5) the Virgin Mary, as Mother of God and Icon of the Church, the spiritual Mother who intercedes for Christ's disciples and for all humanity."

12. I think the same must be said of the little study of Leonardo De Chirico, *A Christian's Pocket Guide to the Papacy: Its Origin and Role in the 21st Century*. For a competing account of the papacy, see Gerhard Cardinal Müller, *The Pope: His Mission and His Task*, trans. Brian McNeil. On the fruits of these dialogues, see the study by Walter Cardinal Kasper, *Harvesting the Fruits: Basic Aspects of Christian Faith in Ecumenical Dialogue*.

13. I am grateful to Msgr. Thomas Guarino, Seton Hall University, for helping me to formulate this dilemma. I consider a solution to this dilemma—again, with his help—in my book, *Pope Francis: The Legacy of Vatican II*.

14. Eduardo Echeverria, "The One Church, the Many Churches: A Catholic Approach to Ecclesial Unity and Diversity—with Special Attention to Abraham Kuyper's Ecclesiastical Epistemology."

15. Vatican II also uses "is" (*est*) when defining the Catholic Church in *Orientalium Ecclesiarum*, §2. For an extensive and insightful discussion of "Subsists In," see Stephen A. Hipp, *The One Church of Christ: Understanding Vatican II*, Chapter 2, "The Church of Christ '*Subsists In*' the Catholic Church," 47–86.

16. Joseph Cardinal Ratzinger, "*Deus Locutus Est Nobis in Filio*: Some Reflections on Subjectivity, Christology, and the Church," in *Proclaiming the Truth of Jesus Christ: Papers from the Vallombrosa Meeting*, at 27.

17. Congregation for the Doctrine of the Faith, Letter *Communionis notio*, 17; cf. Second Vatican Council, Decree *Unitatis redintegratio*, §4.

18. Walter Cardinal Kasper, *Katholische Kirche: Wesen, Wirklichkeit, Sendung*, 233. English translation: *The Catholic Church: Nature, Reality and Mission*, trans. Thomas Hoebel, 158.

19. Eduardo Echeverria, "The One Church, the Many Churches," 239–64.

20. There is also a chapter on *Dei Verbum* in G. C. Berkouwer, *Nabetrachting op het Concilie*. This is Berkouwer's second book on Vatican II, but it remains un-

translated. I am grateful to James A. De Jong for translating into English the untranslated Dutch citations of this book.

21. Furthermore, see Aidan Nichols, OP's two-volume commentary on the *Catechism of the Catholic Church*: Vol. I, *The Splendour of Doctrine: On Christian Believing*; Vol. II, *The Service of Glory: On Worship, Ethics, Spirituality*.

22. E. J. Echeverria, "Hierarchy of Truths Revisited," *Acta Theologica* 35, no. 2 (2015): 11–35. This section is adapted from this article.

23. For Berkouwer's reflections on the ecumenical significance of the hierarchy of truths, see *Nabetrachting op het Concilie*, 106–11.

24. Oscar Cullmann maintained that "this text sets forth for all time *a completely new concept of ecumenism*—new at any rate from the Catholic point of view" ("Comments on the Decree on Ecumenism," *The Ecumenical Review* 17, at 93). Berkouwer cites Cullmann as having said about the hierarchy of truths, "perhaps one of the most promising among all the texts of the council, although curiously so little is said about it" ("vieleicht eine der meistversprechenden unter allen Texten des Konzils, obwohl merkwurdigerweise so wenig von ihr gesprochen wird" (*Nabetrachting op het Concilie*, 102n78). Rahner similarly wrote regarding the "hierarchy of truths" that this notion was "of fundamental importance for the contemporary situation of faith and one of the really great acts of the Council" ("von fundamentaler Wichtigkeit auch fur die gesamte Glaubenssituation der Gegenwart" and "eine der wirklichen Grosztaten des Konzils") (also cited in Berkouwer).

25. If anything, Cullmann went further than Berkouwer, calling this statement "the most revolutionary to be found, not only in the Schema de oecumenismo but in any of the schemas of the present Council" ("Comments," 94).

26. For an account of the historical origin of the term "hierarchy of truths" before Vatican II and twenty years afterwards, see William Henn, OFM Cap., "The Hierarchy of Truths Twenty Years Later," *Theological Studies* 48 (1987): 439–71; idem, "The Hierarchy of Truths," in *Dictionary of Fundamental Theology*, ed. Rene Latourelle and Rino Fisichella, 425–27; Thomas G. Guarino, *Revelation and Truth: Unity and Plurality in Contemporary Theology*, 138–61; Yves Congar, *Diversity and Communion*, trans. John Bowden, 107–33; Karl Rahner, "A Hierarchy of Truths," *Theological Investigations*, Vol. 21, trans. Hugh M. Riley, 162–67; "The Notion of Hierarchy of Truths—An Ecumenical Interpretation," in *Deepening Communion: International Documents with Roman Catholic Participation*, ed. William G. Rusch and Jeffrey Gros, 561–71.

27. I draw on material here presented in Eduardo Echeverria, *Berkouwer and Catholicism: Disputed Questions*, 101–8.

28. See also, *Mysterium Ecclesiae*, Congregation for the Doctrine of the Faith, §4.

29. Secretariat for Christian Unity, "Reflections and Suggestions concerning Ecumenical Dialogue," paragraph IV, 4b; as cited in Congar, *Diversity and Communion*, 128.

30. Helpful in formulating this point is George Vandervelde, "*BEM* [*Baptism, Eucharist, and Ministry*] and the 'Hierarchy of Truths': A Vatican Contribution to

the Reception Process," at 79. This article deals with what some consider to be perhaps the most important document ever produced by the World Council of Churches, *Baptism, Eucharist and Ministry*.

31. James C. Livingston et al., *Modern Christian Thought: The Twentieth Century*, 246–47.

32. See also, Walter Kasper, *An Introduction to Christian Faith*, section entitled "Concentration rather than reduction," 99–104.

33. For Congar's discussion of types of one-sidedness, see *True and False Reform in the Church*, 208–13. For a brief account of Congar's view of the hierarchy of truths, see Henn, "The Hierarchy of Truth Twenty Years Later," 454–55.

34. The Swiss Reformer Ulrich Zwingli (1484–1531) sees the sacraments as a mere outward or empty sign (*nudum signum*), implying the exclusion of grace from the sacrament. Bavinck describes the position of Zwinglians, "True, the sacraments visibly represent the benefits that believers have received from God, but they do this as confessions of our faith and do not impart grace" (*Gereformeerde Dogmatiek*, Vol. IV, 448; translated by John Vriend as *Reformed Dogmatics*, Vol. 4, *Holy Spirit, Church, and New Creation*, ed. John Bolt, 470). For Luther's rejection of Zwinglians or Anabaptists, as he also called them, see his *The Large Catechism*, trans. Robert H. Fischer, Fourth Part: Baptism, 80–101.

35. On this distinction and its sacramental import, see Aquinas, *Summa Theologiae* III, q. 62, a. 1, ad 1, ad 2; and q. 62, a. 5. Roland Millare is right, "The question of causality will be one of the main hermeneutical keys for understanding the differences between Protestant and Catholic theology" ("The Nominalist Justification for Luther's Sacramental Theology," at 170.

36. Automaton: "a machine that performs a function according to a predetermined set of coded instructions, especially one capable of a range of programmed responses to different circumstances" (Oxford Languages).

37. Adam Johann Möhler, *Symbolism*, 218n2: "Now Calvin makes the matter appear, as if the Catholics separated the power working in the sacraments from their primary fountain, and looked upon them as working of themselves."

38. Edward Schillebeeckx, OP, *Christus Sacrament van de Godsontmoeting*, Achtste druk. Translated by Paul Barrett, OP, et al., as *Christ the Sacrament of the Encounter with God*, 88n60. This note, indeed, the whole appendix, "St. Thomas' Christological Interpretation of Sacramental *Ex Opere Operato* Causality" (82–89), is not present in the original Dutch edition.

39. Avery Cardinal Dulles, SJ, reminds us, "The primacy of Christ's role in the sacraments is the true meaning of the frequently misunderstood term, *ex opere operato*" ("The Theology of Worship: Saint Thomas," in *Rediscovering Aquinas and the Sacraments*, ed. Matthew Levering et al., 1–13, at 6).

40. The council is speaking, in this paragraph, about the relationship of Catholicism and Orthodoxy. I am applying this point about complementary theological formulations to Catholicism and Reformed theology. I develop this application to Catholic-Reformed ecumenical dialogue in my book, *Berkouwer and Catholicism*, 20–109.

41. Similarly, Wolfhart Pannenberg, "A Protestant View of the Doctrine of the Lord's Supper," in *The Church*, trans. Keith Crim, at 141: "The promise of the real presence of Jesus Christ himself takes precedence over all theories about what it means. This does not make theoretical reflection superfluous, but, with Edward Schillebeeckx, we must recognize it as indispensable if that which is promised is to be understood as reality."

42. I develop this point at length in *Revelation, History, and Truth*, Chapter 3, "Divine Revelation and Foundationalism: Towards a Historically Conscious Foundationalism," 93–152.

43. Geoffrey Wainwright rightly remarks that "the nature of Christian truth requires that language and substance be held together … in cognitive propositions which hitherto divided churches may together affirm" (*Is the Reformation Over?*, 25).

44. *Unitatis Redintegratio* refers to this connection with John XXIII's opening address at footnote 27.

45. Eduardo Echeverria, "The Accidental Protestant," 41–45.

46. Edward Schillebeeckx, OP, *Christus Tegenwoordigheid in de Eucharistie*, translated by N. D. Smith as *The Eucharist*; idem, "Transubstantiation, Transfinalization, Transignification," 324–38. The latter article is an address delivered in French during the fourth session (1965) of Vatican II to fathers of the council at *Domus Mariae* in Rome.

47. Robert Sokolowski rightly remarks, "In the Eucharistic prayer Christ is quoted not as saying, '*This bread* is my body', but '*This* is my body'. If Christ had said 'this bread' was his body, then the thing referred to would still be bread, but the simple demonstrative pronoun 'this' without a noun implies that it is not bread any longer" ("The Eucharist and Transubstantiation," in *Christian Faith & Human Understanding*, at 105–6.

48. In this context, Schillebeeckx indicates his agreement with Pope Paul's 1965 encyclical, *Mysterium Fidei*: "As a result of transubstantiation, the species of bread and wine undoubtedly take on a new signification and a new finality, for they are no longer ordinary bread and wine but instead a sign of something sacred and a sign of spiritual food; but they take on this new signification, this new finality, precisely because they contain a new 'reality' which we can rightly call ontological" (§46). Says Schillebeeckx, "In other words, the encyclical admits transfinalization and transignification on condition that they are not considered as an extrinsic designation or as a peripheral change, but rather as having a profound and ontological content. That is the very meaning of the dogma of transubstantiation" (338).

49. Pope Francis, *Evangelii Gaudium*, §246: "Through an exchange of gifts, the Spirit can lead us ever more fully into truth and goodness."

50. Helpful on this role, in this instance, is Kasper, *Katholische Kirche: Wesen, Wirklichkeit, Sendung*, 432–33 [306–7].

CHAPTER 3

SCRIPTURE AND TRADITION

[H]owever clear the Bible may be in its doctrine of salvation, and however certainly it is and remains the living voice of God, for a correct understanding it still often requires a wide range of historical, archeological, and geographical skills and information. The times have changed, and with the times people, their life, thought, and feelings, have changed. Therefore, a tradition is needed that preserves the connectedness between Scripture and the religious life of our time. Tradition in its proper sense is the interpretation and application of the eternal truth in the vernacular and life of the present generation. Scripture without such a tradition is impossible.[1]

I regard as alien to Catholicism both any exclusive assertion of the sola scriptura, *the* sola traditio, *or the* solum magisterium, *and similarly any affirmation of two or three parallel and independent sources. Both the scriptures and tradition are necessary to the life of the church. But, on the other hand, scripture and tradition also need the church and each other if they are to be recognized as canonical scriptures and as authentically apostolic tradition.... The church's [normative] supervision of scriptural exegesis does not place it above scripture, but merely points to the church's recognition of the exclusively apostolic principle as the norm of Christian faith and of life in the church.[2]*

Regarding the classical controverted issue of Scripture and tradition, Allison shows no awareness, in *RCTP* or the recent *40 Questions About Roman Catholicism*, nor does De Chirico (*SWDW*, 109), that the "two-source" theory of revelation where Scripture and tradition are two parallel sources of truth—the dominant theory between the sixteenth-century Council of Trent and the nineteenth century in Catholic theology—has undergone severe criticism *within* the Catholic theological tradition. These Catholic critics argue for the integration of the uniquely normative character of Scripture, as the supreme rule of faith, as *Dei Verbum* calls Scripture, or the highest authority in matters of faith (*norma normans non normata*), in an intrinsically and necessarily related way to tradition and the Church, as indispensable to the interpretation of the Word of God. On this view, Scripture must be interpreted in the concrete life of the Church, her living tradition, through the teaching authority of the ecclesiastical Magisterium, which is under the guidance of the Holy Spirit. Arguably, then, when the Second Vatican Council's Constitution on Divine Revelation, *Dei Verbum*, §10 affirms a necessary and intrinsic relatedness of tradition and the Church to Scripture, it also affirms a *prima scriptura* (21–25). I will return to this point below.

Allison continues to insist that Vatican II's *Dei Verbum* affirms the two-source theory of revelation (*40 Questions*, 77, 82–83, 90, 96), as does De Chirico (*SWDW*, 33–34). How, then, does Allison understand the relation between Scripture and tradition in Roman Catholicism?

Let's begin answering this question by locating the discussion of Scripture and tradition in the context of two fundamental modes of revelation. Allison rightly recognizes that Roman Catholicism and Evangelical Protestantism accept general and special revelation (*RCTP*, 75). General revelation is God's revelation of himself in and through the works of creation. Regarding this revelation, God reveals himself to all men at all times and all places such that men, in principle, may know something of God's existence, of his attributes, and of his moral law (Rom 1:20; 2:14–15), and hence this "revelation is not limited to certain people, places, or times, but is truly general" (De Ridder and Van Woudenberg, at 47). It is ubiquitous because "it comes to us through conditions [created realities and conscience] that are present at all times and places" (ibid., 50). Therefore, in principle, all have access to some knowledge of God via his general revelation. By contrast, according to *Dei Verbum*, §2, special revelation is about God revealing himself specially in and through salvation history, a history that runs through the events and people of Israel, culminating in the concentration point of that history in Jesus Christ who is the mediator and fullness of all revelation. Jointly constitutive of God's special revelation are its inseparably connected words (verbal revelation) and deeds, intrinsically bound to each other because neither is complete without the other; the historical realities of redemption are inseparably connected to God's verbal communication of truth in order that we may, as Catholic theologian Francis Martin puts it, "participate more fully in the realities mediated by the words."[3] Allison recognizes that Catholics and Evangelical Protestants agree, "Two modes of divine revelation are divine acts and divine speech" (*40 Questions*, 82). In other words, a core presupposition of the concept of revelation in *Dei Verbum* §2 is that "without God's acts the words would be empty, without His word the acts would be blind,"[4] as was admirably stated by Reformed theologian Geerhardus Vos (1862–1949). Moreover, special revelation, by contrast with general revelation, "is spatiotemporally limited—it comes to us through historical events at special times and places and then through the testimony of others about these events" (De Ridder and Van Woudenberg, 50). In short, special revelation is historical, verbal, and salvific.

Now, before we reach the New Testament writings, special revelation had an oral form. Allison states, "Protestants agree with Catholics that the form of the earliest transmission of apostolic instruction—the *content*, represented here [1 Cor 11:2; 2 Thess 2:15] by [St.] Paul's teachings—was oral" (*40 Questions*, 99). Indeed, the apostolic *paradosis*, tradition (with a small t), "what is handed on," which means the traditionary process, is the form in which the Gospel of Jesus Christ originally comes to us, and hence is transmitted to the Church "under the double form of living kerygma and its written expression in Scripture (cf. 1 Tim 6:20; 2 Tim 1:12 and 14; 2 Tim 3:15)," which is the written prophetic and apostolic testimony to redemptive history with its concentration point in the redeeming act of God in Christ (Geiselmann, *Meaning of Tradition*, 23). In particular, Geiselmann correctly notes, "Holy Scripture is the *paradosis* of the apostolic kerygma, become writing" ("Scripture, Tradition, and the Church," 55). Alternatively put, "New Testament Scripture is the written counterpart of apostolic tradition" (*Meaning of Tradition*, 23; see also 24). Allison agrees (*40 Questions*, 95–96). Regarding Holy Scripture, which is the "literary concretization" (using Karl Rahner's wonderfully apt phrase [*Foundations*, 363]) of the Tradition of the Gospel, *Dei Verbum* writes, "Sacred Scripture is the speech of God as it is put down in writing under the breath of the Holy Spirit." And in regard to tradition, it "transmits in its entirety the Word of God which has been entrusted to the apostles by Christ the Lord and the Holy Spirit." "It transmits it to the successors of the apostles so that," *Dei Verbum* adds, "enlightened by the Spirit of truth, they may faithfully preserve, expound and spread it abroad by their preaching" (§9). Again, to quote *Dei Verbum*, "The commission [given by Christ to the Apostles to preach to all men that Gospel which is the source of all saving truth and moral teaching] was fulfilled, too, by those Apostles and apostolic men who under the inspiration of the same Holy Spirit committed the message of salvation to writing" (§7). In its being so transmitted the apostolic *paradosis* "becomes the *parathêkê*, the apostolic bequest which is committed to the Church's safe-keeping" (*Meaning of Tradition*, 23).[5]

"The Scriptures were given to the Church," adds Geiselmann, "so that it could preserve the Gospel entrusted to it" (ibid., 37). The guardians of the deposit of faith that is handed on are the bishops of the Catholic episcopate, a living teaching authority. As Nichols explains, "[Their] task is to secure the deposit against attempts to corrupt it; and this desire to protect orthodoxy, the integrity of the gospel, against what would later be called heresy is already there in the New Testament" (*Shape of Theology*, 168). Furthermore, the duty of the Catholic episcopate is to transmit the faith "to one's contemporaries across space and to one's successors across time" (*ibid.*).

Moreover, this apostolic *paradosis* is itself divine in origin because it is what God himself hands on. As Nichols correctly states, "Christ himself is engaged and present in the handing on and receiving of tradition. He is not simply the Word found in a book, but the Word found in oral tradition" (ibid.). It is, in this sense, that *Sacred* Tradition (with a capital T) is revelation itself. In other words, the apostolic tradition has its ultimate source in the "original *paradosis*," namely, in God's revelatory self-communication, which revelation culminates in God the Father's handing over his own Son, Jesus Christ, to man, indeed, for us all "because of our offenses" (Rom 4:25; see also 8:32). Here we must emphasize, as Joseph Ratzinger himself does, that Christ himself is present and engaged for his part in the fact that as he is handed over to the world for us by the Father, Christ simultaneously hands himself over (Eph 5:2).[6] "No one takes [my life] from me, but I lay it down of myself" (John 10:18).

To be sure, Roman Catholics and Evangelical Protestants agree, "In the early church, divine revelation was communicated orally and eventually was written down" (*40 Questions*, 96). However, Allison, then, wrongly concludes that Vatican II's *Dei Verbum* holds that "Today, divine revelation continues to be transmitted in two modes: orally, as Tradition, and in writing as Scripture" (*40 Questions*, 96). According to

Allison, "Tradition, then, is the broader of the two modes" (ibid., 96), encompassing Scripture. Tradition is oral, Scripture is written, both are modes of revelation. Of course, given his starting point that *Dei Verbum* continues to affirm the two-source theory of revelation (ibid., 77, 82–83, 90, 96), tradition and Scripture run on separate tracks, as it were, with tradition being a source of continuing revelation whose content is "other than what the apostles communicated in written Scripture. ... [This is] Tradition in terms of the content of divine revelation" (ibid., 99).

Allison is correct that Tradition is a reality larger than the Scripture itself, theologically prior to the Bible, but he mistakenly regards it as an ongoing source of revelation. Rather, as Nichols correctly states, "tradition is the Christian religion itself," namely, "the whole life of the Church in all its essential lines," on the one hand, and "the orthodox faith of that same Church" on the other. He elaborates:

> On the one hand, Tradition is the institutions, rites, and practices that make up the Christian religion in all its concreteness. On the other hand, Tradition is the rule of faith of a Church in continuity with the apostles. Two pairs of Latin words sum up these two complementary senses of tradition. Tradition is the *institutio Christiana*, the "Christian institution," that is, the way of life and worship that is the Church. Tradition is also the *regula fidei*, the normative expression of faith by which theological language, and especially the interpretation of Scripture, are to be judged. Concretely, Tradition is the Church's life; abstractly or reflectively, it is the Church's faith. ... [S]o quite naturally the life and faith of the Church are seen as the proper context in which to read, study, and expound the Scriptures. Tradition as the Christian religion itself, the life and consciousness of the Church considered as a reflection of the Word of God, of God's self-communication, is necessarily a reality at once larger than the Bible and inclusive of it. (*Shape of Theology*, 176)[7]

Tradition envelops the total life and action of the Church, the life and consciousness of the Church, being at once a reality larger than but also inclusive of Scripture, enabling the Church to grasp the deeper meaning of Scripture itself in the development of dogma. This understanding of Tradition integrates the uniquely normative character of Scripture, as the supreme rule of faith, as *Dei Verbum* calls Scripture, in an intrinsically and necessarily related way to traditions.

John Paul II, too, regards Scripture as the *norma non normata*, stressing then the function of tradition as an interpretative source: "the relationship between Sacred Scripture, as the highest authority in matters of faith, and Sacred Tradition, as indispensable to the interpretation of the Word of God." On this view, Scripture must be interpreted in the concrete life of the Church, her living tradition, through the teaching authority of the ecclesiastical Magisterium, which is under the guidance of the Holy Spirit.

The Church's living tradition, on this view, has its own *loci*, but it is more an environment or context in which we properly read Scripture than it is an independent source of revelation in addition to Scripture. "Scripture is the light of the Church, and the Church the life of Scripture," as Bavinck eloquently put it. I will return to this view below.

For now, let us note again that the two-source theory of revelation dominates Allison's interpretation of the Church's teaching on revelation; it even informs his understanding of the Church's Magisterium such that he thinks that the Magisterium "determines the content of Tradition" (*40 Questions*, 104). Allison is mistaken here in his interpretation of *Dei Verbum* because the "Magisterium is not superior to the Word of God, but is its servant." In other words, the teaching office of the Church must be a servant and not master of the Word of God, as *Dei Verbum*, §10 puts it, "in order that the full and living Gospel might always be preserved in the Church through the bishops as the successors of the apostles." As Yves Congar correctly explains:

> The Magisterium is simply the servant, the purveyor of the rule. ...The Magisterium enjoys no autonomy with regard to the deposit [of faith]. There is no moment of its activity as Magisterium—that is, as active tradition—when it is exempt from referring to the deposit and its statement, since the former is merely a witness to the latter. ...The Magisterium does not have an autonomous value: it receives assistance only when it keeps, interprets and defines the *Revelation*, of which it has been made a witness. Similarly, the Church has no power to create truth. (*Meaning of Tradition*, 70–71, 81)

I'll return below to the question regarding the relationship of

Scripture, tradition, the authority of the Magisterium in the concluding section of this chapter.

Regarding the relationship between Scripture and tradition, we can exclude three possibilities that the Council of Trent regarded as dead ends (Nichols, *Shape of Theology*, 176). Allison and De Chirico seem unaware of these exclusions. First, the Council rejected the idea of post-apostolic revelation made to the Church because there is no ongoing public revelation in the Church's teaching on divine revelation. De Chirico is right: "After the revelation of the Christ of the Bible, there can no longer be revelations but only interpretations of the already given revelation" (*SWDW*, 33). De Chirico denies that this is Catholic teaching. He misses out on this because he interprets *Dei Verbum* in light of the two-source theory of revelation suggesting that the Church accepts a post-apostolic revelation in "the living voice of the official teaching of the Roman Catholic Church." He adds, "According to this view, tradition is prior to the Bible, bigger than the Bible, and its present-day voice is not the biblical text but the continuing teaching of the church on whatever it advocates" (*SWDW*, 34). Therefore, he concludes, "[The Bible] is one form of revelation but not the final one" (ibid.). I already argued above against this view, and so I won't repeat myself here.

Unacknowledged by De Chirico and Allison, then, is that the teaching of the Catholic Church in the *Catechism* (§66), which is based on Vatican II's *Dei Verbum*, §4, affirms the finality of biblical revelation. "'The Christian economy, therefore, since it is the new and definitive Covenant, will never pass away; and no new public revelation is to be expected before the glorious manifestation of our Lord Jesus Christ.' Yet even if Revelation is already complete, it has not been made completely explicit; it remains for Christian faith gradually to grasp its full significance over the course of the centuries." This concluding point suggests that there is an historical process of continual interpretation, clarification, and development of doctrinal truths. According to *Dei Verbum*, §8, this apostolic tradition "develops in the Church with the help of the Holy Spirit. For there is a growth in the understanding of the realities and the words which have been handed down." Nichols correctly notes, "There is here *accretion in understanding*. ... There is no suggestion in this text of *accretion in the deposit itself*."[8] *Pace* Allison, tradition is not an autonomous process of generating revelation that bears no relation to the written Word of God. Yves Congar correctly states:

> To imagine that the Church, at a given moment in its history, could hold as of a faith a point which had no stabable support in Scripture, would amount to thinking that an article of faith could exist *without bearing any relation to the centre of revelation,* and thus attributing to the Church and its magisterium a gift equivalent to the charism of revelation, unless we postulate, gratuitously, the existence of an esoteric oral apostolic tradition, for which there exists no evidence whatsoever. *It is an express principle of Catholic teaching that the Church can only define what has been revealed;* faith can only have to do with what is formally guaranteed by God. (*Tradition and Traditions,* 414 [emphasis added])

According to Yves Congar, then, history shows continuity, indeed, identity persisting from the apostolic deposit, which is a determinate revealed datum, revealed truths, taking the form of *didaskalia,* of doctrine, to the developed assertions of Church dogma. God's written revelation necessarily involves propositional revelation in verbalized form. *Dei Verbum* §11 affirms propositional revelation: "Therefore, since everything asserted by the inspired authors or sacred writers must be held to be asserted by the Holy Spirit, it follows that the books of Scripture must be acknowledged as teaching solidly, faithfully and without error that truth which God wanted put into sacred writings for the sake of salvation." Although the revealed truths of the faith may be expressed differently, they must be kept within determinate bounds, or what Oliver Crisp calls a "dogmatic conceptual hard core." That is, we must always determine whether those re-formulations preserve the same meaning and mediate the same judgment of truth—as Vincent of Lérins put it. Authentic dogmatic development must preserve the material continuity, identity, and universality of those truths, unfolding and hence enriching our understanding of the truth.

Second, also rejected by the Council of Trent as a dead end is the gnostic idea that there exists "unwritten apostolic doctrine alongside Scripture," that is, "secret information ... preserved within her [the Church] since the time of the apostles" (*Tradition and Traditions,* 414). Nichols, following Congar, calls this the idea of an "esoteric, non-public apostolic tradition coming out of the closet from time to time" (*Shape of Theology,* 176). Vatican II's *Dei Verbum* (§8) makes no reference to this idea to justify "a growth in the understanding of the realities and the words which have been handed down." Inexplicably, without evidence, Allison ascribes this gnostic idea to Roman Catholicism in its understanding of tradition being the transmitter of revelation (*40 Questions*, 99). He rightly cites Irenaeus (in *Adversus haereses*) opposing this idea of an esoteric oral apostolic tradition "that contains any content other than what the apostles communicated in written Scripture" (*40 Questions*, 99).[9] Ratzinger makes this point in his address to the German-speaking bishops at Vatican II, October 10, 1962:

> An objection arises right away, namely, that some dogmas are proved only by Tradition and not by Scripture. After 1950, one often heard that the dogma [of Mary's assumption] was a typical example of a tenet provable solely through tradition. But such an account in this case really does not help, for it is basically an escape, not an explanation. For tradition clearly knows nothing about the bodily assumption of the Mother of God before the 5th century and when the first accounts do begin to appear they are not at all later records of something handed on orally down to that time. Instead, the insight came to light only after centuries of struggling to understand it, until finally in 1950 the Church declared that the insight was from the Holy Spirit and belongs to the basic content of revelation. Such an approach leads to no proof from tradition as a distinct material principle, but again it appears to be a process of spiritual appropriation and of elaboration of the mystery of Christ amid the Church's historical struggles.[10]

Clearly, Ratzinger here rejects the two-source theory of revelation, which is the view that Allison and De Chirico claim that Vatican II and post-Vatican Catholicism still hold. For Ratzinger it is a question of doctrinal development. Ironically, then, although Allison is correct to cite Irenaeus on this point of an esoteric oral apostolic tradition, Irenaeus, arguably, is an important path, in the same work, opening an appreciation for Mary's place in the plan of salvation. As Manfred Hauke rightly remarks, "Mariology is 'the exemplary case of the development of dogma in Catholicism.'" [11]Allison and De Chirico miss out on this important point since they operate with the presupposition of a two-source theory of revelation in their interpretation of Catholicism. Hence, they never consider approaches to Mariology that deal with dogmatic development.

Finally, also rejected as a dead end is the Protestant position of *sola*

Scriptura when understood as an anti-tradition principle, meaning thereby not only the notion that opposes Scripture and tradition—in other words, "solo Scriptura" or *Scriptura nuda*, "naked Scripture"— but also the idea that Scriptural authority is such that it is epistemically self-sufficient for justifying dogmas. Tradition (e.g., councils, creeds, confessions, catechisms) in no analogous sense whatsoever shares in the authority of Scripture for the purpose of securing certainty about what Scripture actually teaches. Clearly, Allison rejects the idea that the principle of *sola Scriptura* means "that Protestants recognize no authority other than Scripture and denounce any kind of tradition outside of it. This is simply not true" (*40 Questions*, 318; see also, 301–2). Thus, he rejects a monistic principle of authority. "Scripture alone does not mean there is *only* one authority" (*40 Questions*, 91). De Chirico is less clear in rejecting a monistic principle of authority.[12] Allison, however, explicitly states that the Bible is the highest authority but not the only one. He explains: "Protestantism rejects Tradition as a means of divine revelation. At the same time, Protestantism does not reject tradition (small t) in the sense of wisdom from the past. Many Protestant churches embrace the rich legacy of valid biblical interpretation and sound theological formulation handed down from the early church and the medieval church. Examples include the Nicene-Constantinopolitan Creed and the Chalcedonian Creed, [and] Protestant churches consider that tradition to enjoy *presumptive* authority" (*40 Questions*, 83n7; emphasis added). Allison emphatically rejects a monistic principle of authority, attributing "presumptive" authority to creeds and councils. He writes,

> We reject the common misunderstanding that *sola Scriptura* means that as Protestants we can't consult any authority other than the Bible. Rather, we affirm the early church creeds—Nicene-Constantinopolitan, Apostles', Athanasian, Chalcedonian—and the early church councils—Nicea, Constantinople, Ephesus, and Chalcedon—and the stand against the early church heresies as condemned by Scripture and these creeds and councils: Adoptionism, Arianism, Apollinarianism, Nestorianism, Eutychianism, and more. (*40 Questions*, 301)

Since Roman Catholicism and Evangelical Protestantism reject a monistic principle of authority, embracing "multiple authorities," where then is the difference to be found between them, as Allison sees it? It isn't clear. What also isn't clear is why these creeds and councils possess authority, presumptive authority, as Allison attributes to them, or binding authority.

On the one hand, Allison suggests that the difference is found with respect to Catholicism's "insistence on multiple authorities in relationship to divine revelation and its interpretation. In addition to the authority of *Scripture*, the Church relies on the authority of *Tradition* and the authority of *the Magisterium*." He adds, "Authority is not found in Scripture alone, as it is in Protestantism." On the other hand, as I said above, he rejects a monistic principle of authority, for even Protestant churches have multiple authorities. So, where is the difference? It is not over whether Scripture is one among many authorities but whether Scripture has "ultimate authority" (*40 Questions*, 91). De Chirico makes clear as well that the difference is over whether the Bible can be the ultimate authority (*SWDW*, 34). Allison suggests that the problem is over the instability of a "multiple authority structure" (*40 Questions*, 100). But it is not clear that this pertains only to Roman Catholicism since, according to Allison, Evangelical Protestants also reject a monistic principle of authority. Thus, the difference must be over the question of how one settles the conflict between rival interpretations of the Christian faith, given a multiple authority structure? Consider in this connection Vanhoozer's critical statement. "[I]t is one thing to say that Scripture provides the overarching metanarrative and hermeneutical framework for understanding its parts, and quite another to say that the Bible alone authorizes or adjudicates between rival interpretations" (*Biblical Authority*, 116).[13] Allison and De Chirico affirm that "the Bible alone authorizes or adjudicates between rival interpretations." But this position seems implausible. If the Bible alone authorizes a correct interpretation of itself, how then does the presumptive authority of creeds and councils have any real authority to assist in that interpretation, since their authority derives from a presumed correct interpretation of Scripture? Its implausibility derives from the principle of *sola Scriptura*. Aidan Nichols correctly notes:

> Thus, for instance, the faith of a Catholic Christian in the divinity of Christ does not have its rule—its criterion—simply in the Scriptures, for the Scriptures alone did not prevent Arius of Alexandria from teaching that the Son is a created intermediary. Catholic faith in the Son's Godhood has its rule also in an act of the Church's extraordinary magisterium,

the dogma of the *homoousion* proclaimed at Nicaea I (325). (*Figuring Out*, 19–20)

What, then, is the role of tradition in the interpretation and justification of Christian teaching?

The Council of Trent left open the possibility in which Scripture and tradition are viewed as materially incomplete but complementary sources: the two-source theory of revelation. In an address to the German-speaking bishops (October 10, 1962) on the eve of the solemn inauguration of Vatican II, Ratzinger describes this theory that he finds unacceptable, and which, arguably, Vatican II rejected in *Dei Verbum*:

> Scripture and tradition contain revelation and they do this in such a way that parts of revelation are only in tradition. Tradition offers a plus in content over Scripture, because the former is made up of unwritten words passe[d] on solely "from hand to hand" in the Church. ... Clearly this doctrine [of Scripture and tradition as two sources of revelation] has without doubt the backing of most all textbooks of theology[14]

Now, the Tridentine episcopate at Trent "speaks of the gospel as found *both* in the Scriptures *and* in apostolic traditions, insofar as these latter (1) pertain to faith and morals, and (2) are known to be part of the continuous practice of the Church." The key phrase that is the source of a conflict of interpretation is the one in which the episcopate states that both "saving truth and moral discipline are contained in the written books and the unwritten tradition." Nichols adds:

> Over against an earlier draft, revelation is not explicitly said to endure "partly" as Scripture and "partly" as traditions. Though the exact significance of the dropping of the phrase *partim ... partim*, and its replacement by *et ... et* is disputed by historians, we can at least say that Trent closed off certain approaches while leaving others open. (*Shape of Theology*, 176)

I already discussed above the three approaches considered dead ends. Still, there were three interpretations that were left open regarding the relationship between Scripture and tradition.[15] As I have already said, Allison and De Chirico are oblivious to the second and third possibilities left open by Trent. The first possibility, which dominated Catholic theology between the sixteenth and nineteenth centuries, is the one that we have already referred to as the two-source theory of revelation. There are two parallel sources of truth for our knowledge of revelation because "one part of the deposit of faith would come to us in Holy Scripture and the other in the living tradition—which would thus, in a sense, supplement scripture" (Semmelroth, *Preaching Word*, 102). A second interpretation emphasizes "both...and." "This would mean that the two sources, Holy Scripture and tradition, each contained God's entire revelation." However, this interpretation leaves unexplained the particular relation that these two sources have with one another.

The third interpretation strengthens this second interpretation with its explanation of the relation between Scripture and tradition by addressing the question regarding the role of tradition in the interpretation of Scripture. Otto Semmelroth explains:

> According to this view scripture and tradition are seen as joined more or less in the sense expressed by the word "with." Holy Scripture together with the living tradition offers God's revelation to the faithful. In this view the deposit of faith revealed by God is presented through Holy Scripture insofar as it is communicated and interpreted by the church's tradition under the guidance of the Holy Spirit. But the same can just as well be said conversely: God's revelation is transmitted to us through the living tradition, insofar as it bears Holy Scripture in its hands and brings to light from the depths of scripture what God's inspiring Spirit has hidden there. *What tradition has to transmit to later generations, to interpret and to bring to light, is precisely Holy Scripture and Scripture alone.... Scripture and tradition are not the same, nor are they two independent sources.* Rather they are bound together in organic unity. (Ibid., 103–4 [emphasis added])

Semmelroth's position is that tradition interprets and brings to light what is contained in Scripture alone. Yes, Scripture and tradition are not the same but neither are they two sources of revelation. Organic unity, adds Semmelroth, in the sense that "Tradition's function is to unfold and to explicate Scripture in the full depths of its content" (*Church and Christian Belief*, 33). It is this third interpretation that Berkouwer is discussing in his chapter on Scripture and tradition in his first Vatican II book. He summarizes the arguments of Catholic theologians, such as J. R. Geiselmann, who was chiefly responsible for reintroducing the interpretation into the theological discussion where the two-source theory of revelation was rejected. Berkouwer is not suggesting that Trent meant to teach the material sufficiency of Scripture. Still, Trent left this open as a theological possibility, Berkouwer and other Catholic theologians hold, such as Ratzinger, Geiselmann, Congar, Daniélou, Rahner, Semmelroth, and Nichols. Quoting Berkouwer, "That so many now accepted the Geiselmann thesis [at the Second Vatican Council] and see in it the real Catholic teaching about Scripture's unique significance is nothing less than amazing.

A comparable view of Catholic teaching would have been out of the question had the 'partly' phraseology been maintained by Trent. It is possible only because Trent allows at least the possibility of putting an accent on the sufficiency of Scripture" (*VCNT*, 114 [96]). Indeed, Berkouwer adds, "[T]he relationship between Scripture and tradition is a completely open matter" for Trent (ibid., 114 [97]). However, Counter-Reformation Catholics interpreted Trent to have rejected the sufficiency of Scripture, and, in fact, as teaching, clearly and without qualification the first interpretation of the relationship between Scripture and tradition, the doctrine of two parallel and materially incomplete sources of revelation. Hence, the "two-source theory…came to be dominant in the period between the [sixteenth-century] council [of Trent] and the nineteenth century" (ibid.). "On this view," adds Nichols, "there are (alongside Scripture) confessional, liturgical, and ethical traditions in the Church deriving from ancient times and testifying to revelation" (*Shape of Theology*, 176).

Now, Berkouwer sides with those who reject this first view of Trent, taking it to be a misreading by Counter-Reformation Catholics. He says, "Trent said nothing that would put tradition on a par with Scripture in the sense that complements Scripture." Rather, Berkouwer adds, Trent "was content to contradict the Reformation with an expression of great respect for tradition." It left the matter of their mutual relationship an open question. So open, states Berkouwer, "that it is now argued that the text of Trent's decree is not in conflict with the notion that tradition is not a source of revelation on the same level with Scripture, but it is only an interpretative source. Trent, it is argued, leaves Catholics free to identify themselves with the very ancient tradition of the Church according to which all the truth of salvation is contained in Scripture." ([all from] *VCNT*, 114 [96]).

Berkouwer owes the way of thinking of tradition as an interpretative source to Geiselmann who explicitly states, "[W]ith respect to the understanding of Holy Scriptures, [the Church] needs the clarifying tradition of the Fathers in faith and morals. Tradition in these cases exercises the function of *traditio interpretativa*."[16]

On the one hand, then Scripture possesses a material sufficiency; tradition does not play a supplementary or additive role to Scripture, but rather its role is interpretative and explicative. Given that understanding of the role of tradition, the controversy between Rome and the Reformation could no longer be about the issue that tradition was adding to Scripture. Says Berkouwer, "In evaluating this issue, one must first point out that this new interpretation in any case takes a different form in the concreteness of the controversy. Specifically, people can no longer look for another, compensatory source, namely tradition, when certain 'givens' are lacking in Scripture, as frequently occurred earlier. Acceptance of the material sufficiency per force leads to a greater urgency for Scriptural proof" (*De Heilige Schrift*, II, 344).[17]

On the other hand, Berkouwer opined that "even if Geiselmann's interpretation of Trent's decree was correct, that did not mean that the controversy between Rome and the Reformation was resolved" ("Vragen Rondom," 39). Yes, adds Berkouwer, one can see that "there is a remarkable shift in the interpretation of the relation of Scripture and tradition that is connected with a new attention for the normative witness of Scripture." Still, "this shift went from the two-source theory (partim-partim!) to ecclesiology: the ecclesiastical magisterium" (ibid., 39–40). Rather, Scripture and tradition are intrinsically and necessarily related such that Scripture must be interpreted in the concrete life of the Church,[18] its living tradition, through the teaching authority of the ecclesiastical Magisterium, which is under the guidance of the Holy Spirit. So, the chief question is about the relation of Scripture, tradition, and the Church's ecclesiastical Magisterium.

Now, Allison repeatedly cites *Dei Verbum*, §9 throughout his discussion of the Catholic teaching of divine revelation (*40 Questions*, 75, 83, 89–90, 96). "It is not from sacred Scripture alone (*"non per solam Scripturam"*) that the Church draws her certainty about everything which has been revealed. Therefore, both sacred tradition and sacred scripture are to be accepted and venerated with the same sense of devotion and reverence." Allison takes this statement as evidence that Vatican II still holds to the "two-source theory of revelation," as does De Chirico (*SWDW*, 34). Berkouwer disagrees. He, for one, defends Vatican II's Constitution *Dei Verbum*, §9 against the charge that we find here a reassertion of the two-source theory of revelation. He dismisses the charge that *Dei Verbum* reiterates the two-source theory of revelation when it urges to venerate with the same sense of loyalty and reverence both Scripture and tradition.[19] He writes,

> One may not read into this '*non per solam Scripturam*' a pointed choice for the two-source theory (in the sense of *partim-partim*). The perspective is quite pointedly that of a certainty in the church in which tradition plays an important role. One comes to such certainty not by disparaging the voice of the church and its tradition, and by isolating Scripture in the life of the church as a 'sufficient' resource. Much rather, the church—and her tradition—actively functions in understanding the Word rightly, and hence certainty comes not '*per solam Scripturam*'. (*De Heilige Schrift*, II, 342–43)[20]

Hence, in connection with the Church's attaining certainty, *sola Scriptura* has a fundamental and meaningful place as *prima Scriptura*, but only when it is indivisibly connected with tradition and the Church, with tradition being understood as the Church's authoritative interpretation of Scripture (ibid., 344).

Berkouwer, for one, argues that the meaning of "not from Sacred Scripture alone" (*non per solam Scripturam*) need not be taken to question the material completeness of Scripture and opting for the two-source theory in which Scripture must be completed by tradition. He makes the point that the formulation in this passage concerns the certainty of the Church regarding the teachings of Scripture rather than the question of its material sufficiency or insufficiency. In other words, the role of tradition in this passage pertains to the matter of how the Church arrives at the epistemological certainty of the truth. Quoting E. Stakemeier, a German Catholic commentator on *Dei Verbum*, Berkouwer defends this reading on *non per solam Scripturam*.

> Roman Catholic commentators appropriately lay heavy emphasis on this: "One takes note of the word *certitudinem*. This formulation sheds light on the irreplaceable importance of tradition without either exaggerating or minimizing its function." This explains the way in which knowing, the process of knowing within the church, is considered and for which the traditions are indispensable, but not the way in which

the material insufficientia of Scripture is expressed.
These commentators do not want to fix the traditions
as being either complementary or as being merely interpretative.... The council ... limited the significance
of tradition to indicating certitude, *the church's knowledge of the faith*. This is the point at which the *non per
solam Scripturam* functions in the life of the church,
for here the believer is confronted with Scripture in
its connection with tradition and church. But this
does not yet imply that traditions are an independent
source of revelation alongside Holy Scripture. (*Nabetrachting*, 115–16)[21]

Put differently, what is the motive for the assent of faith? Allison
claims that the motive of the act of faith for assenting to divine truth
is obedience to the Church's authority rather than the trustworthi-
ness of God himself. Hence, this conviction leads to his claim that
the Church's position on the matter of ultimate theological authority
is the position of *solum magisterium* (*40 Questions*, 300–4). The position of
solum magisterium is mistaken because it makes the Church's teaching office the supreme norm of faith. In other words, the Catholic
Church does not hold that her authority is the *basis*—"I believe because of the Church's authority"—for intentionally assenting to the
divine truth that is believed, taught, and proclaimed by the Church.
Rather, the Church is a divine instrument *through* which we assent
to that truth. Consider here, for instance, Ratzinger's remarks on the
limits of the Church's authority regarding the ordination of women.
His remarks here pertain to John Paul II's 1994 Apostolic Letter,
Ordinatio Sacerdotalis. Ratzinger writes in respect of this Letter's key
statement:

[Wishing to remain faithful to the Lord's example],
"the Church does not consider herself authorized to
admit women to priestly ordination." In this statement the Church's Magisterium professes the primacy
of obedience and the limits of ecclesiastical authority:
The Church and her Magisterium have authority not
in and of themselves, but rather from the Lord alone.
The believing Church reads the Scriptures and lives
them out ... in the living fellowship of the people of
God in every age; she knows that she is bound by a
will that preceded her, by an act of "institution." This
prevenient will, the will of Christ, is expressed in her
case by the appointing of the Twelve.[22]

And more than thirty years earlier Ratzinger writes in the same vein:

> "Tradition" is indeed never a simple and anonymous handing on of teaching, but is linked to a person, is a living word that has its concrete reality in faith. And, vice versa, [apostolic] succession is never the taking over of some official powers that are then at the disposal of the office-bearer; rather, it is being taken into the service of the Word, the office of testifying to something with which one has been entrusted and which stands above its bearer, so that he fades into the background behind the thing he has taken over and is (to use the marvelous image from Isaiah and John the Baptist) just a voice that enables the Word to be heard aloud in the world.[23]

In other words, the main point that Ratzinger is making here is that the authority of the Church's teaching office is not based on itself and hence the Church is itself not the norm of faith. The Church affirms the primacy of the authority *of God*, of his Word, in short, of divine revelation, over the teaching authority *of the Church*, which is an authority derived from Christ. Certainly, the Church has teaching authority, indeed shares in the authority of Scripture, but it "is only a secondary rule, measured by the primary rule, which is divine Revelation" (Congar, *Meaning of Tradition*, 69).

Consequently, Allison and De Chirico are mistaken in claiming that the Church's teaching office is the motive of the act of faith for assenting to divine truth, for this position would make the teaching office the supreme norm of faith. They can only think this because they think the Church confuses the grounds of faith with the means through which I assent to divine truth. But the Church does not confuse the source of truth, which is divine revelation, with the responsibility of the Church's teaching office to certify divine truth. In other words, the Magisterium is not a source of divine revelation but only an authoritative aid to discerning what belongs to the content of revelation. Only Scripture and tradition are such epistemic sources, but the latter does not play a supplementary or additive role with respect to the former; rather the function of tradition's role is interpretative and explicative for the sake of "making certain of the truth, i.e., [tradition] belongs in the formal and gnoseological sphere—and, in fact, this is the sphere in which the significance of tradition is to be sought."[24]

Perhaps we can make this point clearer by distinguishing between the "formal reason" of faith and the Church's teaching authority. The former is the reason why we believe something, say, that Jesus Christ is true God and true man. We believe it by virtue of divine revelation. "Divine revelation is thus the reason without which there would be no reason to have faith." The latter, Church authority, is the means the Church has "to avoid losing that most precious revelation." The Dominican Cardinal Cajetan (1469–1534) explains what this means:

> And so that no error might appear in the proposal or explanation of things to be believed, the Holy Spirit provided a created rule, which is the sense and the doctrine of the Church, so that the authority of the Church is the infallible rule of the proposition and explanation of things which must be believed by faith. Therefore, two infallible rules concur in faith, namely divine revelation and the authority of the Church; there is between them this difference: divine revelation is the formal reason of the object of faith, and the authority of the Church is the minister of the object of faith.[25]

Furthermore, accepting this pattern of theological authority does not deny that these authorities function together, but, as *Dei Verbum* §10 states, each in its own way exercises its authority in that pattern. Clearly, then, the Reformation decision for *sola Scriptura* did not mean to deny this pattern of theological authority. Thus, one may hold this position that Scripture is not only the final or supreme or primary authority of faith and life, but also that being final is not the same as standing alone and hence that it is intrinsically and necessarily related with tradition and the Church as interdependent authorities.

As Allen and Swain put it, "[T]he Reformers, through intense study of the Bible itself as their final authority, came to believe that the Bible cannot be read by itself, for it warrants or mandates the functioning of other ecclesial authorities. To be more biblical, then, one cannot be biblicistic. To be more biblical, one must also be engaged in the process of traditioning. Thus, the reformers certainly understood and intended *sola Scriptura* to shape engagements of the catholic tradition and the fullness of the riches of the church, all of which are meant to work together to form members of the body for the work of ministry" (Allen and Swain, *Reformed Catholicity*, 84–85). Of course, this sounds like *Dei Verbum* §10.

Ecclesiastical Magisterium, Indefectibility, and Infallibility

In the concluding section of this chapter,[26] I return to Berkouwer's observation that the chief question is now about the relation of Scripture, tradition, and the Church's ecclesiastical Magisterium rather than the relationship of Scripture and tradition.

The responsibility of the Church's teaching office, the Magisterium, is to keep faithfully, to judge authentically, distinguishing between true and false teaching, and to define infallibly the content of the deposit of the faith. The Church is called by the Lord Jesus to be a herald of the apostolic faith, to defend the faith against opposed errors in its judgments, and, as Avery Cardinal Dulles puts it, "to clarify the faith by bringing forth from the treasury 'things new and old.'" He adds, "In answering new questions, as in refuting new errors, the Magisterium sometimes brings out hitherto unnoticed implications of the faith" (*Magisterium*, 62–63). Therefore, the Church's teaching office is the answer to the following question: "Who will defend Scripture when the Church is confronted by two or more contradictory interpretations of Scripture?" Otherwise, who speaks for the Scripture? Are we thrown back on our private judgment? If so, how do we block the move to hermeneutical individualism, subjectivism, and sectarianism?

As Allison asks, "But what of the interpretive chaos into which Protestantism has allegedly thrown us?" He replies: "Importantly, the ultimate arbiter of Scripture is not the individual reader or interpreter. Rather, because of its divine authorship, Scripture itself is its own self-interpreting, ultimate authority. Protestants should understand and apply it with reliance on the illumination of the Holy Spirit." They should work with a proper theological framework, proven interpretive principles, engaging in Bible study, listening to the local church "pastor-teachers," who guide them in their understanding. In sum, "By following the inspired Word of the triune God, the church receives a sure and authoritative message" (*40 Questions*, 303).

As I argued above, Allison rejects a monistic principle of authority; *sola Scriptura* is not an anti-creedal or anti-tradition principle. Still, Allison affirms that "the Bible alone authorizes or adjudicates between rival interpretation." But this position seems implausible. If the Bible alone authorizes a correct interpretation of itself, how then does the presumptive authority of creeds and councils, of a proper theological framework, of proven interpretive principles, have any real authority to assist in that interpretation, since their authority derives from a presumed correct interpretation of Scripture? Its implausibility derives from the principle of *sola Scriptura*.

Will invoking, then, the work of the Spirit help to block the move to hermeneutical individualism, subjectivism, sectarianism, in short, chaos, and thus safeguard the objectivity and authority of Scripture, binding religious subjectivity to the Word of God itself, safeguarding interpretations from these cul-de-sacs and hence from the loss of the authority of Scripture? Karl Rahner gives a Catholic response to this question. Briefly, the difference between Rome and the Reformation is not over whether the Spirit is at work in interpretations made in the light of faith. Rather, the focus of the difference concerns the question as to how the Spirit of God works concretely. According to the Catholic position of faith's living understanding of Scripture, says Rahner, that understanding has itself an ecclesial structure because faith lives on in the Church in a way that makes Scripture a living reality in the power of the Spirit.[27] He explains:

> This does not dethrone Scripture. It does not cease to be the *norma non normata* for the church and also for its teaching office. We did not discover the Bible somewhere by our own curiosity, but rather, as something which awakens faith and brings faith and communicates the Spirit, it comes to us only in the preaching of the concrete church. And this says to us: here is the Word of God, a word which it gives witness to in such a way that according to the Catholic understanding of the faith too it can manifest itself by its own power. … However, faith's living understanding of Scripture, and Scripture's transposition into faith's really pneumatic experience of the reality which Scripture means are processes whose place Scripture itself cannot take, and the process of faith's living understanding of Scripture has itself an ecclesial structure. It is not simply and merely an affair of the individual's religious subjectivity. Rather it is more originally an affair of the Church as such, an affair of the single community of believers within which the individual Christian acquires his concrete understanding of the faith. This community of faith is not only the sum of individual religious subjectivities, but rather it really has a structure, a hierarchical constitution, and an authoritative leadership through

> which the Church's single understanding of the faith
> receives its unambiguous meaning and its binding
> character. (*Foundations of Christian Faith*, 364–65)

As Rahner states admirably well in the above passage, the formative process of faith's understanding of divine revelation, of salvation, of sin, the cross and grace, and so much more, is essentially an ecclesial one, namely, by being members of Christ's historic Church, the Catholic Church. And this ecclesial structure is hierarchically constituted with the official and public teaching of the Church, the Magisterium, consisting of an authoritative leadership, of the pope and the bishops who are in communion with him. This last point is particularly important to counteract what seems like the overwhelming ascendancy of sectarianism and a corresponding congregationalist ecclesiology in contemporary Protestantism. The "magisterial vacuum" in contemporary Protestantism is the unfolding of the logic of Protestantism—separating the Bible from the Church—that has led to a crisis of authority, indeed, a crisis of faith in the authority of Scripture. Let us recall David Lyle Jeffrey's insight, "The loss of the Church's teaching authority has led to the loss of the authority of Scripture" (*"Houses of the Interpreters,"* 30).

This crisis cannot be resolved by reasserting orthodoxy *alone* or the Church's hierarchical teaching office *alone*. Rather what is needed is the teaching and practice of Vatican II's Dogmatic Constitution, *Dei Verbum*, namely, a trilateral conception of authority wherein Scripture, tradition and the Church's teaching office, being intrinsically and necessarily related, operating together, but exercising authority in a way that is unique to each one of them. In other words, to quote Dulles, "nothing is believed on the authority of tradition alone, Scripture alone, or the magisterium alone" (*"Vatican II on the Interpretation,"* 17). This is a crucial point made by Schillebeeckx in the second epigraph to this chapter.

I would like to sum up this Catholic position by using the words of Lutheran theologian Carl Braaten: "Orthodoxy without episcopacy is blind; episcopacy without orthodoxy is empty." In short, adds Braaten, "Without the Bible the church is blind, and without the church the Bible is dumb" (*Mother Church,* 97). The indefectibility of the Church's teaching authority in truth, indeed, the very authentic exercise of her authority, is derived from her submission in faith and hope to the Word of the living and ever-present Lord of the Church,

Jesus Christ. Only her ongoing submission to the prophetic-apostolic witness of the Scripture can preserve her in the continuity of the Gospel, orthodoxy, as it were. It is not the fact that the Church as such has authority to teach through a hierarchical constitution and authoritative leadership, papacy and episcopacy, that preserves her in the promise of perpetuity or indefectibility. For papacy and episcopacy without orthodoxy is empty. The realization of this promise in her teaching authority is neither automatically guaranteed nor self-evident. Rather, it is based in the Lord's divine assistance, who preserves her in the truth by his Spirit (John 14:26, 16:13) to the extent that the Church remains faithful to the promise of the Spirit to be with her until "the closing of the ages" (Matt 28:20), such that not even the "gates of hell will overcome her" (Matt 16:18).

The source of this guarantee is found in the Church's ongoing obedience manifested in her living "in coherence with love, faith and walking in the truth," indefectibility thus being "the fruit of her confidence in God's gracious promise, in *timore et tremore*" (Schillebeeckx, "Ecclesia Semper Purificanda," 228). How then is the Church preserved from errors that would contradict the truth of the Gospel? According to the Catholic faith, "The Magisterium is one of the means whereby God preserves the Church in the truth of the gospel" (Dulles, *Magisterium*, 65). Furthermore, in reply to the question of how it does so, the brief answer is simply, though significantly, that by exercising its teaching authority the Magisterium of the Church teaches infallibly, and the latter is "at the service of the Church's indefectibility." On this view, infallibility cannot be reduced to indefectibility, meaning by the latter that the Church "will remain in truth in spite of all the errors that are always possible."[28] "Properly understood," as Hans Küng explains, infallibility, now reduced to indefectibility, "means the confidence of faith that, in spite of many errors in detail, intrinsically the Church is maintained in the truth of the gospel by the Spirit of God."[29]

This reductionist view of infallibility is rejected by the Church. On Dulles's non-reductionist view of infallibility, by contrast, "Thanks to the promised assistance of the Holy Spirit and the created means of grace, the Church as a whole has what Vatican II speaks of as a 'charism of infallibility' [*LG*, §25]. Putting this idea in a positive form, one may say that the Church is gifted with what Vatican I calls a 'charism of unfailing truth and faith'" (*Magisterium*, 65). In particular, this means that "infallibility in the traditional sense," as Rahner correctly puts it, "includes the *truth of individual defined statements* and not merely in the sense that Hans Küng…seems to advance, namely that the indefectibility of the Church's faith ultimately refers to the continuing union of the Church with its Lord—a union which allows, even in 'definitions', many remediable errors" ("A Century of Infallibility," 216).

Of course, the Church's teaching function derives its justification from the truth of Christian doctrine and the proclamation of the true Word of God. As Ratzinger correctly sees, "The function of the Magisterium is not, then, something extrinsic to Christian truth nor is it above the faith. It arises directly from the economy of faith itself, inasmuch as the Magisterium is, in its service to the Word of God, an institution positively willed by Christ as a constitutive element of his Church. The service to Christian truth which the Magisterium renders is thus for the benefit of the whole People of God called to enter the liberty of the truth revealed by God in Christ."[30]

I think we can now understand why the Catholic Church, in its understanding of indefectibility, requires as one of the conditions of indefectibility "that those preaching and teaching the faith on the highest authoritative level be not mistaken about what pertains essentially to revelation." Moreover, Dulles adds, "as defined at Vatican I and reaffirmed at Vatican II, the supreme Magisterium, in its definitive teaching about matters of faith and morals, is divinely protected against error" (*Magisterium*, 66). In other words, infallibility is a necessary condition even if not a sufficient one of the Church's indefectibility. It is therefore necessary for the Magisterium's activity of teaching what the truth of the faith is in "an infallible homogeneity and continuity between the divinely revealed deposit of faith revealed once and for all by the apostles, on the one hand, and its actual preservation through the ages by means of a divinely assisted teaching office, on the other" (*Primacy of Peter*, 57). In sum, Dulles is right that the notion of infallibility makes good theological sense when seen in light of other Christian beliefs:

1. God provides for the Church effective means by which it may and will in fact remain in the truth of the gospel till the end of time.

2. Among these means are not only the canonical Scriptures but also, as an essential counterpart to the Scriptures, the pastoral of-

fice. Without such a pastoral office the Christian community would not be adequately protected against corruptions of the gospel.

3. The pastoral office is exercised for the universal Church by the bearer of the Petrine office (which means, for Catholics, by the pope). It is therefore reasonable to suppose that the pope is equipped by God with a special charism (or grace of office) for correctly interpreting the gospel to the universal Church, as circumstances may require.

4. In order that the papacy may adequately discharge its function of preserving unity in the faith and exposing dangerous errors, the papal charism must include the power to assert the truth of the gospel and to condemn contrary errors in a decisive and obligatory manner. Authoritative pronouncements from the Petrine office that are seriously binding on all the faithful must have adequately certified truth, for there could be no obligation to believe what could probably be error. (Dulles, "Moderate Infallibilism," 83)

Pace Allison and De Chirico, the teaching function of the Magisterium is not extrinsic to the discernment of Christian truth nor is it above the faith. A dogma, says the International Theological Commission, is "a teaching in which the Church proposes a revealed truth definitively, and in a way that is binding for the universal Church."[31] John Paul II makes this point about dogmatic statements in his 1998 encyclical letter, *Fides et Ratio*: "Dogmatic statements, while reflecting at times the culture of the period in which they were defined, formulate an unchanging and ultimate truth" (§95). Elsewhere in that same encyclical, he states: "The Bible, and the New Testament in particular, contain texts and statements which have genuinely ontological content. The inspired authors intended to formulate true statements capable, that is, of expressing objective reality." Doctrinal assertions are, then, such that they "may be considered irrevocable, continuous, universal, materially identical, and objectively true" (§82). If doctrinal assertions do not possess these properties, then, does this not imply that all Christian teaching, particularly doctrine, is reversible? If so, what is it that gives continuity, material identity, and therefore intelligibility to dogma? But is that so? How could the Nicene Creed claim that Jesus is the incarnate Son of God, *homoousion* with the Father, be reversible? In other words, is it admissible to deny that Jesus Christ is the incarnate Word of God? I dare say not. "For the historic and orthodox Christian faith," as Guarino rightly says, "this assertion is universally and enduringly true, mediating an actual state of affairs" (Guarino, *Systematic Theology*, 129).

"On the other hand, adds Guarino, "a qualified fallibilism is always endorsable if one means by this that every statement requires further thought and elucidation, that every assertion is open to reconceptualization and reformulation, and that no statement comprehensively exhausts truth, much less divine truth" (ibid., 139n59). But this qualified fallibilism is not inconsistent with the teaching of the Catholic Church that God has graciously bestowed upon his Church, through the gift of the Holy Spirit, a participation in his own infallibility and hence that the property of infallibility belongs to the Magisterium's activity of teaching. I conclude this section with this very point that is made by the *Catechism of the Catholic Church*: "In order to preserve the Church in the purity of the faith handed on by the apostles, Christ who is the Truth willed to confer on her a share in his own infallibility" (§889).

NOTES

1. Herman Bavinck, *Gereformeerde Dogmatiek*, Vol. I, 356. Translated by John Vriend as *Reformed Dogmatics*, Vol. 1, *Prolegomena*, ed. John Bolt, 493.

2. Edward Schillebeeckx, OP, "De Openbaring en haar 'Overlevering'," and this quote, 20. English translation: "Revelation, Scripture, Tradition, and Teaching Authority," this quote, 23–24 (the italics are in the Dutch version).

3. Fr. Francis Martin, "Some Directions in Catholic Biblical Theology," at 67–68.

4. As Geerhardus Vos says in his address, "The Idea of Biblical Theology as a Science and as a Theological Discipline," Inaugural Address as Professor of Biblical Theology, Princeton Theological Seminary, delivered at the First Presbyterian Church, Princeton on May 8, 1894. Reprinted in *Redemptive History and Biblical Interpretation: The Shorter Writings of Geerhardus Vos*, 3–24.

5. Geiselmann adds, "Holy Scripture as the guardian of the Gospel is the dowry of the Holy Spirit to the Bride of Christ, the most precious jewel in which the *Spiritus creator* endowed her subsequent life with the word of Christ" (37). See also, *Dei Verbum*, §7.

6. Ratzinger, "Revelation and Tradition," in *Revelation and Tradition*, at 46; Hermann Pottmeyer, "Tradition," in *Dictionary of Fundamental Theology*, at 1124.

7. See also Yves Congar's statement, "the essential idea is that of the transmission of a body of truths and principles of life, both normative and efficacious for salvation," in *Tradition and Traditions*, 26, as cited by Nichols, *The Shape of Catholic Theology*, 169n16.

8. Moyra Doorly and Aidan Nichols, OP, *The Council in Question*, 43.

9. Although Allison correctly refers to St. Irenaeus's *Adversus haereses*, he neglects to mention that Irenaeus has a teaching, in the same book (III, c. 24, 4), regarding Mary's place in the plan of salvation and the communion of saints. "Irenaeus describes Eve's disobedience as the universal cause of 'death' and Mary's obedience as the cause of 'salvation' (*causa salutis*) 'for herself and for the whole human race.' The image appears of the knot tied by Eve loosed by Mary. ... 'What Eve bound through her unbelief, Mary loosed by her faith.' 'And just as through a disobedient virgin man was stricken down and fell into death, so through the Virgin who was obedient to the Word of God man was reanimated and received life'" (as cited by Hauke, *Introduction to Mariology*, 80–81).

10. Ratzinger, "Six Texts by Prof. Joseph Ratzinger as Peritus Before and During Vatican Council II," at 275.

11. Manfred Hauke, *Introduction to Mariology*, 77, and on Irenaeus, 79–82.

12. See his discussion of *sola Scriptura* in Leonardo De Chirico, *"Fides et Ratio* (1998): Three Theses on the Roman Catholic Synthesis between Faith and Reason,"* Section 3. His discussion presumes that the two-source theory of revelation informs *Dei Verbum* and, hence, John Paul II's *Fides et Ratio*, §§55, 65.

13. I discuss at length Vanhoozer's view of the relationship between Scripture, tradition, and ecclesial authority in my book, *Revelation, History, and Truth: A Hermeneutics of Dogma*, Chapter 2, "The Nature of Revelation," 47–92.

14. Ratzinger, "Six Texts by Prof. Joseph Ratzinger as Peritus," 273.

15. I am here indebted not only to Aidan Nichols, *The Shape of Catholic Theology*, 169, 176–77, but also Otto Semmelroth, SJ, *The Preaching Word: On the Theology of Proclamation*, 102–8; idem, *The Church and Christian Belief*, 32–36.

16. Geiselmann, *Die Heilige Schrift und die tradition*, 282.

17. This passage is not in the English translation, *Holy Scripture*.

18. On the matter of the relation between Scripture and the Church, Herman Bavinck stresses their reciprocal interrelationship even while affirming the subordination of the latter to the former. In other words, Bavinck seems to affirm that Scripture and the Church are interrelated and joined together such that one cannot maintain itself without the other. He writes eloquently, "In applying [objective] revelation, illumination and regeneration, Scripture and church are linked to each other. ... Revelation in this dispensation is continued jointly in Scripture and in the church. In this context the two are most intimately connected. Scripture is the light of the church, the church the life of Scripture. Apart from the church, Scripture is an enigma and an offense. Without rebirth no one can know it. Those who do not participate in its life cannot understand its meaning and point of view. Conversely, the life of the church is a complex mystery unless Scripture sheds its light upon it. Scripture explains the church; the church understands Scripture. In the church Scripture confirms and seals its revelation, and in Scripture the Christian—and the church—learn to understand themselves in their relation to God and the world, in their past, present, and future" (*Gereformeerde Dogmatiek*, I, 356 [384]).

19. Although Berkouwer rejects the claim that *Dei Verbum* §9 is a return to the two-source theory of revelation, he is correct that "One can expect with certainty that the problem of the connection between the 'pari pietatis affectu ac reverentia' [with the same sense of reverence and devotion] and the 'norma normans non normata' [a norm that norms but is not itself normed] will remain one of the most gripping questions in the future" (*Nabetrachting*, 130n72).

20. This passage is not in the English translation, *Holy Scripture*.

21. This, too, is the view of Ratzinger in his commentary on the meaning of *non per solam Scripturam*: "The function of tradition is seen here as a making certain of the truth, i.e., it belongs in the formal and gnoseological sphere—and, in fact, this is the sphere in which the significance of tradition is to be sought" (Ratzinger, *Commentary on Dogmatic Constitution on Divine Revelation*, at 195).

22. Joseph Ratzinger, "Grenzen kirchlicher Vollmacht: Das neue Dokument von Papst Johannes Paul II: zur Frage der Frauenordination," Internationale katholische Zeitschrift 23 (1994): 337–45, at 338; as cited in Gerhard Müller, *Priesthood and Diaconate*, trans. Michael J. Miller, 65n3.

23. Joseph Ratzinger, "Primacy, Episcopacy, and Successio Apostolica," in *God's Word: Scripture—Tradition—Office*, trans. Henry Taylor, at 23.

24. Ratzinger in his commentary on *Dei Verbum*, 195.

25. Cajetan, In Summ. Theol., Iia, Iiae, q.1, a.1, no. X; as cited in Charles Morerod, OP, *The Church and the Human Quest for Truth*, 47.

26. Some paragraphs in this section are from my book, *Berkouwer and Catholicism*, 339–43.

27. The following paragraphs are adapted from Echeverria, *Berkouwer and Catholicism*, 332–45.

28. Anglican-Roman Catholic International Commission, September 3, 1998, "The Gift of Authority," §41.1.

29. As Hans Küng, the prominent defender of "ecclesial indefectibility" rather than "magisterial infallibility," put it in his controversial book, *Infallible? An Inquiry*, 144 (italics added).

30. *Donum Veritatis*, Instruction on the Ecclesial Vocation of the Theologian, Congregation for the Doctrine of the Faith, §14. The Prefect for the Congregation at that time was Joseph Cardinal Ratzinger, who was Pope Benedict XVI, 2005–2013.

31. International Theological Commission, "On the Interpretation of Dogmas," *Origins* 20 (May 17, 1990): 9; as cited in Thomas Guarino, *Foundations of Systematic Theology*, 3. See also, Müller, *Priesthood and Diaconate*, "Dogma is the linguistic form assumed by the Word as a result of God's will to communicate himself—that same Word which, in the Church's verbal profession of faith, is God and has become flesh" (190).

CHAPTER 4

EVANGELICAL HERMENEUTICS OF CATHOLICISM

The most fundamental weakness in Allison's studies *(RCTP, 40 Questions)* is his uncritical dependence on Leonardo De Chirico's 2003 study on the hermeneutics of post-Vatican II Roman Catholicism from an Evangelical theological perspective. I have great respect for De Chirico himself and his work, even though I reject his interpretation and conclusions about Catholicism. De Chirico claims to provide a hermeneutics of Catholicism as a coherent, all-encompassing system that is grounded in two first principles. Allison shares De Chirico's hermeneutics that identifies these first principles: "the nature-grace interdependence, that is, a strong continuity between nature and grace; and the Christ-Church interconnection, that is, an ecclesiology ... that views the Catholic Church as the ongoing incarnation of Jesus Christ" *(RCTP, 31; 40 Questions, 47–58)*.

This hermeneutics deserves far more critical attention than I can give here in this chapter and the next. So, my critical comments on each of the first principles will be substantive but succinct.

Nature and Grace

> "*Gratia praesupponit naturam*": This axiom is correct and fully biblical in saying that grace, the encounter of man with the God who calls him, does not destroy what is truly human but, rather, salvages and fulfills it. This genuine humanity of man, the created order "man," is completely extinguished in no man; it lies at the basis of every single human person and in many different ways continuously has its effects on man's concrete existence, summoning and guiding him. But of course, in no man is it present without warping or falsification; instead, in every individual it is caked

with the layer of filth that Pascal once aptly called the "second nature" of man.[1]

> [A]part from the paramount importance of the relationship between nature and grace for any theological current, the Roman Catholic tradition is perhaps the one which has more extensively cultivated and willingly promoted reflection on the issue to the extent that its tradition as a whole may be thought of as being largely shaped along the lines of the nature-grace motif. (*ETP*, 221)

How are we to understand the distinction and relation of nature and grace? How should we understand the impact that the fall has had upon human nature? De Chirico gives a response to these questions that I shall sum up (*ETP*, 219–41). Pared down for my purpose here, regarding the first question De Chirico distinguishes between "rigid Thomism" (*ETP*, 224), or what I would call "hard dualism," from what I also call "soft dualism." Hard dualism conceives of nature first in terms of its own finality, to which is then "superadded," as a matter of grace, a second, supernatural finality; grace superimposes a supernatural reality upon nature. Says De Chirico, "Because of the sharp differentiation between the two orders, this [view] is characterized by a thoroughgoing extrinsicism, as if, at least potentially, they could function independently" (*ETP*, 224). De Chirico's description of "rigid Thomism" resembles the late medieval dualism where, as Herman Dooyeweerd more accurately stated, the "Thomistic synthesis of nature and grace [is] replaced by a sharp antithesis. Any point of connection between the natural and the supernatural sphere [is] denied." "This was the introduction to the shifting of primacy to the nature [level of the nature and grace] motive" (Dooyeweerd, *Twilight*, 44–45). The Thomistic synthesis of nature and grace is a *softer dualism*: primacy is ascribed to grace, and grace is thought to perfect nature rather than replace it altogether. This more subtle dualism accepts that there is only one ultimate end for nature, a supernatural one. Dooyeweerd elaborates:

> The inner dialectic of the ground-motive of nature and grace drove scholastic thought in the 14th century from the Thomistic (pseudo) synthesis (*Natura praembula gratiae*) to the Occamist antithesis (no point of contact between nature and grace according to William of Occam, the leader of the nominalist scholasticism of the 14th century). ... In the

> later-medieval scholasticism of William of Occam,
> which had become keenly conscious of the antago-
> nism between the "nature" and the "grace-motive,"
> "natural reason" has become entirely tarnished. There
> is no longer place here for a metaphysics and a natu-
> ral theology, although the autonomy of natural reason
> is maintained to the utmost. The grace-motive retains
> the primacy, but not in a synthetic hierarchical sense
> as in Thomism. (*De Wijsbegeerte der Wetsidee*, Vol. I, 66–67)

The Occamist antagonism between "nature" and "grace" resembles
the position of Allison and De Chirico where there is no "substantial continuity between the order of nature and that of grace" (*ETP*,
236). Contrary to Catholicism, De Chirico argues that sin has disen-
tangled the continuity between nature and grace. Allison says that
"grace has nothing to work with in nature because creation has been
devastatingly tainted by sin" (*RCTP*, 253). He adds, "Scripture does not
present nature [the structures of reality] in a positive light [after the
fall], as a realm that is open to grace and that can serve as a conduit
between God and human beings" (*RCTP*, 53). Given this view, they
seem to envisage a "relationship between a holy God and a sinful
world in terms of an ontological opposition" (*ETP*, 238). This position seems more Barthian than Evangelical or Reformed. Here, too,
Dooyeweerd's point is relevant.

> In the most recent time [the inner dialectic motive of
> nature and grace] has disclosed its polar tendencies in
> the "dialectical theology." The conflict between Karl
> Barth and Emil Brunner was entirely dominated by
> the question whether in "nature" there may be accept-
> ed a "point of contact" for "grace." Against Brunner's
> "yes," going in the synthetic direction, Barth set his
> inexorable "no." (*A New Critique*, I, 66-67)

I'll return to this point below when analyzing what I call Position I.
For now, two other positions of "nature" and grace" need description.
One is described by De Chirico stating that there is "a reciprocal
relation between nature and grace, as if the world and the elevating
operations of divine dealings with it were part of the same, though
composite, order of reality" (*ETP*, 224).

Now, almost a century past, Jacques Maritain significantly re-
marked regarding the question of the relation of nature and grace
that it is erroneous to ignore both the distinction between nature
and grace as well as their union.[2] Although Maritain maintains the

distinction between nature and grace, he rejects dualism both of a "hard" and "soft" sort. Both sorts fail to grasp the intrinsic relation between the supernatural end and nature by failing to consider that this end directs and orders nature and all its intermediate ends, from within rather than alongside of or above nature. Thus, the key idea in Maritain's theology of nature and grace is that grace restores nature from within so that nature may attain its own proper ends. On Maritain's view human nature is integrally wounded by sin: original sin does have an impact on the whole of human nature. Maritain writes, "The original sin, however, did not only deprive human nature of the supernatural gifts proper to the state of adamic innocence; it also wounded human nature. That is a theological datum on which St. Thomas lays particular stress. And these wounds of our nature are a reality always present in the human race" (*Philosophy of History*, 80). Hence, *grace neither replaces nature* (because human nature is so corrupt that grace, no longer able to transform it, replaces it altogether), *nor leaves nature untouched*. In other words, Maritain argues that it is from within that grace forms nature, and, far from replacing it altogether, or leaving it untouched, raises nature up, in order to make it serve its own ends. I'll return to this position when considering Position II below.

There is one final position that De Chirico describes and which he thinks is the contemporary Catholic position of nature and grace. "Grace is now being thought of as being immanent to nature whereas nature is being seen as interspersed with grace. In this view which favours a holistic approach, the notion of *natura pura* is categorically rejected in that nature is never considered as mere nature but always as graced nature" (*ETP*, 225). The problem with this view of nature and grace, of an intrinsically graced nature, is that it tends to conflate human nature and divine grace, threatening, as Romanus Cessario puts it, "to confuse God's creative presence to the human creature with the realization of the same person's call to beatitude" (*Christian Faith*, 28). This statement requires explanation.

God's creative presence refers to man having been created by God and for God. Man is a creature of God such that he is "totally dependent for his existence on the incessant creative activity of the self-existent God" (Mascall, *The Openness of Being*, 150).[3] And the importance of this is that, having been created for God, the meaning of man's existence is such that his relation to God is constitutive of his existence. The

Compendium of the Social Doctrine of the Church expresses well this first principle of Christian anthropology. "This is a relationship that exists in itself, it is therefore not something that comes afterwards and is not added from the outside. ... The human being is a personal being created by God to be in relationship with him; man finds life and self-expression only in [that] relationship, and tends naturally to God" (§109). The *Compendium's* formulation here avoids the dualistic and hence extrinsic construal of the relation of nature and grace (in which grace is a "plus factor" or an "add-on") discussed above.

Now, one of the fundamental implications of this constitutive relationship is that man has, by nature, that is, by virtue of being created, a "capacity for God" (*homo est Dei capax*) (ibid.). Put differently, "man has, by nature, some *potentia oboedientialis*, some receptive capacity ... for the supernatural"; otherwise, "God will be unable to communicate with man because, even if God speaks, man will be unable to hear him" (Mascall, *The Openness of Being*, 143). This "capacity for God" is a matter of divine grace; not the special grace of redemption but rather the universal gift due to God's common grace resulting in our having been created with this capacity. It is argued, moreover, that man cannot actualize this capacity by his own powers. Thus, he has been endowed by God with a "supernatural existential," which is the offer of God's grace, a supernatural gift not given in and with man's nature (Nichols, *Catholic Thought*, 142–43). As a consequence of God's universal saving will this offer is, nonetheless, universally bestowed so that man might respond to God, given that he is powerless to save himself. Cessario is right, however, that the "danger here is the risk of emphasizing the pervasive and inclusive character of divine grace in a way that practically eliminates the need for a real grace of justification—one that effectively transforms an impious person into a holy one" (*Christian Faith*, 28). Or as Pius XII was to state this risk, "Others destroy the gratuity of the supernatural order, since God, they say, cannot create intellectual beings without ordering and calling them to the beatific vision" (*Humani Generis*, §26). Put differently, entirely missing from this picture is, as the *Compendium* pointedly states, the fact that "this relationship with God can be ignored or even forgotten or dismissed"—even if "it can never be eliminated" (§109).

Thus, because of original sin, indeed human sinfulness, man is wounded in the sense that at the very core of his being there is an act of separation from God, resulting in alienation and estrangement "not only from God but also from [man] himself, from other men and from the world around him" (ibid.). Man's "capacity for God" has, then, been defectively and frustratedly hindered because of his sinful human condition. We can, therefore, understand why "the New Testament makes it exceedingly difficult to glide over the fact that the justification won by the blood of Christ really involves a movement from our being 'by nature children of wrath, like everyone else' to our being 'alive together with Christ—by grace you have been saved' (Eph 2:3–5)" (Cessario, *Christian Faith*, 28–29). Therefore, we must avoid conflating human nature and divine grace because created reality's structures are in a fallen state and in need of redemption; otherwise, we run the risk of "overlook[ing] God's judgment on the world rendered dramatically in the cross of Christ" (Guarino, *Foundations*, 20).

At this point it becomes necessary to consider the standard Calvinist objection that nature is not just wounded, but corrupted. This objection is also made by De Chirico. "The Evangelical point of view is that the hamartiological breach which occurred at the fall has a significance which is much more far-reaching than a mere wound or stain. …The seriousness with which sin is considered is shown by the fact that between creation and redemption there is the breach of the fall which, because of the *corruptio totalis* brought by it, becomes a constituent part of the over-arching scheme" (*ETP*, 237). Is this now a distinction without a difference? I think so, and my argument is as follows. Herman Dooyeweerd, for one, holds that the state of corruption has neither destroyed the goodness of creation nor has it incapacitated our proper functioning altogether. This, too, is the position of John Paul II. In the pope's own words:

> As a result of that mysterious original sin, committed at the prompting of Satan, the one who is a "liar and the father of lies" (John 8:44), man is constantly tempted to turn his gaze away from the living and true God in order to direct it toward idols (cf. 1 Thes 1:9), exchanging "the truth about God for a lie" (Rom 1:25). Man's capacity to know the truth is also darkened, and his will to submit to it is weakened. Thus, giving himself over to relativism and skepticism (cf. John 18:38), he goes off in search of an illusory freedom apart from truth itself. (*Veritatis Splendor*, §1)

And yet, the pope continues, "[N]o darkness of error or of sin can totally take away from man the light of God the Creator. In the depths of his heart there always remains a yearning for absolute truth and a thirst to attain full knowledge of it" (ibid.). That the result of original sin is not merely the loss of a supernatural addition to our human nature is already alluded to in the above passage; it also affected human nature and hence our ability to know ourselves, others, and God. Furthermore, it is not man's actual goodness that makes possible the proper functioning of reason's powers. It is fundamentally the reality that "no darkness of error or sin can totally take away from man the light of God the Creator," as John Paul expresses it above. Yet reason's powers are fallen and pervaded by sin resulting in "gnoseological concupiscence" (Col 2:18), which is that sinful inclination that sets us against God, as Dooyeweerd states. This, too, is the position of John Paul II. He writes:

> The blindness of pride deceived our first parents into thinking themselves sovereign and autonomous, and into thinking that they could ignore the knowledge which comes from God. All men and women were caught up in this primal disobedience, which so wounded reason that from then on its path to full truth would be strewn with obstacles. From that time onward the human capacity to know the truth was impaired by an aversion to the One who is the source and origin of truth. It is again the Apostle [Paul] who reveals just how far human thinking, because of sin, became "empty," and human reasoning became distorted and inclined to falsehood (cf. Rom 1:21–22). The eyes of the mind were no longer able to see clearly: reason became more and more a prisoner to itself. *The coming of Christ was the saving event which redeemed reason from its weakness, setting it free from the shackles in which it had imprisoned itself.* (*FR* §22, emphasis added)

De Chirico overlooks the significance of passages like the above in his criticism of John Paul II's *Fides et Ratio*. De Chirico states that the pope recognizes in his encyclical "The fragility, fragmentation, and limitations of reason (§§13 and 43), as well as an inner weakness (§75) and a certain imperfection (§83)." He adds, "Sin intervenes on the structure of reason, bringing wounds, obstacles, obfuscation, debilitation, and disorder (§§23, 82, 71)" (De Chirico, "*Fides et Ratio*," 2.2). Still, he charges John Paul with an "unwarranted autonomy of reason," reflecting an "autonomy of the creature."

De Chirico's claim that John Paul II affirms an autonomy of the creature is confusing. If De Chirico means to say that John Paul affirms a creature's self-sufficiency, then he is wrong. In *Fides et Ratio*,

John Paul denies the very claim that De Chirico makes. "From the Bible there emerges also a vision of man as *imago Dei*. This vision offers indications regarding man's life, his freedom and the immortality of the human spirit. Since the created world is not self-sufficient, every illusion of autonomy which would deny the essential dependence on God of every creature—the human being included—leads to dramatic situations which subvert the rational search for the harmony and the meaning of human life." (*FR* §80)

Furthermore, what is reason, according to John Paul? This question is especially important since John Paul affirms the noetic effects of sin in the above passage. De Chirico recognizes that but thinks that the total depravity of human nature entails reason's incapacity to grasp reality, truth, and so, God, rendering it unreliable, reflecting an extreme pessimism about nature (Nichols, *Shape of Theology*, 45–46). De Chirico thinks that since John Paul says that since human reason is still able to grasp truth, even about God, then his view of reason weakens the noetic effects of sin. He is wrong, again. What, then, is human reason, according to John Paul?

To answer this question requires making some distinctions.[4] Following Aidan Nichols, I distinguish between "absolute reason," "pure reason," and "natural reason" (Nichols, *Epiphany*, 10). [1] "Absolute reason, refuses all revelation, as of set purpose." De Chirico seems to charge John Paul with this view of reason. [2] Neo-scholastics of the nineteenth and twentieth centuries, who held that the unaided reason of natural theology could reason about God, of course did not subscribe to a notion of "absolute reason" that "refuses all revelation, as of set purpose." In other words, they were not "pure rationalists." "While the pure rationalist puts philosophy [and hence reason] in the highest place, and identifies it with wisdom, the neo-scholastic subordinates it to theology which alone, as he holds, fully deserves that name." Still, the neo-scholastics subscribed to a notion of "'pure reason,' beloved of rationalism, [which] belongs only with a state of pure nature." The notion of "pure nature" prescinds from all concrete conditions and circumstances under which human reason actually functions. Gilson correctly notes that even though these neo-scholastics subordinate philosophical reason to theology, divine wisdom, as it were, in their view "philosophy [and hence reason] remains precisely of the same nature as any other that recognizes no Wisdom higher than itself" (Gilson, *Spirit of Medieval Philosophy*, 4). But this means that neo-scholastics do not recognize in the order of nature, as Vatican I stated, that "created reason is wholly subordinate to uncreated Truth" (Denzinger, §3008), even in the natural activity of human reason. On this view, human reason is autonomous, self-sufficient, and the ultimate authority in the order of nature, which is precisely what Reformed and Evangelical critics, such as Berkouwer, Allison, and De Chirico, repudiate.

De Chirico and Allison are oblivious to Catholic critics of the neo-scholastic conception of human reason, such as Gilson, Maritain, Balthasar, Ratzinger, Nichols, et al. These critics argue that—in Nichols' words—the "state of pure nature…has never, in the concrete, existed" (*Epiphany*, 10).

As I understand these critics, "pure reason" does not, concretely, exist because the natural reasoning of actual human beings is a religious act, as it were, being already directed in the actual conditions of fact under which it operates by the central disposition of the heart, whether fallen or renewed, either for or against God. Indeed, instead of absolute reason, or pure reason, these Catholic critics subscribe to a notion of "natural reason," according to Nichols, which "remains open and disponible where revelation is concerned: it is able to enter into a relation with some historically realized situation of [humanity], whether fallen or redeemed" (ibid.). Nichols's view, then, is that men seek a natural knowledge of God in the actual conditions in which they have already made a choice either for or against God, and hence they are in either a state of grace or of sin. This, too, is Hans Urs von Balthasar's view: "The outlook of his reason will not be the outlook of a *ratio pura* but of a reason that already stands within the teleology of faith or unbelief." He adds,

> In the light of faith, both a pure nature and a pure reason appear as abstractions which indeed need not be false as such, but which lack any corresponding detached and separate reality in the concrete world-order. The human person, as he exists *de facto*, is always *a priori* one who has taken a position for or against the God of grace, because the entire order of nature has been set *a priori* by the revelation of Christ at the service of his supernatural kingdom. Thus, too, the concrete eye of reason is always an eye that is purified and made keener by the light of faith and love, or else an eye that is obscured by original sin or personal guilt.[5]

Balthasar's view is consistent with Vatican I as long as one affirms at the same time that we can have certain knowledge of God by the natural light of reason. "[A]ccording to Vatican I," argues Balthasar, "all natural knowledge of God occurs de facto within the positive and negative conditions of the supernatural order. Thomas Aquinas was of the opinion that in corresponding to the fact that man possesses only one single supernatural goal, every human being who had reached the age of reason must make a choice either for or against the God of grace" (Balthasar, *Theo-Logic*, 30).

In other words, man himself within the actual history of salvation is always *de facto* the man who has either turned away from God in sin or turned toward God in the light of grace and faith. This turn toward God always occurs with his prevenient grace, or, in the words of Vatican I: "For the most merciful Lord stirs up those who go astray and helps them by his grace so that they may come to the knowledge of the truth [see 1 Tim 2:4]; and also confirms by his grace those whom he has translated into his admirable light [cf. 1 Pet 2:9; Col 1:13], so that they may persevere in this light" (Denzinger, §3005). Still, on this view, the natural capacity of human reason to grasp, in some degree, the truth about God continues to function because "the intellectual character of [natural reason] or the clear evidence it perceives" has not been called into question by being called to total submission to the Creator and Lord. Rather than destroy or turn human nature and hence human reasoning into its opposite, grace transforms it by calling "on reason to fulfill the most natural aspects of its identity" (Balthasar, *Theo-Logic*, 30).

Given this understanding of human reason and hence of human nature and the noetic influences of sin, isn't it enough to say, then, as John Paul II does above and St. Thomas did before him, that original sin wounded human nature? St. Thomas makes clear that original sin involves the dissolution of a natural harmony pertaining to human nature that he also calls a "sickness of nature." As he puts it, "original justice was taken away by the sin of the first parents. As a result, all the powers of the soul are in a sense lacking the order proper to them, their natural order to virtue, and the deprivation is called the 'wounding of nature' ... In so far as reason is deprived of its direction towards truth, we have the 'wound of ignorance.'"[6] Thus, reason is, as Etienne Gilson puts it, "stripped of its disposition for truth." Importantly, St. Thomas does not say that reason merely lost a supernatural addition to our rational capacities. No, what was lost was suffered by our natural reason. "To be sure," adds Gilson, "the very essence of human reason was left intact and even the natural aptitude of man to know the truth has suffered less from original sin than his aptitude to will the good; but nevertheless, because our reason is the knowing power of a human nature wounded by sin, it did suffer from it, and it still suffers from each supplementary wound that new sins inflict on it" (*Christianity and Philosophy*, 80). Dooyeweerd agrees with John Paul II that we have retained the power to reason and understand in its fallen state. They agree as well that our entire being has been disordered by sin, hampering our employment of the human capacity to know the truth. Thus, I ask once again, is it not enough that human reason is wounded and weakened by sin? Could Evangelical Protestants, such as Allison and De Chirico, ask for more?

In what follows, I distinguish Position I and Position II in Allison's and De Chirico's theology of nature and grace. Position I is the stance they take when criticizing Catholicism on the relation of nature and grace. Position II qualifies that stance, in terms of common grace, and the distinction between structure and direction, and hence comes within the orbit of a Catholic theology of nature and grace.

Position I on Nature and Grace

Regarding Position I, Allison claims that Catholicism denies that "original sin impacts every aspect of human nature" (*RCTP*, 129). De Chirico agrees: "the Thomist tradition has been able to summarize its own worldview with the adage: 'grace does not remove nature, but perfects it'; between nature and grace there is a distinction of order, *but not a breach caused by sin*."[7] I have already refuted that claim above. But I would like to pursue further their position. De Chirico explains:

> The Evangelical point of view is that the hamartiological breach which occurred at the fall has a significance which is much more far-reaching than a mere wound or stain: in that tradition, sin has a far more serious theological status which impinges on the whole orientation of its worldview, to the extent that nature has definitely lost that inner capacity to correspond with divine grace and has radically changed its protological status into a sin-driven, and utterly corrupted reality. (*ETP*, 237)

Allison agrees, "Nature and grace are the two constitutive elements of the Catholic system, with sin as a serious yet not devastating secondary element. Nature, while wounded by sin, retains a capacity for grace [i.e., to receive, transmit, and cooperate with grace, he says elsewhere], and grace elevates or perfects nature. The two continue to operate interdependently" (*RCTP*, 47). By contrast, according to Allison:

> [E]vangelical theology has three poles: creation, fall/ sin, and redemption/grace. In this system, sin is taken more seriously, and its corrupting impact on the creation is not mitigated by its being part of nature. … Indeed, evangelical theology has three constitutive elements, with the fall or sin a primary, rather than secondary element of its system. Because of the devastatingly deep impact of sin on creation, the notion of nature as possessing some capacity for grace is nonsensical in the evangelical system. … For Catholic theology, nature and grace are interdependent; for evangelical theology, nature and grace are at odds because of the devastating impact of sin on nature. … According to evangelical theology, [consequently] grace has *nothing* [emphasis added] to work with in nature because creation has been devastatingly tainted by sin (*RCTP*, 48–49).

First, then, Allison and De Chirico claim that Evangelical theology holds that human nature is fallen and devastatingly tainted by sin in the sense of being *obliterated* and, consequently, irreclaimable. As Allison states in the concluding sentence of the above paragraph, "grace has *nothing* [emphasis added] to work with in nature because creation has been devastatingly tainted by sin." Such a view however would suggest that post-fall human nature is simply a corrupt vessel needing to be replaced by something altogether new. Such a position seems inevitable if Allison and De Chirico deny that there exists any continuity whatsoever between nature and grace in view of the fall/sin. This emphasis on discontinuity between nature and grace reflects pessimism and hence an ontological opposition between nature and grace after the fall—despite De Chirico's disclaimer to the contrary. This, too, is De Chirico's view upon which Allison demonstrates an uncritical overreliance. In the postlapsarian situation, De Chirico says, the "protological status" of the structures of creation "has radically changed … into a sin-driven, and utterly corrupted reality." Again, he says, "Creation is therefore a fallen creation which has irreversibly lost its primordial prerogatives and exists in a state of separation from God" (*ETP*, 237). Concurring again with De Chirico, Allison repeats throughout his books that Evangelical theology rejects the "Catholic system's axiom of the nature grace interdependence, specifically ... grace must be embodied in nature" (*RCTP*, 253), or "that grace be manifested concretely in nature" (*RCTP*, 194; 170). Says De Chirico, "The Roman Catholic system is therefore based on a bipolar scheme in which nature is related to grace but where sin, though taken seriously, is nonetheless included in the sphere of nature, and in [sic] its negative effects are therefore relativized" (*ETP*, 236). So, there is no sense whatsoever in which we can say that grace builds upon nature. Yet this would mean that grace has no point of contact whatsoever with nature (read: enduring structures of created reality). This position seems more Barthian than Evangelical or Reformed, as I argued above.

It is important to consider here, even if only briefly, Berkouwer's rejection of the idea that human nature, even after the fall, and hence human reason possess a "principled capacity and openness to the revelation of God."[8] In his 1949 work on Catholicism, *Conflict met Rome*, Berkouwer critically discusses the view of Dutch Catholic theologian Jan C. Groot (1908–1994) who held that human nature remained intact even after the fall.[9] Says Berkouwer, "It consists in the rational moral nature of man owing to which, even after the fall, man has retained a certain openness to God. There is no other possibility, according to Rome, for this is the basis of man's susceptibility to the Word of God." In sum, according to Groot, "Human nature should not be conceived as totally closed to God. ... For this reason there must be a 'positive point of contact,' a positive possibility on the 'part of nature.'"[10] The denial of this Catholic view, argued Groot, results in the separation of "nature from grace, not recognizing any point of contact, and making grace a new creation hovering in a vacuum" (*Conflict met Rome*, 135 [100]). On this view, grace replaces nature in us *de novo*; man is a new creation in that sense for there is nothing already existing in human nature, no previous analogies, to which the gospel might appeal. Groot aligns the Calvinist view, as he understands it, with Barth's claim that "[Revelation] comes to us as a datum with no point of connection with any previous datum."[11]

In response to Groot, and to his charge that revelation must result in an overcoming of the order of creation such that it is replaced altogether by something entirely new, Berkouwer defends the view that human nature is preserved even after the fall because of common grace—the latter is a kind of grace that restrains sin and evil from having its full way with the whole creation.[12] He explicitly rejects the charge, which he associates with the early dialectical theology of Barth, "that faith is a *donum superadditum*, a *donum novum* in God's hands, which remains external to concrete existence."[13] Barth's view would make it difficult to account for faith as a human act (Berkouwer, *Geloof en Rechtvaardiging*, 187 [178]). As *CCC* states, "Believing is possible only by grace and the interior helps of the Holy Spirit. But it is no less true that believing is an authentically human act. Trusting in God and cleaving to the truths that he has revealed are contrary neither to human freedom nor to human reason" (§154). Thus, the substance of human nature, its deepest structure, in short, the order of creation, remains the same as God intended it even under the regime of sin. Rather than the structure of human nature having changed, needing to be replaced altogether by something entirely new, "a new world apart from human nature," as Berkouwer describes this view, what has changed, according to Berkouwer is man's *direction*. "Direction" here may also be referred to as "the order of sin and redemption." Berkouwer explains: "The moment of 'direction,' of the being directed of man in obedience or in apostasy, plays a decisive role...for the entire way of Reformed thought about man after the fall." Significantly, Berkouwer adds, "That is why, without any supra-naturalistic exaggeration, and recognizing the universal revelation [in creation], Reformed theology could deny any positiveness and susceptibility in man in relation to the true God, and was able more than Rome to profess the absolute miracle of God's grace and the opening of man's heart by the Holy Spirit" (*Conflict met Rome*, 137 [101]). Elsewhere Berkouwer writes in the same vein, "Grace does not mean an ontological cutting-off of a part of human life" (*Geloof en Rechtvaardiging*, 187–88 [179]). Berkouwer is arguing here that grace does not replace human nature altogether with something new but rather restores nature to fulfill its ordained ends. He explains:

> The new man—that is the mighty change which in Christ comes over human nature. It is not a change in the sense of a "transubstantiation," a change from one essence to another. Rather, man comes to his true nature, his nature as God intended it to be. (*De Mens Het Beeld Gods*, 102 [99])[14]

But this emphasis on structure—the order of creation—and direction—the order of sin and redemption—does not really get at the issue that divides Catholics and Reformed thinkers, like Berkouwer. I show below that this is actually close to the Catholic view when I consider Position II that qualifies Position I; the former comes within the orbit of a Catholic theology of nature and grace. For now, we more properly get at the division between Catholics and Reformed thinkers with Berkouwer's rejection of "all such notions as capacity, point of contact, susceptibility, fitness [that] in the Roman view have an ontological accent" (*Conflict met Rome*, 137 [101]). By "ontological accent" Berkouwer means that, on the Roman Catholic view, man remains a human being such that he is responsible and addressable, in short, *capax Dei*, providing a point of contact—*Anknüpfungspunkt*—between the gospel and human nature, a natural access point of entry, which is the condition of the possibility of the reception of revelation. For Berkouwer, the ontological accent of these notions presupposes a relative optimism in a Catholic view of human nature, predisposing man favorably to God's redemptive revelation. This criticism is also the view of Allison and De Chirico.

I want to respond to this criticism by considering the question regarding the relation between nature and grace, or structure and direction, as Berkouwer, at least in *Conflict met Rome*, and other neo-Calvinists prefer to phrase it, and the corresponding question of the *capax Dei*, namely, the question of the condition for the reception of revelation. As we saw above, Berkouwer distinguished between "structure" and "direction," or, alternatively put, between "the order of creation" and the "order of sin and redemption." Albert Wolters succinctly states the meaning of this categorical distinction in neo-Calvinism:

> "Structure" refers to the created cosmos as it was meant to be; "direction" refers to that cosmos as it is misdirected by sin and redemptively redirected by Christ. Because sin and redemption, in the Calvinist understanding, are cosmic in scope, this distinction holds in principle for all the earthly creation, including natural, cultural and societal life as well as morality and piety. Here the Calvinist stress on the radical and comprehensive scope of man's Fall, as well as the equally radical and comprehensive scope of Christ's redemption, finds expression in a succinct categorical formulation. At the same time, this fundamental

distinction reflects the basic Calvinist intuition that salvation is re-creation, that is, that grace does not destroy or supplement, but rather restores nature.[15]

We find this understanding of the relation of nature and grace, creation and re-creation, in Berkouwer's 1932 doctoral dissertation, *Geloof en Openbaring in Nieuwere Duitsche Theologie,* as well as in his 1949 work, *Conflict met Rome.* In the former work, this relation is especially evident in regard to the question of the basis of the believing subject in both the order of creation and redemption. Berkouwer writes, "The connection between the believing subject and creation, and in this connection between the believing subject and general revelation, opens the possibility for subjectivity to come fully into its own" (*Geloof en Openbaring,* 238). Indeed, he adds, "The perspective on subjectivity comes into its own in light of Scripture's teaching regarding creation and re-creation" (ibid.). Berkouwer elaborates:

> Man is God's creature and through general revelation is thus never a revelation-less being. Furthermore, the created being of man remains intact, not having been abolished by the fall, and hence the subjective possibility exists for special revelation to find a point of contact in man's nature. ... The denial of this subjective possibility of revelation in man seems to be a plea for the glory of God, but it actually negates the principle that the creation is a work of God's hands. ... Recreation then is the restoration of what was wrongly directed through sin. ... The recognition of this actual human subjectivity in creation is in no sense a denial of the freedom of God's self-revelation, but results from the recognition of the believing subject in creation and hence the continued existence of its being despite the impact of sin. *(Ibid., 239)*

Therefore, the relation between special revelation and general revelation, re-creation and creation, is such that the former is inseparably connected to the latter. Summarily stated, "Revelation follows this law: re-creation is adapted to creation."[16]

I have argued in several works that the theology of nature and grace expressed in neo-Calvinism is similar to Gilson's Catholic theology of nature and grace.[17] Gilson explains: "Grace presupposes nature, whether to restore or to enrich it. When grace restores nature, it does not substitute itself for it, but re-establishes it; when nature, thus re-established by grace, accomplishes its proper operations, they are indeed natural operations which it performs" (*Christianity and Philosophy*, 24). So, grace does not overcome the natural operations of creation; indeed, it restores them from within. Elsewhere Gilson writes, "Catholicism teaches before everything the restoration of wounded nature by the grace of Jesus Christ. The restoration of nature: so that there must be a nature, and of what value, since it is the work of God, Who created it and re-created it by repurchasing it at the price of His own Blood! Thus, grace presupposes nature, and the excellence of nature which it comes to heal and transfigure" (ibid., 111).[18] In sum, my argument here is that the neo-Calvinist theology of nature and grace is consistent with the Thomistic axiom that grace neither abolishes nor leaves nature untouched: our nature was created by God, it exists in the state of fallen nature as a consequence of Adam's sin, but in Christ it is marvelously restored, and so now exists in a state of redeemed nature. So, the difference between Berkouwer and Catholicism is not as such in respect of that theology. The real difference is seen clearly when we ask whether the natural capacity for God remains intact even after the fall and, if so, in what sense and to what degree.

I now argue that humans lack the spiritual tendency or predisposition to free themselves by their own powers from their rejection of God; the alienation between God and humanity is too deep to suggest that man possesses a tendency or predisposition in favor of God's revelation. As Trent's Decree on Justification states, "On the Inability of Nature and of the Law to Justify Man":

> First the holy council declares that for a correct and clear understanding of the doctrine of Justification it is necessary that each one admits and confesses that all men, having lost innocence through the sin Adam [cf. Rom 5:12; 1 Cor 15:22], "became unclean," and, according to the apostle, were "by nature children of wrath," [Eph 2:3], as the council taught in its decree on original sin. So completely were they the slaves of sin [cf. Rom 6:20] and under the power of the devil and of death that not only the Gentiles by the power of nature but even the Jews by means of the law of Moses were unable to liberate themselves and to rise from the state. (Denzinger, §1521)

Accordingly, God's grace renews the direction of the whole man's existence, with his gracious initiative and activity having priority given humanity's inability to redeem itself; in this point Berkouwer is right that man has lost his spiritual disposition for God. There is no difference here with the Catholic tradition. As the *Catechism of the Catholic Church* states: "For man to be able to enter into real intimacy with him [a personal God], God willed both to reveal himself to man and to give him the grace of being able to welcome this revelation in faith" (§35).

There is a difference between "capacity" and "tendency or predisposition." But this difference does not entail that sinful humanity does not have a *capax Dei*, a natural capacity for God's self-revelation even in his postlapsarian condition. Indeed, the *Catechism* locates the "point of contact" for man to receive God's self-revelation in grace and faith in "man's capacity for God," that is, the faculties that "make him capable of coming to a knowledge of the existence of a personal God." "Without this capacity," adds the *Catechism*, "man would not be able to welcome God's revelation. Man has this capacity because he is created 'in the image of God'" (§35). Isn't this natural capacity the condition for its reception even after the fall?

If man was created by God and for God, if the desire for him is written in the human heart and God never ceases to draw man to himself, if all of this is given with the structure of humanity's creation, sustained even in the regime of sin by God's grace and mercy, then the structure of creation, in particular, humanity's natural capacity for God remains intact even after the fall. What man lost after the fall is his spiritual disposition for God, his direction, as Berkouwer puts it. Gilson explains this point admirably well:

> The first thing to find out, therefore, is whether our nature, wounded by original sin, can wisely neglect the remedy supplied by God Himself for its wound. Saint Thomas constantly justifies the necessity of Revelation by the weakness of human reason which, left to itself, would inevitably become entangled in the grossest errors. Since when is the human reason so weak? When St. Thomas enumerates the wounds inflicted on human nature by the sin of Adam, he never forgets to mention ignorance, by which reason is stripped of its disposition for truth. We could not of ourselves remedy this loss suffered by our natural reason.

On the one hand, actually functioning human reason suffers the noetic effects of original sin. Given these effects, particularly, human reason has been stripped of the disposition for truth; man experiences many difficulties in knowing God by the light of reason alone. Hence, divine revelation makes available to us truths that are rationally knowable truths "so that even in the present condition of the human race, they can be known by all men with ease, with firm certainty and with no admixture of error."[19] Gilson continues:

> To be sure, the very essence [read: structure] of human reason was left intact and even the natural aptitude of man to know the truth has suffered less from original sin than his aptitude to will the good; but neverthe-less, because our reason is the knowing power of a human nature wounded by sin, it did suffer from it, and it still suffers from each supplementary wound that new sins inflict on it. We have therefore come back to that fundamental Catholic postulate, namely, that fallen nature, although it can do something, can, however, no longer do all the good connatural to it so that it never fails in any way (*totum bonum sibi con-naturale ita quod in nullo deficiat*).... (*Christianity and Phi-losophy*, 80)

The deepest foundation, structure, of human reason is still what God made it, despite it being savagely wounded and seriously dam-aged by the fall. Furthermore, says Gilson:

> [So] the detriment suffered by his nature remains and only a divine intervention can remove it. Faith in the divine Word brings this grace to us.... To forget what good remains in nature is fatal to Catholicism, but to forget what nature has suffered and the remedies which its weakness calls for would be none the less fatal to it.

Fatal to Catholicism is forgetting that the deepest foundation of nature persists even in the regime of sin, on the one hand, and for-getting the noetic effects of sin on the other.

In this light, we can ask what, then, are the conditions of possibil-ity for the reception of revelation? In this connection, we need to consider whether Berkouwer has satisfactorily addressed the issue of the point of contact (*anknüpfungspunkt*) for divine revelation in some sense within human nature. He still leaves us wondering how that revelation is received, and what the conditions are for its recep-tion by the receiver. Does this natural capacity for God mean that human nature should not be conceived as totally closed to him? I would answer this question affirmatively, but I would quickly add that it is a matter of God's grace that it is not completely closed.

That is, it is a matter of God's grace that he never ceases to draw man to himself even after the fall. If so, isn't this natural capacity, this *capax Dei*—as the Dutch Catholic theologian Jan Groot, Berkouwer's contemporary, once put it—"the reason why there is a 'positive point of contact,' a positive possibility on the part of nature."[20] This natural capacity for God, which remains intact even after the fall, and which is the condition for the possibility of humanity's intimate and vital bond to God, of course does not mean that humanity by nature, or naturally, by its own powers, responds to God. Not at all, humanity has lost the spiritual disposition for God, which is evident in that "God can be forgotten, overlooked, or even explicitly rejected by man" (*CCC* §30). Still, "Although man can forget God or reject him, He [God] never ceases to call every man to seek him, so as to find life and happiness." This is the case "even after losing through his sin his likeness to God, [for] man remains an image of the Creator, and retains the desire for the one who calls him into existence." Significantly, "this search for God demands of man every effort of intellect, a sound will, an 'upright heart,' as well as the witness of others who teach him to seek God" (*CCC* §30). In keeping with the truth that man lost after the fall his spiritual disposition for God, his direction, one must add here, in order to avoid any misinterpretation, that this all is a work of grace: "The preparation of man for the reception of [justifying] grace [in Christ and by the Holy Spirit] is already a work of [prevenient] grace" (*CCC* §2001). The question I now want to put to Allison and De Chirico is whether they have pushed the *non capax* too far, given their emphasis on divine transcendence and the fact that humanity is justified in believing in God only because of revelation, of the *Deus dixit*? Revelation is a complete and utter *novum* by the power of the Holy Spirit with no prior conditions for the possibility of its reception, except the conditions that God himself has created in his act of self-revelation.

One such condition is, then, human nature's natural capacity for God, a *capax Dei*, which should not be conceived as *totally* closed to him. Natural theology, then, plays a role in creating a space in which the possibility of divine revelation is allowed. Of course, the Catholic tradition does hold that truths like the existence of God are within the capacity of natural reason in itself to grasp through theistic arguments. And such arguments contribute to the "motives of credibility" that should make the reception of revelation in faith epistemically responsible. As the *Catechism of the Catholic Church* states, "The proofs of God's existence…can predispose one to faith and help one to see that faith is not opposed to reason" (§35).

Allison and De Chirico, given their view of nature and grace, and the impact of sin upon nature, reject natural theology. Here, too, Allison acknowledges that there does not exist unanimity among Evangelicals concerning theistic arguments (*RCTP*, 76). Given the diversity of views among Evangelicals, with some, like William Lane Craig,[21] sharing Catholicism's affirmation of the legitimacy of natural theology, it is not clear why he identifies his view as Evangelical and antithetical to Catholicism.

Be that as it may, Allison rejects *CCC*'s support for natural theology because the "deceitfulness and destructiveness of sin … extends to human rationality and corrupts its ability to gain sure knowledge of God through the created order" (*RCTP*, 77). His reasoning is this: given human nature's total corruption, then, human rationality, as an integral part of human nature, is grossly unreliable as an even subordinate source of knowledge of God's general revelation and the enduring structures of creation and natural law, and hence cannot be of much service to the gospel. Allison, then, claims that given Catholicism's view of a "nature-grace continuum" and hence its inadequate attention to human rationality being "thoroughly devastated by sin" (*RCTP*, 77), *CCC* has a "rather hopeful attitude toward general revelation" (*RCTP*, 76). Hopeful in the sense, he claims, that for Catholicism general revelation is "enough for salvation to take place." But this claim is false. I have refuted it elsewhere.[22] For now, it suffices to note that "evangelical theology would agree with *CCC* that the mere knowledge of the existence of God is insufficient for a personal relationship with him" (*RCTP*, 76).

For now, I want to emphasize the point made by *CCC* that "for man to be able to enter into real intimacy with him, God willed both to reveal himself to man, and to give him the grace of being able to welcome this revelation in faith" (§35). Thus, it adds, "This is why man stands in need of being enlightened by God's revelation, not only about those things that exceed his understanding, but also 'about those religious and moral truths which of themselves are not beyond the grasp of human reason, so that even in the present condition of the human race, they can be known by all men with ease, with firm certainty and with no admixture of error'" (§38).[23] And again, *CCC* states: "there is another order of knowledge, which man cannot possibly arrive at by his own powers: the order of divine Revelation. Through an utterly free decision, God has revealed himself and given himself to man. This he does by revealing the mystery, his plan of loving goodness, formed from all eternity in Christ, for the benefit of all men. God has fully revealed this plan by sending us his beloved Son, our Lord Jesus Christ, and the Holy Spirit" (§50). Allison inexplicably overlooks all these passages from *CCC*. Be that as it may, the Catholic tradition agrees with Allison that the knowledge of God by means of general revelation is insufficient to give us a saving knowledge of God. He is right: "general revelation was not designed to foster a personal relationship with God; special revelation serves that role" (*RCTP*, 76).

Furthermore, Allison repeats the same—as I will argue, faulty—argument in the context of the knowledge of the natural law. He acknowledges that Catholic theology affirms not only the noetic influences of sin upon man's knowledge of natural law principles but also that man needs grace and revelation to overcome these influences. But then he draws the bewildering conclusion that for Catholicism "humanity's problem is … just an epistemological one—the failure to know natural law's precepts." Allison insists, however, that man's "plight is moral—the culpable failure to obey those precepts" (*RCTP*, 427).

But Allison could not be further from the mark on both counts. Regarding man's plight as allegedly merely epistemic, Allison offers no evidence that the failure to grasp natural law precepts is, according to Catholicism, the source of man's alienation from God. He has reversed the order: man's alienation from God is not merely noetic—even of the natural law—but religious because of sin. It is sin that is man's plight. *CCC* states: "He freely sinned. By refusing God's plan of love, he deceived himself and became a slave to sin. This first alienation engendered a multitude of others. From its outset, human history attests the wretchedness and oppression born of the human heart in consequence of the abuse of freedom" (§1739). *CCC* explains:

> Sin is present in human history; any attempt to ignore it or to give this dark reality other names would be futile. To try to understand what sin is, one must first recognize the profound relation of man to God, for only in this relationship is the evil of sin unmasked in its true identity as humanity's rejection of God and

opposition to him, even as it continues to weigh heavy on human life and history [including man's epistemic grasp of natural law precepts]. Only the light of divine Revelation clarifies the reality of sin and particularly of the sin committed at mankind's origins [i.e., original sin]. Without the knowledge Revelation gives of God we cannot recognize sin clearly and are tempted to explain it as merely a developmental flaw, a psychological weakness, a mistake, or the necessary consequence of an inadequate social structure, etc. Only in the knowledge of God's plan for man can we grasp that sin is an abuse of the freedom that God gives to created persons so that they are capable of loving him and loving one another (§§386–87).[24]

In sum, *pace* Allison, it is divine revelation, not the natural law, which illuminates the reality of sin by disclosing that man's plight is his alienation from God. Says John Paul II, "Moreover, man, who was created for freedom, bears within himself the wound of original sin, which constantly draws him towards evil and puts him in need of redemption. Not only is *this doctrine an integral part of Christian revelation*; it also has great hermeneutical value insofar as it helps one to understand human reality. Man tends towards good, but he is also capable of evil" (*Centesimus Annus*, §25). *CCC* explains, "But this 'intimate and vital bond of man to God' (GS §19) can be forgotten, overlooked, or even explicitly rejected by man. Such attitudes can have different causes: revolt against evil in the world; religious ignorance or indifference; the cares and riches of this world; the scandal of bad example on the part of believers; currents of thought hostile to religion; finally, that attitude of sinful man which makes him hide from God out of fear and flee his call" (§29). Clearly, Allison's interpretation of Catholicism on this point is reductionist and is not borne out by what *CCC* actually says.

Now, regarding natural theology, what sets Allison off in the wrong direction is his misinterpretation of *CCC*'s statement:

Man's faculties make him capable of coming to knowledge of the existence of a personal God. But for man to be able to enter into real intimacy with him, God willed both to reveal himself to man, and to give him the grace of being able to welcome this revelation in faith. The proofs of God's existence, however, can predispose one to faith and help one to see that faith is not opposed to reason. (§35)

In addition to his inaccurate claim that general revelation discloses to us a saving knowledge of God, Allison claims that *CCC* affirms that general revelation "dispose nonbelievers to faith." But how is this possible "when they [nonbelievers] so steadily and *completely* reject general revelation" (RCTP, 76; emphasis added)? Allison's answer to this question returns him to the "nature-grace interdependence, one of the axioms of the Catholic theological system" in which "while sin has seriously influenced nature, it has not so corrupted it that a *positive human response* to general revelation is *precluded* " (RCTP, 76; emphasis added).

Although Allison underscores his conviction that "Evangelical theology strongly dissents from this position," he would be more accurate that *his* version of Evangelical theology strongly dissents. For instance, because of God's common grace, Dutch neo-Calvinists like Kuyper and Herman Bavinck find truth and goodness in pagan religions.[25] Also, the Canons of Dort (1619) state: "There remains, however, in man since the fall, the glimmerings of natural light, whereby he retains some knowledge of God, of natural things, and of the difference between good and evil, and shows some regard for virtue and for good outward behavior."[26] So, even according to the Reformed tradition, clearly man does not completely reject general revelation but also there is a positive human response, albeit non-salvific one, to that revelation.

Furthermore, Allison misunderstands the role of theistic arguments concerning faith's knowledge of God. *CCC* says such arguments predispose one to faith in the sense of showing that "faith is not opposed to reason." Does Allison deny this claim? I can't imagine that he denies that faith is reasonable in that sense. Moreover, *CCC* does not claim that theistic arguments, although available, are necessary to come to knowledge of God's existence. Indeed, it says the very opposite. "In the historical conditions in which he finds himself, however, man experiences many difficulties in coming to know God by the light of reason alone" (§37). It follows up this claim by quoting Pius XII, *Humani Generis*, who emphasizes, among other obstacles to gaining a natural knowledge of God, the noetic influences of sin:

> Though human reason is, strictly speaking, truly capable by its own natural power and light of attaining to a true and certain knowledge of the one personal God, who watches over and controls the world by his providence, and of the natural law written in our

hearts by the Creator; yet there are many obstacles which prevent reason from the effective and fruitful use of this inborn faculty. For the truths that concern the relations between God and man wholly transcend the visible order of things, and, if they are translated into human action and influence it, they call for self-surrender and abnegation. The human mind, in its turn, is hampered in the attaining of such truths, not only by the impact of the senses and the imagination, but also by disordered appetites which are the consequences of original sin. So it happens that men in such matters easily persuade themselves that what they would not like to be true is false or at least doubtful. (Denzinger, §3875)

Now, it isn't that Allison rejects God's general revelation. He affirms God's objective revelation of himself in and through the works of creation. This general revelation still persists despite the fall into sin. But no sooner does he affirm general revelation that he claims that we have no reliable access via natural reason to grasp the works of God (*RCTP*, 75–76) to certain knowledge of him. This means a rejection of natural theology, theistic arguments, or reasons for belief in God. Allison acknowledges that this conclusion is not unanimously held by all Evangelicals (*RCTP*, 76). Why, then, does he take an antithetical stance only toward Catholicism?

Moreover, according to the Catholic tradition, the knowledge of God that is in principle possible to gain through general revelation is inadequate, distorted, incomplete, non-salvific knowledge, but nonetheless true. The noetic influences of sin suppress and impede the functioning of natural reason's capacity to acquire knowledge of God through general revelation. Significantly, this knowledge of all such truth "must ultimately be disciplined by, and incorporated into, the revelatory narrative [of creation, fall, and redemption]. Athens, whatever its own insights into truth, must ultimately be chastened by Jerusalem" (Guarino, *Foundations*, 269) if it is to be of any service in deepening our intimate knowledge of the Trinity.

I call Allison's view "epistemic supernaturalism," or fideism, because the *sole* source, not just the ultimate or primary source of our reliable knowledge of God is special revelation. What about general revelation? I return to this point in the next paragraph. For now, let us take note that at the root of this so-called "hopeful attitude" (*RCTP*, 76) concerning natural theology's ability to grasp God through general revelation is, according to Allison, "the Catholic system's axiom of a nature-grace continuum that is not *thoroughly* devastated by sin" (*RCTP*, 77; emphasis added). Thoroughly devasted means totally incapacitated, reflecting an extreme pessimism about nature, as I argued above. Of course, the Catholic tradition holds that after the fall, according to Nichols, "human nature has been savagely wounded by the Fall; its powers, and thus its activities, have been seriously damaged by sin." Still, adds Nichols rightly, "its deepest foundation is still what God made it" (*Shape of Theology*, 45). What, then, is grace restoring? On Allison's *unqualified* view of the relation between nature and grace, there is nothing to restore because human nature in its fallen condition is, says Allison, "thoroughly devastated by sin" (*RCTP*, 77), and hence is essentially, *irreclaimable*. Human nature is just a corrupt vessel as a consequence of the fall into sin and hence it needs replacing by something entirely new by God's grace. On this view, human nature is taken to be completely closed to God and hence as capable of nothing but sin, with the accompanying loss or destruction of natural reason's response to the enduring structures of creation and general revelation.

In this connection, Allison's epistemic supernaturalism appears to be a corollary of his understanding of *sola Scriptura*. He assures us that the principle of *sola Scriptura* does not mean Scripture *alone*, that is, *Scriptura nuda*, "naked Scripture," and hence it is not an anti-tradition or anti-creedal principle, but rather that "Scripture enjoys primary authority," but "is not the only authority—indeed, the principle is not a rejection of other authorities" (*RCTP*, 92). Notwithstanding Allison's claim about *sola Scriptura*, Scripture *alone* actually functions for him as a *self-sufficient* authority for Christian faith and thought. I have already refuted his view in Chapter 3, and hence will not return to my arguments here. For now, I just want to emphasize that, of course, *pace* Allison and De Chirico, in fact, it is not Scripture alone that he uses as the standard of theological judgment, it is "Scripture and evangelical theology" (*RCTP*, 18; emphasis added), the latter refracted at times through, for example, a congregationalist ecclesiology (*RCTP*, 182; 192), quasi-Zwinglian sacramental theology (*RCTP*, 230; 243), and a particular understanding of the relation between grace and freedom (*RCTP*, 404n75).

Such an ecclesiology, sacramental theology, and understanding of grace and freedom are not held by all Evangelicals. Evangelicals that are Lutheran or Reformed (or Catholic!) have either an episcopal or synodical/presbyterian form of church governance, taking the universal church to be a visible, concrete, actual reality (*RCTP*, 170), rather than only local churches that are autonomous and self-governing congregations. These, adds Allison, "local churches are *divinely* designed to be the [only] instruments of salvation as their parents and members proclaim the gospel, disciple, worship, baptize, celebrate the Lord's Supper, pray, educate, fellowship, provide care, exercise spiritual gifts, and the like" (*RCTP*, 169). Allison thinks that episcopal forms of church governance lead to the papacy and hence "departs from the sufficiency of Scripture because it is dependent on developments in the following centuries for its justification" (*RCTP*, 182). Of course, Presbyterian, Reformed, Lutheran, Anglican, Orthodox—not to say, Catholic—would disagree that the only divinely designed instrument of salvation is the local church. The principle of *sola Scriptura* has not overcome the theological differences on ecclesiology, not merely between Protestants and the Catholic Church, but among Protestants themselves.

Furthermore, regarding Allison and De Chirico's tilt toward Zwinglian sacramentology, as to the question of, not whether but how the sacraments are means of grace, the Catholic tradition agrees with Calvin that the sacraments are the "pillars of our faith."[27] Intriguingly, Allison does not share Calvin's view of the sacraments. In his recent book, *Embodied*, the chapter "The Worshipping Body" does not connect the sacramental life of the Church to embodied worship. Be that as it may, by contrast there is much that Reformed and Catholic theologies have in common when it comes to the doctrine of the sacraments. They agree that the sacraments are means of grace, rather than merely outward and empty signs.[28] In short, they agree that God really does impart his grace by sacramental means. They also agree, as Bavinck states, that God alone is the author, initiator, and efficient cause[29] of the sacraments (*Gereformeerde Dogmatiek*, IV, 451 [474]). On this question, according to Kuyper, "The Reformed stand with Rome, Luther, and Calvin against Zwingli in their adherence to a divine working of grace in the sacraments."[30] Briefly, here, too, Allison acknowledges that "While one large segment of Protestant theology continued to embrace the sacraments as means of grace, another large segment moved to a view far removed from any notion of means of grace. Evangelical theology, therefore, encompasses these two positions" (*RCTP*, 243). Again, given the diversity of positions, how then can Allison continue to insist that his position represents Evangelical theology? I'll return to Allison and De Chirico's Evangelical sacramentology in Chapter 5.

On the matter of grace and freedom, Allison acknowledges that "Evangelical theology embraces a number of views of human freedom, including libertarian freedom, dovetailing with indeterminism and with much overlap with Catholic theology's position, and compatibilistic freedom, dovetailing with (soft) determinism" (*RCTP*, 404n75).[31]

Clearly, the diverse Evangelical positions on these matters and others are not, according to Allison, fellowship-dividing issues between Evangelicals. Conceding that point, however, makes it obvious that *sola Scriptura* does not settle the question of justified theological interpretations of these matters briefly sketched above.

Yet such a view—a perennial problem for any Protestant interpretation of Scripture—conflicts with one of the "solas" of Protestantism: "*sola Scriptura* (only Scripture), not Scripture *and* Tradition" (*RCTP*, 44). Be that as it may, evidence of my claim that Allison's position on *sola Scriptura* is indistinguishable from *Scriptura nuda*—despite his disclaimer to the contrary when rejecting a monistic principle of authority—is clear from his judgment that Part III of the *CCC* that deals with the moral life in Christ, theological anthropology, moral theology, social and political dimensions of that life, the natural law, and much more, cannot be considered "definitive and binding." Why? Because the claims made in Part III are "neither explicitly biblical nor explicitly unbiblical" (*RCTP*, 412; see also 404). Yes, Allison affirms that the views expressed there "may be welcomed as a possible contribution to discussions on corporate dimensions of human existence" *(RCTP, 412)*. But that is all they are, being unable to be justified by Scripture alone. His "epistemic supernaturalism" is at work here. It is reflected in his ambivalence about the enduring structures of creation and about the reality of general revelation, which all these reflections purport to be grounded in. This is evident from his judgment that *CCC*'s teaching on the moral life in Christ is flawed because it lacks attention to "any explicit role of Scripture for Christian living." This "criticism reflects what evangelical theology is known for—the Word of God and its authority, sufficiency, and necessity for life in Christ" (*RCTP*, 408). But Allison's claim that *CCC*'s teaching on the moral life in Christ lacks attention to "any explicit role of Scripture for Christian living" is inaccurate, not to say, false. Indeed, I am bewildered by his claim since *CCC*, Part III, Section Two, The Ten Commandments, devotes several hundred paragraphs (§§2052–57) to the explicit role of Scripture for Christian living. Furthermore, *CCC*, Part I, Chapter Two, Article 3, recapitulates the teaching of *Dei Verbum* (§§21–25) on the nature, scope, and necessity of biblical authority—*prima Scriptura*—in the Christian life.[32] What is more, Allison rejects a monistic principle of authority and a corresponding biblicistic purism because he affirms two modes of divine revelation: special and general revelation. The former is historical, verbal, and salvific; the latter refers to God's general revelation of himself in and through the works of creation, which entails a normative creation order or structures of creation, and a natural moral law (Rom 1:18ff; 2:14ff). Special and general revelation must be read in light of each other. But special revelation has a *cognitive priority*—again, *prima Scriptura*—over God's revelation in creation via the very structures of creation, such as marriage and family.

Position II on Nature and Grace

Secondly, I turn now to Position II on Allison's theology of nature and grace. Having opposed "the" Evangelical theological view of nature and grace by insisting that it has been "thoroughly devastated by sin" and all that this claim entails about an *unqualified* opposition between nature and grace, Allison *qualifies* his claim about the discontinuity between nature and grace (*RCTP*, 48n36) by adding references to common grace and the distinction between structure and direction. He derives this idea of qualifying the discontinuity from De Chirico (*ETP*, 238–240), which De Chirico himself gets from the Canadian neo-Calvinist theologian Albert Wolters, who posits and develops this distinction in his well-known book, *Creation Regained* (1985, 1st edition). The upshot of these distinctions is to limit the impact of the fall/sin upon nature (i.e., the structures of reality) such that the fall/sin disordered human nature but human nature itself, its deepest foundations, remained in place after the fall/sin. In other words, metaphysically speaking, what human nature lost because of the fall/sin was accidental, not substantial or essential to being a human being, for the fall/sin did not literally turn the human being into a different kind of creature. The distinction here is between substance/

accident. Paul Helm appeals to this very distinction: "So there are essential features of being a human being—whatever they are—and also accidental features, those lost in the fall, and those restored in Christ" (*Faith, Form, and Fashion*, 28).

Indeed, Calvin himself appeals to this very distinction in his response to Albert Pighius, found in *The Bondage and Liberation of the Will*.[33] And this distinction is traceable to Augustine's *City of God*, Book XIV, Chapter XI,[34] which is applied by *CCC* (see §§1603, 1606–9, 1614–15). Augustine writes: "The natures in which evil exists, in so far as they are natures, are good. And evil is removed, not by removing any nature, or part of a nature but by healing and correcting that which had been vitiated and depraved." So, the essential feature of human nature remains the same, being primary, and hence sin is a secondary element (to use the language of De Chirico) such that it is accidental to human nature. *Pace* De Chirico, in this Augustinian perspective, the "negative effects [of sin] are therefore relativized" (*ETP*, 236). In sum, as Berkouwer argues:

> Reformed theology has been particularly inclined to walk this road [of distinguishing substance and accident]. Calvin, for example, in his commentary on 2 Peter 3:10, distinguishes between substance and quality. The cleansing of heaven and earth 'so that they may be fit for the kingdom of Christ' is not a matter of annihilation, but a judgment in which something will remain. The things will be consumed 'only in order to receive a new quality, while their substance remains the same.' According to Bavinck, the annihilation of substance is an impossibility, but the world, her appearance laid waste by sin, will vanish. There will not be a new, second creation, but a re-creation of what exists, a renaissance. Substantially, nothing will be lost. (*Wederkomst van Christus*, I, 279 [225])

In a passage worth quoting in full from volume 4 of Bavinck's *Reformed Dogmatics*, he succinctly describes this consummation and its substantial continuity with the original creation. This, too, is the position of the Catholic Church, as expressed in *CCC*.

> All that is true, honorable, just, pure, pleasing, and commendable in the whole of creation, in heaven and on earth, is gathered up in the future city of God—renewed, re-created, boosted to its highest glory. The substance [of the city of God] is present in the creation. Just as the caterpillar becomes a butterfly,

as carbon is converted into diamond, as the grain of wheat upon dying in the ground produces other grains of wheat, as all of nature revives in the spring and dresses up in celebrative clothing, as the believing community is formed out of Adam's fallen race, as the resurrection body is raised from the body that is dead and buried in the earth, so too, by the re-creating power of Christ, the new heaven and the new earth will one day emerge from the fire-purged elements of this world, radiant in enduring glory and forever set free from the "bondage to decay" ... [Rom. 8:21]. More glorious than this beautiful earth, more glorious than the earthly Jerusalem, more glorious even than paradise will be the glory of the new Jerusalem, whose architect and builder is God himself. The state of glory (*status gloriae*) will be no mere restoration (*restauratie*) of the state of nature (status naturae), but a re-formation that, thanks to the power of Christ, transforms all matter ... into form, all potency into actuality (*potentia, actus*), and presents the entire creation before the face of God, brilliant in unfading splendor and blossoming in a springtime of eternal youth. *Substantially* nothing is lost. (*Gereformeerde Dogmatiek*, IV, 702 [720])[35]

De Chirico and Allison are obliged to revise their thinking on the Church's understanding of nature and grace in view of the similarities between the Reformed and Catholic traditions. For both traditions grace neither abolishes nature nor leaves it untouched but rather transforms it from within its own order; and grace presupposes nature because it is "the very material through which grace works and for whose ultimate perfection grace itself exists."[36]

What I just described above in my second point as Allison's qualified view of the nature-grace continuum is, ironically, the position of the Catholic Church. Significantly, Allison does not bring his critique of the Catholic system's axiom of a nature-grace continuum to bear on *CCC*'s exposition of marriage. Consider *CCC*, §§29, 400, 405, 407 where the fall/sin's impact upon the totality of human nature is described.

Consider also *CCC*, §§1601–5, where marriage is considered from the perspective of creation, fall/sin, and redemption, with redemption/grace restoring and renewing the fallen creation from within. By nature *CCC* understands the deepest foundations of human nature that remain in place after the fall, a nature that has been savagely wounded or seriously disturbed by the fall/sin, but still remains what God originally made them to be. Admittedly, De Chirico states: "Of course, the Evangelical meaning of creation does not exclude what is conveyed in part by the Roman Catholic understanding of nature [structures of creation]; on the contrary, there are important parallels and some overlapping, indeed, these terms can be used as synonyms if nature is considered as the primordial state of the world and humanity" (*ETP*, 235). Still, the crucial question is whether the deepest foundation of nature is still what God made it to be even in the regime of sin where nature has been savagely wounded and seriously disturbed by the fall. The Catholic answer is yes. But so, too, is the answer of the neo-Kuyperian philosopher, Herman Dooyeweerd. He states:

> The Fall has brought about spiritual death in the root-unity, the radix [root] of our temporal world, and can manifest its operations in this world in the first place from the human heart. As soon as we posit, while following the speculative theological train of thought, that we actually cannot know the divine laws as those have been grounded in the creation order, because we do not know whether they have begun to function in an entirely different way as a result of the Fall, then the biblical creation motif loses its central grip on our thinking, and we begin to view it in a dialectical, and thus unbiblical, tension with the manifestation of the Fall, because we ascribe to sin a power that is independent from the creation order and thus independent from God. ("Van Peursen's critische...New Critique," 115)[37]

Thus, the order of creation remains valid, indeed, normative, even in the regime of sin. Furthermore, this normative order is knowable.

> To be sure, it is entirely true that we cannot ascertain the meaning of these ordinances apart from God's revelation in Christ Jesus, but this is still altogether different from arguing that as a result of the Fall they would have begun to function in an entirely different way apart from humanity [*ook buiten de mens*]. When dealing with the divorce question, Christ himself pointed to the unalterable requirement of the creation order. And when this is applied to the normative ordinances that are identified in terms of their human construction, then there is surely no reason to accept that the natural laws grounded in the creation order have been altered by the Fall. (Ibid.)

In this light, we can easily understand the teaching of *CCC* on the relation between sin and nature:

> According to faith the disorder we notice so painfully [in marriage] does not stem from the nature of man and woman, nor from the nature of their relations, but from sin. ... Nevertheless, the order of creation [of marriage] persists, though seriously disturbed. ... In his mercy God has not forsaken sinful man. ... After the fall, marriage helps to overcome self-absorption, egoism, pursuit of one's own pleasure, to open oneself to the other, to mutual aid and to self-giving (§1607).

De Chirico is right, according to *CCC*, that the fallen creation is "incapable of restoring the relationship [with God] in its own strength, nor is it even willing to do so" (*ETP*, 237). Furthermore, "In his preaching Jesus unequivocally taught the original [i.e., creational, from the order of nature] meaning of the union of man and woman as the Creator willed it from the beginning. ... By coming to restore the original order of creation disturbed by sin, [Jesus] himself gives the strength and grace to live marriage in the new dimension of the Reign of God" (*CCC*, §§1603, 1606–9, 1614–15). Grace restores nature to function properly according to its divinely intended ends.

As Evangelical and Catholic theologians, our starting point is the written Word of God (Gen 1:27; 2:24) that reveals to us the marital order of the created world as an objective reality. Marriage is a normative structure of creation in which the male-female prerequisite—gendered sexuality—of the "twoness" of the sexes, ordained by God "in the beginning," is necessary for the reality of becoming "one flesh" in marriage. The normative grounding of marriage in the created order is held by Luther,[38] Calvin,[39] leaping over a few centuries, Kuyper (*De Gemeene Gratie*, Vol. III, 295–374), Bavinck,[40] and Berkouwer, to name just a few representative thinkers of the Protestant tradition, on the one hand, and on the other hand the Catholic tradition,[41] e.g., M. J. Scheeben (*Mysteries*, 593–610), Walter Kasper (*Gospel of Family*, 5–12), John Paul II (*Man and Woman*),[42] as well as magisterial documents such as the Doctrine and Canons on the Sacrament of Marriage of the Council of Trent (Denzinger, §§1797–1816), *Gaudium et Spes* (§48),[43] the *Catechism of the Catholic Church* (§§1601–66), and the *Code of Canon Law* (Latin-English Edition, can. 1055).

How does Scripture frame its understanding of marriage? In Matthew 19:3–8, the words of Jesus Christ refer back to the Genesis texts of 1:27 and 2:24. "Back-to-creation" is the *leitmotif* in Jesus' teaching. In his own teaching regarding marital monogamy and indissolubility (Mark 10:6–9; Matt 19:4–6), creation texts in Genesis 1–2 have foundational importance, in particular Genesis 1:27 and 2:24: "Male and female he created them" and "for this reason ... a man will be joined to his wife and the two will become one flesh." These texts are absolutely normative for marriage, indeed, for sexual ethics.[44] Jesus unites into an inextricable nexus the concepts of permanence, twoness, and sexual complementarity.[45] Sexual differentiation is a fundamental prerequisite for the two to become "one flesh." Yes, Genesis 2:24 is about the permanence of marriage; it is also about the exclusivity of the relationship: "twoness";[46] but it also about the fundamental prerequisite of complementary sexual differentiation for effecting the "two-in-one-flesh" union of man and woman. "So then they are no longer two but one flesh" (Mark 10:8).[47] Indeed, as Pruss rightly notes, "the text [Gen 2:24] is a seminal scriptural text on the nature of human sexuality" (*One Body*, 94–95). In short, marriage is a comprehensive spiritual unity founded on (and given expression in) a singular act of physical unity.

Catholics and Reformed Christians should agree on the import of these Genesis texts. Briefly, "Integral sexual complementarity" must be distinguished from "fractional complementarity" (to use terms coined by Sr. Prudence Allen[48]); the former holds that biological gender complementarity is integral to the ability of a man and a woman to fulfill their marital role within creation, as Reformed theologian David Crump puts it (*Review*, at 291). This is not the same thing as saying that without each other a man and a woman would not each be a complete being, that is, be whole as a person. Furthermore, we should resist the interpretative move suggesting that the response of the man Adam when he meets the woman Eve (Gen 2:23) is merely one of discovering sameness, not difference. "This at last is bone of my bones and flesh of my flesh." Yes, both man and woman have the same dignity. "But man and woman are not simply identical," as Kasper correctly notes. "Their equality in dignity, as well as their difference, is grounded in creation. ...Being man and being woman are ontologically grounded in creation" (*Gospel of the Family*, 8). This is not just a Catholic position. Crump correctly states, "By seeing only the similarity between man and woman at the expense of their differences in Genesis 2—and thereby continuing to discount any overtones of sexual complementarity—[one] posits an either/or equation where none exists." He adds: "Similarity always entails difference or different things would not be similar; they would be identical. Man and woman are not identical; they are similar (both human) while being different (male and female)" (Crump, 291–92).

Further, the Word of God teaches that the redemptive work of Christ reaffirms and simultaneously renews the goodness of creation and hence of marriage, of the human body sharing in the dignity of the image of God, of the complementary sexual differentiation of man and woman, and of a faithful, reciprocal, and fruitful love. Yes, in light of the redemptive work of Christ, the Catholic sacramental tradition teaches that the sacrament of marriage renews and restores the reality of marriage—given that it is savagely wounded by the fall and our own personal sin—from within its order. Redemption of the body: grace penetrating fallen nature and renewing it from within (*gratia intra naturam*); there is an essential continuity in man and a link between creation and redemption.[49] Kasper rightly says, "The order of salvation takes up the order of creation. It is not inimical to the body or sexuality; it includes sex, eros, and human friendship; it purifies and perfects them" (*Gospel of Family*, 18). As the *Catechism of the Catholic Church* puts it, "Jesus came to restore creation to the purity of its origins" (*CCC* §2336).

Elsewhere the *Catechism* explains, "In his preaching Jesus unequivocally taught the original meaning of the union of man and woman as the Creator willed it from the beginning. ... *By coming to restore the original order of creation disturbed by sin*, [Jesus] himself gives the strength and grace to live marriage in the new dimension of the Reign of God" (§§1614–15 [emphasis added]).[50] But this sacrament not only recovers the order of creation, but also while reaffirming this ordinance of creation it simultaneously deepens, indeed, fulfills the reality of marriage in a reciprocal self-giving, a joining of two in a one-flesh union that is a visible sign of the mystery of the union of Christ with the Church (see Eph 5:31–32). This joining is such that, according to Pruss, it "provides the crucial link between the theological conception of the Church as the bride of Christ and the Church as an organic unity with Christ as head" (*One Body*, 90). One must ask why sexual union would possess the symbolic significance of the union between Christ and the Church. Pruss rightly answers: "what makes [sexual union] fit is a union as one body, and the unitive nature of sexuality reflects a spiritual union" (ibid., 129). Of course, "This [symbolic significance] is a great mystery," according to St. Paul, namely, this two-in-one-flesh-union of a man with his wife, "and I mean in reference to Christ and the Church" (Eph 5:32). In other words, M. J. Scheeben rightly notes that "the sense in which marriage is said to be so great a mystery clearly depends on the meaning apprehended in its relationship to Christ and to the Church" (*Mysteries of Christianity*, 601).

Marriage and family are, then, grounded in the order of creation, seriously disrupted by the fall into sin, integrally redeemed by salvation in Christ, and attain the fullness of redemption in Christ when creation reaches its final goal. Within this comprehensive scope is the Thomistic insight that grace restores nature rather than abolishes or leaves it untouched and hence that grace presupposes nature in order to build on it, being the "very material in which grace works and for whose ultimate perfection grace itself exists" (Mascall, 153). But also, forasmuch as grace's restoration is not a mere recovery of the deepest foundations of created reality, in some sense those foundations are raised to a "higher level" in the eschatological consummation of God's plan of salvation for the whole creation. The exact sense in which "the redemption by grace of created reality, the reformation of nature, is not merely repristination, *but raises the natural to a higher level than it originally occupied*" is a hotly disputed matter, especially in Reformed and Catholic thought.[51] Berkouwer summarizes the disputed issue clearly:

> The meaning and extent of redemption are the heart of the issue. Is God's Kingdom something more than just a restoration of what has been lost? Is not the deepest meaning of the eschatological mystery this, that it will supersede and transcend the original created nature of man? ... It is as if according to God's intention the glory of creatureliness sets up certain boundaries that cannot be transgressed, and any effort to attribute something more to man in the eschaton runs against these boundaries. Those who defy these boundaries need to be reminded that it "does not yet appear what we shall be" (1 John 3:2). This remark by John sets the limit to our penetration of the eschatological mystery. When we speak of that mystery, then, we cannot, in the very nature of the case make a simple identification of end-time and original time. (*Wederkomst van Christus*, II, 267–68 [449–50])

In this light, we can understand Henri de Lubac's point about the essence of Christianity:

> The supernatural does not merely *elevate* nature (this traditional term is correct, but it is inadequate by itself); it does not penetrate nature merely to help it prolong its momentum ... and bring it to a successful conclusion. It *transforms* it. ... 'Behold, I make all things new!' (Rev 21:4). Christianity is 'a doctrine of transformation because the Spirit of Christ comes to permeate the first creation and make of it a 'new creature.' (*Brief Catechesis*, 81)

Thus, Allison and hence De Chirico are criticizing a straw man in Position I concerning the relationship between nature and grace. Their criticism of Catholicism from the standpoint of a unqualified emphasis on sin and hence a discontinuity between nature and grace brings with it problems that I have critically discussed. But the qualification made by them concerning the nature-grace continuum brings their position within the orbit of a Catholic theology of nature and grace, and consequently of *CCC*.

NOTES

1. Benedict XVI/Joseph Ratzinger, "*Gratia Praesupponit Naturam*, Grace Presupposes Nature," in *Dogma and Preaching*, Unabridged Edition, at 158. For an instructive analysis of Benedict XVI's view of the relation of nature and grace, see Msgr. Thomas G. Guarino, "Nature and Grace: Seeking the Delicate Balance," 1–13.

2. Jacques Maritain states, "There is one error that consists in ignoring [the] distinction between nature and grace. There is another that consists in ignoring their union," *Clairvoyance de Rome*, 222. Cited in Henri de Lubac, "Apologetics and Theology," in *Theological Fragments*, at 103n28.

3. See also, "Scripture, Tradition and Traditions," in *The Fourth World Conference on Faith and Order, Montreal 1963*, ed. P. C. Rodger and Lukas Vischer).

4. The following paragraphs are adapted from Echeverria, *Berkouwer and Catholicism*, 165, 223–29.

5. "On the Task of Catholic Philosophy in Our Time," (first published 1946), *Communio* 20, no. 1 (Spring 1993), at 151–52.

6. St. Thomas Aquinas, *Summa Theologiae*, IaIIae, q. 85, a. 3, Resp. St. Thomas describes the wound of human nature as a sickness in *Summa Theologiae*, IaIIae, q. 82, a. 1, Resp.

7. Leonardo De Chirico, "A Biography of Thomas Aquinas' *Summa Theologiae*: Is

It Also a Radiography of Roman Catholicism?"

8. The following paragraphs are adapted from Echeverria, *Berkouwer and Catholicism*, 155–59.

9. Berkouwer engages Groot's 1945 work on theological epistemology, *Karl Barth en het theologische kenprobleem, in Conflict met Rome*, Tweede Druk, 134–38. Translated as *The Conflict with Rome* by David Freeman, 99–102.

10. Cited in Berkouwer, *Conflict met Rome*, 135 [99].

11. Karl Barth, *Church Dogmatics* I/2, 172–73, as cited in Michael Horton, "Meeting a Stranger: A Covenantal Epistemology," *Westminster Theological Journal* 66 (2004): 337–55, at 339n17.

12. The following paragraphs are adapted from Echeverria, *Berkouwer and Catholicism*, 157–60.

13. G. C. Berkouwer, *Geloof en Rechtvaardiging*, 182. Translated by Lewis B. Smedes as *Faith and Justification*, 175. Similarly, Berkouwer already in his Vrije Universiteit dissertation, Geloof en Openbaring in de Nieuwere Duitsche Theologie, 104–33, 193–226, extensively criticizes early Barth's conception of faith. Dooyeweerd aligns himself with Berkouwer's criticism of early Barth's dialectical theology and its corresponding conception of faith in *De Wijsbegeerte der Wetsidee*, Vol. II, *De Functioneele Zin-Structuur Der Tijdelijke Werkelijkheid and het Probleem der Kennis*, 228–29. In the English translation and revised edition of this volume, *A New Critique of Theoretical Thought*, Vol. II, *The General Theory of the Modal Spheres*, trans. D. H. Freeman and H. De Jongste, Dooyeweerd gives a more extensive critique of the early Barthian conception of faith, 300–302. For my discussion of Dooyeweerd's critique of Barth, see Echeverria, *Berkouwer and Catholicism*, 228-32, especially 230n154.

14. G. C. Berkouwer, *De Mens Het Beeld Gods*, 102. Translated by Dirk W. Jellema as *Man: The Image of God*, 99.

15. Albert Wolters, "Dutch Neo-Calvinism: Worldview, Philosophy and Rationality," in *Rationality in the Calvinian Tradition*, ed. Hendrik Hart, Johan van der Hoeven, and Nicholas Wolterstorff, at 8–9.

16. Bavinck, *Gereformeerde Dogmatiek*, I, 351 [380], as cited by Berkouwer, *Geloof en Openbaring*, 241.

17. For example, Eduardo Echeverria, *"In the Beginning…": A Theology of the Body*, chapter 5.

18. See also, "The true Catholic position consists in maintaining that nature was created good, that it has been wounded, but that it can be at least partially healed by grace if God so wishes. This instauration, that is to say, this renewal, this re-establishment, this restoration of nature to its primitive goodness, is on this point the program of authentic Catholicism" (ibid., 21–22).

19. Pius XII, *Humani Generis*, as quoted in *CCC*, §38.

20. Cited in Berkouwer, *Conflict met Rome*, 135 [99].

21. For example, William Lane Craig, "God Is Not Dead Yet: How Current Phi-

losophers Argue for His Existence," *Christianity Today*. See also, idem., *Reasonable Faith: Truth and Apologetics*, Third Edition.

22. I refute this claim in Eduardo Echeverria, "The Salvation of Non-Christians? Reflections on Vatican II's *Gaudium et Spes* 22, *Lumen Gentium* 16, Gerald O'Collins, SJ, and St. John Paul II," in *Angelicum* 94 (2017): 93–142.

23. *CCC* cites in the note attached to this quotation from Pius XII, references to Vatican I, *Dei Filius*, §2; Vatican II, *Dei Verbum*, §6; and St. Thomas Aquinas, *Summa Theologiae* I, q. 1, a. 1. For an in-depth study of the issues raised here, see Echeverria, *Berkouwer and Catholicism*, 110–272.

24. See Eduardo Echeverria, "Original Sin, Preterition, and Its Implications for Evangelization," *Perichoresis* 18, no. 6 (2020): 73–101; idem, "The New Man: Nature, Sin, and Grace in St. Paul," in *St. Paul, the Natural Law, and Contemporary Legal Theory*, ed. Jane Adolphe et al., 89–111.

25. Kuyper, *Encyclopaedie der Heilige Godgeleerdheid*, Vol. II, 254–55; see also 227, 231. English translation: *Encyclopedia of Sacred Theology: Its Principles*, 301–2; see also 275, 279. *Gereformeerde Dogmatiek*, I, 290–91 [318–19].

26. The Canons of Dort (1618–1619), in *Reformed Confessions of the 16th and 17th Centuries in English Translation*, Vol. 4, *1600–1693*, compiled with Introduction by James T. Dennison Jr., at 135, Article 4, Third and Fourth Heads of Doctrine.

27. Calvin, *Institutes*, IV, trans. Henry Beveridge, XIV, 6: "We might refer to other similitudes, by which sacraments are more plainly designated, as when they are called the pillars of our faith. For just as a building stands and leans on its foundation, and yet is rendered more stable when supported by pillars, so faith leans on the word of God as its proper foundation, and yet when sacraments are added leans more firmly, as if resting on pillars. Or we may call them mirrors, in which we may contemplate the riches of the grace which God bestows upon us. For then, as has been said, he manifests himself to us in as far as our dullness can enable us to recognize him, and testifies his love and kindness to us more expressly than by word."

28. The Swiss Reformer Ulrich Zwingli (1484–1531) sees the sacraments as a mere outward or empty sign (*nudum signum*), implying the exclusion of grace from the sacrament. Bavinck describes the position of Zwinglians, "True, the sacraments visibly represent the benefits that believers have received from God, but they do this as confessions of our faith and do not impart grace" (*Gereformeerde Dogmatiek*, IV, 448 [470]. For Luther's rejection of Zwinglians or Anabaptists, as he also called them, see his *The Large Catechism*, Fourth Part: Baptism, 80–101.

29. God is the principal efficient cause and the sacraments are examples of instrumental efficient causality. On this distinction and its sacramental import, see Aquinas, *Summa Theologiae* III, q. 62, a. 1, ad 1, ad 2; and q. 62, a. 5.

30. Cited by Berkouwer, *De Sacramenten*, 101–2 [84].

31. On grace and freedom in Calvin, Scheeben, Barth, Berkouwer, Bavinck, and Von Balthasar, see my study, *Divine Election: A Catholic Orientation in Dogmatic*

and Ecumenical Perspective.

32. In Chapter 2 of my book, *Revelation, History, and Truth*, I defend in critical conversation with Kevin Vanhoozer a Catholic view of the relationship between Scripture and Tradition that affirms the epistemic primacy of Holy Scripture, and refutes many of the objections raised by Evangelicals like Allison.

33. See *Bondage and Liberation of the Will*, 2.263 (at n. 58), 264 (at nn. 63, 65), 284 (at n. 213), 290 (at n. 259); 4.331 (at n. 45); 5.361 (at n. 100); 6.381 (at n. 59). G. C. Berkouwer, *Wederkomst van Christus*, Vol. I, 279, translated by James van Oosterom as *The Return of Christ*, 225). For a critical discussion of Calvin on grace and freedom, and his corresponding notion of nature and grace, see chapter 2 of my book, *Divine Election*.

34. Trans. Marcus Dods, *Nicene and Post-Nicene Fathers* 1/2, ed. Philip Schaff.

35. See also American editor's note, 697.

36. In the words of the Anglican Thomist, E. L. Mascall, *The Openness of Being*, 153.

37. Van Peursen's critische vragen bij 'A New Critique of Theoretical Thought,'" 115. My hearty thanks to Nelson Kloosterman for the translation.

38. Martin Luther speaks of marriage as an "ordinance of creation." See Luther's "The Estate of Marriage" (1522): Part I, http://pages.uoregon.edu/dluebke/Reformations441/LutherMarriage.htm. See also, idem., "A Sermon on the Estate of Marriage" (1519). Luther says as much in his much later 1535 *Commentary on Genesis 2.22*, "For the lawful joining of a man and a woman is a divine ordinance and institution" (*Luther's Works*, vol. 1, 134).

39. For the relevant sources of Calvin's sacramentology and his view of marriage, see the entries in *The Calvin Handbook*, ed. Herman J. Selderhuis, trans. H. J. Baron, et al., 344–55, 455–65.

40. Herman Bavinck, *Het Christelijke Huisgezin*, 2nd rev. edn. Translated by N. D. Kloosterman as *The Christian Family*. See also, Eduardo J. Echeverria, "Review Essay: Bavinck on the Family and Integral Human Development," 219–37.

41. Colman E. O'Neill, OP, *Sacramental Realism*, "The Catholic tradition thinks the way it does about marriage and affirms it to be a sacrament, not because of a positive act of 'institution' attributed to Jesus, but because it understands salvation in terms of creation. It regards marriage as the most fundamental form of human association and, in that sense, as an 'institution' given by God the Creator. It sees it, consequently, as blemished by sin, just as all human relations are; and it sees Christ's redemptive work as a force acting towards the restoration of marriage to its pristine ideal. To call this a sacrament is equivalent to a whole theology about the relation of Christ to creation, of grace to the human task" (29).

42. Also see Benedict XVI, *Verbum Domini*, §85; Pope Francis, *Lumen Fidei*, §52.

43. See also, Pius XI, *Casti Connubii*.

44. Alexander Pruss, *One Body: An Essay in Christian Sexual Ethics*, "They are seminal texts, ones that the biblical and postbiblical traditions take very seriously. They are, Christians should believe, true, and true in a deep way" (155).

45. Robert A. J. Gagnon, "Marriage in Scripture," June 5, 2013, a paper presented at a Meeting of Evangelical and Catholics Together. See also his *magnum opus, The Bible and Homosexual Practice: Texts and Hermeneutics*.

46. Edward Schillebeeckx, OP, *Het Huwelijk, Aardse Werkelijkheid en Heilsmysterie*, Eerste Deel, 34. Translated by N. D. Smith as *Marriage, Human Reality and Saving Mystery*: "What cannot be justified from the texts [Gen 2:24; Eph 5:31] is that Genesis as a whole refers merely to the creation of woman and man, and not directly to marriage. The intention of the whole text was to restore the social fact of marriage to a divine institution. With a deliberately pointed reference to monogamous marriage, that is, to marriage between one man and one woman, the Samaritan Pentateuch and the Septuagint translated the Hebrew "and they become one flesh" interpretatively as "and *these two* become one flesh" (Gen 2:24). This ideal of marriage, based on a belief in God's creation, was not stated by the sacred writer without a certain element of conscious polemic against the ancient oriental views concerning marriage [namely, polygamy] which had tainted the Israelites. ... Although polygamy was officially tolerated by the Law, it was in no sense an expression of the deepest experience of the Israelite ethic. The purest expression of this ethic of married life is to be found in Genesis and in the commentary of the Book of Sirach upon it" (20–21).

47. Matthew Levering, *Biblical Natural Law: A Theocentric and Teleological Approach*, 59: "This instruction to be 'fruitful and multiply' [Gen 1:28] is not merely an extrinsic command, but an internal inclination toward the good [of union], as is manifest in Eve's rejoicing, 'I have gotten a man with the help of the Lord' (Gen 4:1). God creates human beings with an inclination toward the good of living in society: 'male and female he created them' (Gen 1:27) and 'It is not good that the man should be alone' (Gen 2:18)." Levering adds: "In this regard recall, too, Adam's wonderful statement, 'This at last is bone of my bones and flesh of my flesh; she shall be called Woman, because she was taken out of Man' (Gen 2:23). Nor is this inclination, in human beings, merely animal: marital intercourse is a 'knowing' (Gen 4:1)." See Eduardo Echeverria, "A Catholic Perspective on Marriage and the Gift of Children—With Special Attention to Herman Dooyeweerd's Social Ontology of Marriage," 1–14.

48. Prudence Allen, RSM, "Man-Woman Complementarity: The Catholic Inspiration."

49. "Endowment with grace is in some sense a 'new creation'," says John Paul. "New creation" does not, however, mean that grace is a plus-factor, a superadded gift, to the order of creation. Rather, nature and grace, creation and re-creation, the sacrament of creation and redemption are united such that God's grace affirms and simultaneously renews the fallen creation from within its own internal order. Thus: "Marriage is organically inscribed in this new sacrament of redemption, just as it was inscribed in the original sacrament of creation" (*Man and Woman He Created Them*, 97.3, 102.7, respectively). This major claim along with

its undergirding theology of nature and grace is developed throughout John Paul II's *Man and Woman*, especially 93.1, 95.7, 96, 97.3, 98, 99.7, and 100. I discuss this matter thoroughly in my book, *"In the Beginning…": A Theology of the Body*.

50. See also, §2382. Bavinck claims that in Catholic sacramentology grace is a superadded gift that is added to nature (*donum superadditum*), such that grace supervenes upon the natural, but does not inwardly penetrate and sanctify it. Yet, Bavinck's own description of the relation between nature and grace with respect to marriage wherein "marriage is restored and renewed in its own natural order" (*Gereformeerde Dogmatiek*, IV, 473 [495]) is remarkably similar to the *Catechism*.

51. For this quote, see Jan Veenhof, "Nature and Grace in Bavinck," at 22; see also *Gereformeerde Dogmatiek*, IV, 702 [720], see also editor's note, 697.

Chapter 5

Christ-Church Interconnection
PROLONGING THE INCARNATION

A broadly defined law of Incarnation is something that belongs to every classic and orthodox form of Christianity and not exclusively to Roman Catholicism. While it is true that each tradition articulates differently its understanding of this law, the significance of the incarnation of the Son of God is generally thought of as being a divine-human act which is not reducible to a merely historical event. It is rather envisaged as the pattern for the Church to accomplish her mission so that the Christian gospel may be witnessed and practiced in concrete, embodied forms in real situations. Even the less sacramentally oriented Evangelical tradition would strongly uphold some kind of law of Incarnation resulting in a corresponding theology of mediation, even though it would interpret it in an utterly different way from Roman Catholicism. … The law of incarnation is not central for Roman Catholicism alone, even though, in the Roman Catholic tradition, it is elaborated in a way that is not found in the Protestant tradition, especially as far as the strongly Christological connotation of the Roman Catholic theology of the Church is concerned. (ETP, 250)

I turn now to the second principle of De Chirico's Evangelical hermeneutics of Catholicism: the Christ-Church interconnection concerning the unity of Christ and the Church in a single body such that the Catholic Church is the continuation of the Incarnation of Jesus Christ (*RCTP*, 56). Hans Urs von Balthasar expresses this view: "The Church, in this perspective, is the broadest 'incarnation [of the Logos] … since she has as her goal leading all of humanity to God.'"[1] Accordingly, says Allison, "the Church is a prolongation of the incarnation of the Son of God, mediating the grace of God to the world as the incarnate Christ mediated the divine grace to the world" (*RCTP*, 58). De Chirico calls the Christ-Church interconnection, with the Church's role being that of a mediating agent, the "law of Incarnation." Unlike Allison who claims "Protestants find no biblical support for a law of incarnation" (*40 Questions*, 64), De Chirico makes clear in the epigraph to this chapter that the Evangelical objection is not to this law of Incarnation as such.

Although Allison neither explicitly refers to this important passage from De Chirico nor gives an endorsement of a "law of Incarnation," something like it is evident from his claim "that the salvation accomplished by Christ, revealed through the gospel, is and must be applied in a continuous fashion is certainly true" (*RCTP*, 230). So, it isn't clear at all why De Chirico and Allison object to the "law of Incarnation." The Incarnation is about the Word of God, the eternal Son of the Father, becoming man. The "teleology of the Incarnation" (to borrow a term from Robert Sokolowski) moves to the sacrificial Death, Resurrection, and Ascension of Jesus Christ. As De Chirico rightly notes in the above passage, this work of God is not an event that recedes into the past because it was meant to transform creation and history, indeed, the whole of life. What, then, is their objection to the Catholic teleology of the Incarnation, that is, its prolongation such that the Catholic Church is the continuation of the Incarnation of Jesus Christ?

Their objection is twofold. For one thing, they object to the Church as an agent of mediation of nature and grace, and, for another, that its mediation is sacramental, indeed, the "sacramental economy." Regarding the former, De Chirico states the reason "why it is impossible for the Roman Catholic system to think of Christ in isolation from the Church and, vice-versa, and therefore the utter theological implausibility, in Roman Catholic eyes, of the Protestant cry *solus Christus* if it implies a potential breach of the organic bond that unites Christ and the Church ... reinforcing the centrality of the Church as the mediating agent of the system" (*ETP*, 262). Hence:

> [T]he theological rationale provided by the concept of the Church as the prolongation of the incarnation in the context of the indissoluble union between Christ and the Church ... is the basis on which the Roman Catholic system argues for the mediating agency of the Church whose centrality for the system is utterly fundamental. (*ETP*, 266)

Regarding the sacraments, Allison's and De Chirico's charge against Roman Catholicism is—in Vanhoozer's words—that "of the

Catholic concept of the church as a continuation of Christ's Incarnation and thus an instrument in mediating grace to fallen nature through *the sacraments*." ("Protestant Response," 219 [emphasis added)]). Both these objections are grounded in a more basic objection regarding "the hermeneutic of the Ascension for the Church's self-understanding" (*ETP*, 275). Says De Chirico, "[T]he ascension is the Christological locus from which the two ecclesiological perspectives depart, developing into two divergent systems" (*ETP*, 276). Before turning to the two objections of the Church as a mediating agent, and the sacramental mediation of grace, I will examine their hermeneutic of the Ascension.

Their interpretation of Christ's ascension into heaven sees, according to De Chirico: "[A] stronger element of *discontinuity* [emphasis added] between the pre-ascension enactment of the law associated with the earthly ministry of Jesus Christ and its post-ascension prolongation within the life of the Church. ... So, the ascension is the Christological *locus* from which the two ecclesiological perspectives depart, developing into two divergent systems." He explains:

> The theological hermeneutic of the ascension has therefore a systemic value for it decides the paramount questions: what kind of embodiment of the law of Incarnation comes to an end with the departing of Jesus Christ from the earth and what kind of embodiment of the same law continues in the Church even after His departure? The Roman Catholic system looks at the ascension within the *continuity* [emphasis added] of the pattern established with the Incarnation, even though it recognizes the newness of the post-ascension period of the same law. ... The Evangelical system tends to view the ascension in more abrupt, radical ways in that it conceives it as the coming to an end of the earthly ministry of Jesus Christ which cannot be extended or prolonged in any form because of its uniqueness within the economy of salvation and its once and for all soteriological significance. The demarcation between 'before' the ascension and 'after' it does not leave enough room to shape an ecclesiology in terms of the prolongation of the Incarnation. ... [T]he leaning it attributes to the ascension is much more marked by an element of *discontinuity* [emphasis added] within the unfolding of God's redemptive plan (*ETP*, 275–277; *RCTP*, 64–65).

Doesn't the unfolding of God's redemptive plan include creation, the full spectrum of culture, indeed, all of life? Allison and De Chirico would surely agree—given Position II on the relationship of nature and grace. I think it is, however, important here to see that the nature-grace interconnection and the Christ-Church interconnection are corollaries. Allison and De Chirico reject the latter because they reject the former. In fact, Allison claims that there is an intrinsic connection between these two axioms. "If there is no nature-grace interdependence as conceived by Catholicism, then the reason for the Christ-Church interconnection evaporates. If nature is not capable of receiving and transmitting divine grace ... then the Christ-Church interconnection is not needed as the go-between that links the two realms" (*40 Questions*, 67). Allison elaborates on the connection between the two axioms in the following way. He quotes De Chirico: "Between the orders of nature and grace, a mediating subject is needed to represent nature to grace and grace to nature, so that nature will progressively and more fully be graced and grace will eventually achieve its final goal of elevating nature. That mediation is the theological *raison d'etre* ... of the Roman Catholic Church and the chief role of the Church within the wider Roman Catholic system" (*ETP*, 247; Allison, *RCTP*, 56). Since I have already criticized their view of nature and grace above, I won't repeat my criticism here except to say that their view of the Ascension reinforces the *discontinuity* between nature and grace, what I called Position I, resulting in their rejection of the Church as a mediator of grace.

Furthermore, their emphasis on discontinuity between Christ and the Church, Christ and the world, raises the question of how to maintain the dialectic between Christ's presence and absence in the Church given his Ascension, and, with it, the proper relation between the Church and the world, Christ and culture, indeed, the calling of the sanctified laity, and, in consequence, nature and grace. De Chirico is right: "the ascension is the Christological *locus* from which the two ecclesiological perspectives [Evangelical and Catholic] depart, developing into two divergent systems." How, then, is the Kingdom of God present in history, according to Allison and De Chirico, given their emphasis on discontinuity, on Christ's absence? In particular, De Chirico claims that in Roman Catholic thought "the ascension does not represent a definitive end of Christ's work in salvation which confirms its uniqueness and completeness" (*SWDW*,

109). I will say something about each of these points in rebuttal of their views of Catholic thought.

First, with Allison's and De Chirico's emphasis on discontinuity and Christ's absence, which rests on Position I regarding the relationship of nature and grace, what could it mean to say that the Holy Spirit "engages in the ongoing application of the saving work of the Son" (*40 Questions,* 66)? Given their emphasis on discontinuity and Christ's absence, what could the ongoing application of Christ's redemptive work mean now in history for the calling of the laity, for Christ and culture, and for the cosmic significance of Christ in creation and redemption?

I dare say that Allison's and De Chirico's emphasis on discontinuity, on Christ's absence (*40 Questions,* 66), is not the view of the Reformed tradition, or even of the Evangelical theological tradition as such. Christ is Lord of all areas of life, of history, indeed, of creation, and hence, according to the late Evangelical theologian George Eldon Ladd, "God is King and acts in history to bring history to a divinely directed goal." He explains, "The Christian gospel is concerned about mankind as well as about individual men. Its God is the Lord of history who acts in history and who will surely establish his Kingdom at the end of history."[2] Furthermore, the late leading Reformed theologian Herman Ridderbos explains, "[The Kingdom of God] has a much more comprehensive content. It represents the all-embracing perspective, it denotes the consummation of all history, brings both grace and judgment, has cosmic dimensions, [and] fills time and eternity" (*Coming of Kingdom,* 354). In my view, and arguably the view of the Second Vatican Council, and John Paul II, Jesus Christ makes the Kingdom present, bringing God's plan to fulfillment. "Jesus gradually reveals the characteristic and demands of the kingdom through his words, his actions, and his own person" (John Paul II, *Redemptoris Missio,* §14). Although the concentration point of the Kingdom of God is the Church, it is not identical with it, but also is not separate from the Kingdom; the kingdom must be detached neither from Christ nor from the Church. Still, the Kingdom encompasses the whole creation. Hence, the realization of that Kingdom is an enactment of the great divine work of redemption in its recapitulation—fulfillment and consummation—of all the fallen creation in Christ. "Working for the kingdom means acknowledging and promoting God's activity, which is present in human history and transforms it." "In a word," as John Paul II adds, "the Kingdom of God is the manifestation and the realization of God's plan of salvation in all its fullness" (ibid., §15). In all its fullness, I would say, refers to the restoration or renewal of creation, as Congar puts it, "in the redemptive plan and in the redemptive power of Jesus Christ."[3] That this, too, is the teaching of the Council is clear from the following passages. For example, regarding the calling of the laity:

> But the laity, by their very vocation, seek the kingdom of God by engaging in temporal affairs and by ordering them according to the plan of God. ... They are called there by God so that by exercising their proper function and being led by the spirit of the gospel they can work for the sanctification of the world from within. ...It is therefore his [the layman's] special task to illumine and organize [temporal] affairs in such a way that they may always start out, develop, and persist according to Christ's mind, to the praise of the Creator and the Redeemer. (LG, §31)[4]

Furthermore, regarding the relation between Christ and culture:

> The good news of Christ constantly renews the life and culture of fallen man. It combats and removes the errors and evils resulting from sinful allurements which are a perpetual threat. It never ceases to purify and elevate the morality of peoples. By riches coming from above, it makes fruitful, as it were from within, the spiritual qualities and gifts of every people and of every age. It strengthens, perfects, and restores them in Christ. Thus, by the very fulfillment of its own mission the Church stimulates and advances the human and civic culture. (GS §58, italics added)

More generally, the Council makes crystal clear the cosmic significance of Christ in creation and redemption:

> [T]he Church has a single intention: that God's kingdom may come, and that the salvation of the whole human race may come to pass. For every benefit which the People of God during its earthly pilgrimage can offer to the human family stems from the fact that the Church is "the universal sacrament of salvation," simultaneously manifesting and exercising the mystery of God's love for man. For God's Word, by whom all things were made, was Himself made flesh so that as a perfect man He might save all men and sum up all things in Himself. The Lord is the

goal of human history, the focal point of the longings of history and civilization, the center of the human race, the joy of every heart, and the answer to all its yearnings. He it is whom the Father raised from the dead, lifted on high, and stationed at His right hand, making Him judge of the living and the dead. Enlivened and united in His Spirit, we journey toward the consummation of human history, one which fully accords with the counsel of God's love: "To re-establish all things in Christ, both those in the heavens and those on the earth (Eph 1:10)." (*GS* §45)

Second, De Chirico is mistaken that Catholic thought does not affirm the uniqueness and completeness of Christ's salvific work in as much as the Ascension does not represent a definitive end of that work. Now, *CCC* states, "Christ's ascension marks the definitive entrance of Jesus's humanity into God's heavenly domain" (§665). The Catholic tradition agrees that "since the Ascension God's plan [of salvation] has entered into its fulfillment" (*CCC* §670). "As Lord, Christ is also head of the Church, which is his Body. Taken up to heaven and glorified after he had thus fully accomplished his mission, Christ dwells on earth in his Church" (§669). It is the definitive end of his saving work but not its consummation; the already accomplished work of salvation but not yet its eschatological fulfillment. In that light, the following account of *CCC* (§§670–71) makes sense:

> Since the Ascension God's plan has entered into its fulfillment. We are already at "the last hour." "Already the final age of the world is with us, and the renewal of the world is irrevocably under way; it is even now anticipated in a certain real way, for the Church on earth is endowed *already* with a sanctity that is real but imperfect." Christ's kingdom already manifests its presence through the miraculous signs that attend its proclamation by the Church. ... *until* all things are subjected to him.
>
> Though already present in his Church, Christ's reign is nevertheless yet to be fulfilled "with power and great glory" by the King's return to earth. This reign is still under attack by the evil powers, even though they have been defeated definitively by Christ's Passover. Until everything is subject to him, "until there be realized new heavens and a new earth in which justice dwells, the pilgrim Church, in her sacraments and institutions, which belong to this present age, carries

the mark of this world which will pass, and she her-
self takes her place among the creatures which groan
and travail yet and await the revelation of the sons of
God." That is why Christians pray, above all in the
Eucharist, to hasten Christ's return by saying to him:
Maranatha! "Our Lord, come!"

The teleology of the Incarnation is realized from the first moment
that the Word became flesh and this teleology unfolds all the way
to the Ascension. *Pace* De Chirico, Journet refutes the claim that
Catholic thought does not represent the Ascension as a definitive
end of Christ's saving work. "The mystery of the Incarnation is accomplished. Jesus is fully himself, true God and true man, without
possible progress in the line of this union, at each moment of his
earthly life, from the moment of his conception to that of his Ascension. ... [T]he mystery of the Incarnation is in a state of becoming
with respect to its unfolding. It is complete only with the Ascension"
(*Theology of the Church*, 331). In particular, God's plan of salvation comes
to fulfillment in the Ascension of Jesus Christ because of the "irreversible entry of his humanity into divine glory" (*CCC* §659). Christ's
Ascension truly affirms the humanity of Christ, but also "completes
the formation of man and perfects his image in man. In bearing our
humanity home to the Father, Jesus brings human nature as such to
its true end and to its fullest potential in the Holy Spirit" (*Farrow*, xii,
122). Says *CCC*, §668:

> Christ's Ascension into heaven signifies his participa-
> tion, in his humanity, in God's power and authority.
> Jesus Christ is Lord: he possesses all power in heaven
> and on earth. He is "far above all rule and authority
> and power and dominion," for the Father "has put all
> things under his feet." [Eph 1:20–22] Christ is Lord of
> the cosmos and of history. In him human history and
> indeed all creation are "set forth" and transcendently
> fulfilled. [Eph 1:10; cf. Eph 4:10; 1 Cor 15:24, 27–28]

When Allison and De Chirico are criticizing Catholicism from
the standpoint of an unqualified emphasis on sin and hence a discontinuity between nature and grace, they miss out theologically on
this important understanding of the Ascension of Jesus Christ where
it is an act of perfecting grace of the creation itself. By contrast, their
qualified view, which I called Position II, is open to this interpretation where the Ascension is the goal of the Incarnation. The Catholic
view of nature and grace, as I sketched it above, fits well with this un-

derstanding of the Ascension. For the understanding of nature and grace presupposed in this view is none other than Aquinas's teaching that grace perfects nature, neither abolishing nor suppressing nature, or leaving it untouched, but rather elevating as well as perfecting or completing it from *within* its own order.

The Church as the Body of Christ

I said in Chapter One, De Chirico criticizes the Catholic Church's ecclesiology for its alleged tendency, in the words of Kevin Vanhoozer, "to assimilate Christology into ecclesiology," or make "the church … constitutive of the Son's identity as are the Father and the Spirit" (*Biblical Authority*, 152). In particular, he criticizes Catholic thought for the quasi-divine status it ascribes to the Church. I won't repeat my rebuttal here. For my purpose here, I think we can quickly dismiss Vanhoozer's charge that the inherent incarnational relationship between Christ and the Church is substantival, such that there is an *unqualified* identification between the two, according to Catholic teaching. *Pace* Vanhoozer, his understanding of this teaching cannot align itself either with De Chirico's interpretation, or with Vatican II. De Chirico rightly sees that "Vatican II [*Lumen Gentium* 8], while substantially restating the inherent incarnational link between Christ and the Church, has relaxed the quasi-identification between the incarnation of the Son of God and its ecclesial prolongation, and redefined it in terms of an 'excellent analogy' ('*Ideo ob non mediocrem analogiam incarnati Verbi mysterio assimilatur*', ['For this reason, by no weak analogy, it is compared to the mystery of the incarnate Word'])" (*ETP*, 255).

Still, De Chirico is less nuanced, ignoring completely the role of analogy, in a more recent article. He writes: "It is obvious that Roman Catholicism maintains a series of distinctions between Christ and the church that prevent an indiscriminate and wooden identification. Nevertheless, despite all the subtle distinctions that are introduced, a substantial continuity remains between the incarnation of the Son and the work of the Church and that has serious consequences" ("Blurring of Time," 42). What is a "substantial continuity?" For one thing, De Chirico claims it blurs the distinction between what God has done (*hapax*), the finished work of Christ, and what he is doing (*mallon*). "The act of having blurred the unique and definitive nature of the incarnation with its glorious conclusion at the ascension implies the transferal of the mission of the Son from Christ to the Church. ... The unique mediation of Christ yields to the mediation of the Church" (*SWDW*, 109). I have already argued against De Chirico's criticism of Catholic thought that it allegedly does not hold the Ascension to be representative of a definitive end of Christ's saving work. So, the Church is not an extension of the Incarnation since the teleology of the latter was fulfilled in the Ascension.

Nevertheless, in the earlier work he clearly notes the significant difference between the mystery of the Incarnation, which is a mystery of "filiation," whereas the mystery of the relationship between Christ and the Church is a mystery of "spiration," that is, a work of the Holy Spirit, is made clear in the sentence following the one that De Chirico cites (*ETP*, 258n57). "As the assumed nature inseparably united to Him, serves the divine Word as a living organ of salvation, so, in a similar way, does the visible social structure of the Church serve the Spirit of Christ, who vivifies it, in the building up of the body."[5] De Chirico summarizes the Christ-Church interconnection in light of Vatican II:

> The cautious teaching of Vatican II stressing the relationship between Christ and the Church in terms of 'analogy' (LG 8) is an indication of the magisterial awareness of the problem of [the strong incarnational continuity] and its willingness to provide a theological category which is better suited to exegeting the incarnational view of the Church in a Roman Catholic way. Apart from being grounded in the classic Thomist tradition, the analogical pattern maintains the nexus between the incarnation and its prolongation while suggesting a safer way of arguing it theologically. ... According to an analogical understanding of the relationship, the mystery of the Church appears first of all as a distinct *mystery*... but also connected ... with the mystery of Incarnation.
>
> More precisely, ... it is not the incarnation as such ... that continues in the Church; however, it is something of Christ himself ... that continues to live in her. The recourse to analogical thinking makes it possible to underline the presence of the God-man Jesus Christ in the Church in which He continues to live so as to give the Church divine and human aspects, rather than the ontological divinity and humanity of the Incarnate One which is shared with the organ which prolongs the incarnation throughout history.

… Within an analogical framework, continuities as well as discontinuities are envisaged between the two forms of Incarnation (*ETP*, 257–58).

In particular, Vanhoozer continues by claiming that Catholic teaching threatens to undermine the finality of God's revelation (word) and redemption (work) in Christ. "De Chirico's contention is that the Roman Catholic theological framework is guilty of a 'blurring' of time, namely the distinction between 'once for all' and 'more and more'; 'Roman Catholic ecclesiology rests on the idea of the continuation of the incarnation of the Son of God in his mystical body, that is, the Church.' In other words, Roman Catholics view the incarnation in ongoing *mallon* ["more and more"] rather than definitive *hapax* ["once and for all"] terms: 'The unique mediation of Christ yields to the mediation of the Church'. … [T]his blurring of the time results in the *totus Christus* whereby Christ and the church make up the 'whole Christ's' person and work" ("Protestant Response," 219–20).[6] A key example offered by De Chirico regarding this blurring is the sacramental economy. Here, in particular, De Chirico claims that the saving work of Christ "is considered definitive but not final. Above all, it is unable to actualize its own efficacy without the active participation of the church in making it [redemptive grace] present" (*SWDW*, 39; see also 110).

Regarding the sacraments, then, Allison's and De Chirico's charge against Roman Catholicism is—in Vanhoozer's words—that "of the Catholic concept of the church as a continuation of Christ's incarnation and thus an instrument in mediating grace to fallen nature through *the sacraments*" ("Protestant Response," 219 [emphasis added]). I've already argued against their view that Catholic thought does not hold the Ascension to be representative of a definitive end of Christ's saving work. So, I argued, the Church is not an extension of the Incarnation since the teleology of the latter was fulfilled in the Ascension. The issue here pertains to their interpretation of "sacramental efficacy." They are wrong in their interpretation.

Pared down for my purpose here, I'd like to concentrate on Allison's total rejection of the idea that the Church is "the mediatorial agent between the grace of God and the world of nature" (*RCTP*, 57; 194). This is not De Chirico's view. He qualifies the rejection of "mediation" because there is, he says, "the preaching of the Word and the administration of the sacraments" (*ETP*, 248). But insofar as De

Chirico grants that grace comes to us through the meditation of the Church and through the preaching of the Word and the sacraments, he has no ground for making an in-principle objection to the Catholic doctrine of the "law of the Incarnation." Still, he nevertheless rejects the ecclesiological claim of the Catholic Church that she is "the mediating agency between nature and grace" (*ETP*, 249). He adds, "The Roman Catholic Church stands in continuity with the Incarnation and is the new enactment of the law of Incarnation, being the post-ascension mediating agent which embodies the aspirations of nature to which the mission of grace is entrusted" (*ETP*, 249).

Consider here briefly the view of Charles Journet as to the sense in which Christ is incarnate in the Church. According to the Catholic concept regarding the origin of Christianity, which is an ontological concept, it "is marked by a unique impulse, a *hapax*, in Christ himself, who represents a unique and incomparable entry of eternity into time, the immediate counter-effect of which is the inauguration of a continuous presence of eternity in time, in the Church, which is his body" (*Primacy of Peter*, 11). He adds in a gloss on Ephesians 1:22–23, Colossians 1:18–20, and Colossians 2:9–10 regarding Christ and the Church: the Catholic Church is the *totus Christus*.

> And he put all things under his feet and gave him as head over all things to the church which is his body, the fullness [*pleroma*] of him who fills all in all.

> And he is the head of the body, the church. He is the beginning, the firstborn from the dead, that in everything he might be preeminent. For in him all the fullness [*pleroma*] of God was pleased to dwell, and through him to reconcile to himself all things, whether on earth or in heaven, making peace by the blood of his cross.

> For in him the whole fullness [*pleroma*] of deity dwells bodily, and you have been filled in him, who is the head of all rule and authority.

Accordingly, "Christ is the *pleroma* of Deity in the midst of us and the Church is the pleroma of Christ. It completes Christ, not intrinsically of course, extrinsically." Not intrinsically, I said in Chapter One, because Christ's uniqueness is incomparable, belonging to the hypostatic order, whereas "the Church belongs to the order of created grace and the indwelling of the Holy Spirit" (*Primacy of Peter*, 17). Moreover, there is a connection to be made between unity, catholicity, and fullness. The Catholic Church alone is given the *fullness* of all means of salvation. Berkouwer's reflections on "fullness in Christ" (*De Kerk*, I, 135–39 [112–15]) and the Church's participation in that fullness in Christ, having been entrusted to the Church of Christ in its concrete form, are very helpful for gaining a proper perspective on this ecclesiastical sticking point—scandal of particularity—for Protestants in general. The catholicity of the Church cannot be adequately understood except in light of Christ's fullness. Regarding Jesus Christ, he is full of grace and truth (John 1:14), full of the Holy Spirit (Luke 4:1), with the fullness of God pleased to dwell in him (Col 1:19), and "in him the whole fullness of deity dwells bodily" (Col 2:9). "Jesus Christ is, so to speak, the concrete universal, for in the particularity and contingency of his human existence the plenitude of divine life is made available to all who will receive it" (Dulles, *Catholicity*, 9). Now, in what way is the Church related to the fullness of Christ and the fullness of God?[7]

Significantly, "fullness [in Christ] and fulfillment" are a gift to the Church's being, entailing a task as well since this gift does "not describe a tensionless 'being,' as if the Church had already achieved the final purpose of all her ways; rather they appear in living and relevant connection with her concrete life on earth" (*De Kerk*, I, 135–136 [113]). Thus, Berkouwer rightly says, "In the fullness [of Christ] that the Church received, she is directed toward fullness. That is the fantastic dynamic characterizing Paul's view of the Church, and through it he wants to make the Church rest in Christ's self-sufficient work" (ibid.). Furthermore, we cannot abstract the fullness that the Church received from Christ and his all-sufficient work from the calling to preserve this relatedness to him. Christology is not assimilated into ecclesiology as if we are left with a deistic conception of the Church, meaning thereby that she is "left to her own, independent existence, as if her acquisition of fullness meant that she could find and go her own way" (ibid., 137 [114]). What Berkouwer calls the "correlative language of the Scriptures" must be attended to so that we might see the Church in the light of the fullness of Christ: "Therefore, the Church, after receiving this fullness, must set her mind on and seek many things [Col 3:1f.]; and from the fullness, the whole life becomes visible in a radical, utterly concrete admonition [Col 3: 5f.; cf. Eph 4:17ff]" (ibid.).

The limits of this study will only allow me to give one brief example to illustrate that dynamic correlation between Christ and the

Church, and hence between fullness in Christ, the concrete universal, and fulfillment. *Ressourcement* is at the heart of this dynamic correlation. *Lumen Gentium* 8 states that the Church "is at one and the
same time holy and always in need of being purified [*sancta simul
et semper purificanda*], and incessantly pursues the path of penance
and renewal." In *Unitatis Redintegratio* 6 the Council states that
the Church is called "to continual reformation [*ad hance perennem
reformationem*]." Furthermore, several other paragraphs of *Lumen
Gentium* make clear that purification, renewal, and reformation of
the Church are the work of the Holy Spirit: "The Spirit guides the
Church into the fullness of truth. ... By the power of the gospel He
makes the Church grow, perpetually renews her [*Ecclesiae eamque
perpetuo renovat*], and leads her to perfect unity with her Spouse. (*LG*,
§4)" In *Lumen Gentium* 7, the Church is subject to her Head, Christ
"in order that we may be unceasingly renewed in Him [*Ut autem in
illo incessanter renovemur*] ... so that she may grow and reach all the
fulfillment of God." It is said about the Church in *Lumen Gentium* 9,
"that moved by the Holy Spirit she may never cease to renew herself
[*seipsam renovare non desinat*], until, through the cross, she arrives at
the light which knows no setting." Finally, *Lumen Gentium* 12 states
that the gifts of the Spirit among Christ's faithful "renders them fit
and ready to undertake the various tasks and offices which help the
renewal and up building of the Church [*pro renovation et aedifican-
tione ecclesiae*]."

Hence, there is not a complete identification of Christ and his
Church. The relationship here may be understood as an analogy.
Things may be predicated univocally, equivocally, and analogically.
The first means that what is predicated of something has the same
meaning in each instance of application. The second means that
what is predicated of something has a different meaning in each
instance of application. "Finally, analogical predication always refers
to something common in the predicated things, either in respect
to something third (not predicated) or some relation between the
predicated things. According to St. Thomas Aquinas, only the latter
form of analogy is applicable when speaking of God."[8] Regarding
"analogy," the Fourth Lateran Council in 1215 stated: "For between
Creator and creature no similitude can be expressed without implying a greater dissimilitude" (Denzinger, §806). Benedict XVI draws out
the implication in "The Regensburg Lecture": "unlikeness remains

infinitely greater than likeness, yet not to the point of abolishing analogy and its language." In this light, Allison is correct that the relationship between Christ and the Church is "an analogous relationship that features far more discontinuity than continuity between the two" (*40 Questions*, 65). Still, Allison is mistaken in his understanding of analogy. He denies that analogical predication is a realistic predication, and hence an essential relationship, a realistic organic unity between Christ and the Church.

Accordingly, says Kasper in *Katholische Kirche* in more precise language: "If these specifications [analogy, similarity, priority of Christ] are taken seriously, then we cannot say that the Church was the present and continuously effective Christ and the continuation of the incarnation. It is more correct to state that Christ is efficaciously present in the Church. *One must take care that Jesus Christ remains the subject of the statement, and that the subject Jesus Christ must not be replaced by the subject Church* [emphasis added]." Otherwise, Christology is mistakenly assimilated or reduced to ecclesiology, and the Church is wrongly taken to be substantially constitutive in her relationship to Christ, hence making the Church the "subject." No, says Kasper, "'In Christ' we are simultaneously under Christ. That is why we call in the liturgy Jesus Christ our Lord and worship him: 'you alone are the Holy One, you alone the Lord, you alone the Most High: Jesus Christ' (*Gloria*, Order of Mass)." Kasper adds, "This makes clear that," *pace* Vanhoozer, "there is not only a Protestant but also a Catholic '*solus Christus*'! However, the Catholic *solus Christus* always includes the Church and that means the *totus Christus* with head and members" (*Katholische Kirche*, 196 [131]).

I return in conclusion of this chapter to the question of whether the Church is a continuation of the Incarnation, according to Walter Cardinal Kasper. He helpfully addresses it by arguing that the Catholic tradition does not assimilate or reduce Christology to ecclesiology, as if to suggest that the Church is now the "subject" rather than Christ. Christ precedes the Church as its Head; the Church mediates the light of the nations that is Christ. Kasper explains:

> What the captivity letters [of St. Paul] mainly express is the superordination of Jesus Christ as head over the Church. Therefore, the Church cannot be identified with Jesus Christ and it cannot tout court be called the Christ living-on. It depends on what is respectively subject in such a statement and what is

the predicate object; not the Church is Christ, but Christ is present in the Church as his body; he lives and works in it. (Ibid., 191 [127])

Kasper continues, "[Still], the [Second Vatican] Council emphatically stresses that Jesus Christ himself is the head of the Church's body. It refrains therefore from speaking of the continuation of the incarnation in the Church and the identification of the Church as Christ's body with Christ himself. It says, rather, that the Church, which is a complex reality growing together out of a divine and human element, is 'by no weak analogy, [...] compared to the mystery of the incarnate Word. As the assumed nature, inseparably united to Him, serves the divine Word as a living organ of salvation, so also, in a similar way, does the visible social structure of the Church serve the Spirit of Christ, who vivifies it in the building up of the body'" (ibid., 196 [131]).

Elsewhere Kasper adds: "It is not the Church, it is Christ who is the way, the truth and the life (Jn 14:6). ... The Church is not itself the light of the nations. The light of the nations is Jesus Christ whose human face reflects the image of the living God" (ibid., 111 [68]). This Christological consciousness is at the core of the ecclesiology of Vatican II's *Lumen Gentium*.

The Sacramental Economy

The Church was made manifest to the world on the day of Pentecost by the outpouring of the Holy Spirit. The gift of the Spirit ushers in a new era in the "dispensation of the mystery"—the age of the Church, during which Christ manifests, makes present, and communicates his work of salvation through the liturgy [and sacraments] of his Church, "until he comes." In this age of the Church Christ now lives and acts in and with his Church, in a new way appropriate to this new age. He acts through the sacraments in what the common Tradition of the East and the West calls "the sacramental economy"; this is the communication (or "dispensation") of the fruits of Christ's Paschal mystery in the celebration of the Church's "sacramental" liturgy (*CCC*, §1076).

[H]ow are we to think of the presence of Christ in the Lord's Supper [?] This question is often ignored in discussions of the doctrine of the Lord's Supper in Protestant and especially Lutheran theology of the present day [1977]. It is easy to restrict oneself to Christ's promise contained in the words of institution [Matt 26: 26-28; 1 Cor 11: 23-25] and to regard the question of the "how' of his presence in the Eucharist as more or less superfluous. ... [But] we will be unable to avoid the question of how that which the words of institution state as a promise can become a reality for us, how it can be related to an understanding of reality which is at all accessible to us. (Pannenberg, "A Protestant View," 141)

Now, aside from Allison's explicit rejection of Vatican II's basic claim that the Catholic Church possesses "the fullness of the means of salvation" (*RCTP*, 175), the only other reason that I can see why he rejects the idea that the Church mediates grace is because he, like De Chirico, is deeply distressed by the tendency of substituting "'the church in the place of its absent Lord'" (*RCTP*, 65). Moreover, the Catholic view of the mediation of the Church involves the sacramental actions of the Church because those actions are, as Allison rightly sees but categorically rejects, "instruments of grace that operate concretely through these visible means" (*RCTP*, 230; 245). But ecclesial mediation is, according to *CCC*, analogical and participatory, and hence not the primary source of grace, not even when it comes to the sacraments, but only an instrumental means of grace. As Berkouwer rightly understands, "God is the cause of grace, as *causa principalis*, and ... he is this *causa principalis* in the sacraments as *causa instrumentalis*. ... Ultimately God, as *causa principalis*, is the worker of grace. (*SAC*, 75 [65])" Allison and De Chirico completely ignore this distinction between causes and the fundamental point that the sacraments do not communicate grace in themselves and apart from God. Although he pays some attention to "analogy," he does not take seriously *CCC*'s understanding of the Church's Christological consciousness, in other words, her awareness that the Catholic Church is the Church "of Christ": "*Lumen gentium cum sit Christus*" (*LG* §1).

Now, Allison is confused about simile, metaphor, and analogy in describing St. Paul's head-body relationship. He rejects Augustine's realistic interpretation. "The Protestant perspective holds that Paul's metaphor is to be understood as an analogy: like or similar to the relationship between a human head and its body, so the relationship between Christ and his Church" (*40 Questions*, 64). Now, is the formal comparison—using "as … so" or "like" to express resemblance—that St. Paul makes between the love and faithfulness of Christ's giving of himself to the Church on the one hand, and the love that exists between husbands and wives on the other, a simile, metaphor, or analogy?

E. W. Bullinger explains the difference between simile and metaphor: "Simile differs from metaphor in that it merely states resemblance, while metaphor boldly transfers the representation," and again, "while the simile gently states that one thing is like or resembles another, the metaphor boldly and warmly declares that one thing is the other."[9] *Pace* Allison, the resemblance here cannot be a mere comparison—a simile. For then St. Paul's statement that marriage—the two-in-one-flesh-union of husband and wife—is a mystery, indeed a profound mystery, could not be anything but "an extravagant hyperbole" (Scheeben, 602).

The Greek word *mysterion* ("mystery") has been given three different interpretations: one, it refers to the hidden meaning of Gen 2:24 that St. Paul cites in Eph 5:31; two, it refers to marriage itself; and three, it refers to the "connection between Christ and his Church."[10] The widespread view of biblical scholars and theologians is that *mysterion* means the last interpretation, namely, the "revelation and realization in time of the mystery of salvation, of the election of love 'hidden' from eternity in God" (Eph 1:9–10), which is "expressed and realized in time through the relationship of Christ with the Church" (John Paul II, *Man and Woman*, 90.1).[11]

Still, the second interpretation—i.e., *mysterion* refers to marriage itself—is included in this revelation and realization of the reality of salvation. How so? The loving union of husband and wife signifies the redemptive love of Christ for his Church. So there really is a divinely instituted sign in marriage. "In this revelation and realization, the mystery of salvation includes the particular feature of spousal love in the relationship of Christ with the Church, and for this reason one can express it most adequately by going back to the analogy of the relationship that exists—that should exist—between husband and wife in marriage" (ibid.). On this view, the union of husband and wife as members of the body of Christ is an offshoot of the union between Christ and the Church, and hence marriage really, essentially, and intrinsically refers to the mystery of Christ's relationship with his Church such that "the mystery proves active and operative in [marriage]" (Scheeben, 602).[12] How does this take place?[13] Sacramentally?

Briefly, there are three senses of "sacramental" I will employ, only the last sense being fully Catholic but able to integrate the two other senses. First, sacramental in a more general sense in which marriage is sanctified, meaning thereby, according to James V. Brownson, that "the call to live 'one flesh' [in Christ] can be the school in which we learn more deeply 'what is the breadth and length and height and depth, and to know the love of Christ that surpasses knowledge, so that you may be filled with all the fullness of God' (Eph. 3:18–19)." Brownson continues, "In seeking to imitate the pattern of Christ's faithfulness to us in the context of marriage, we are forced, again and again, to die with Christ to our selfish ways and our self-centered identity, and to rise with Christ to a deeper expression of love and faithfulness in union with another. In this wide 'sacramental' sense, marriage—like many forms of human community—becomes the context in which we learn and live out our union with Christ and enter more deeply into its riches" (Bible, Gender, Sexuality, 101).

There is a second sense of sacrament that I will refer to here and that may be applied to the idea that marriage is a sacrament because the symbols—the love between a man and a woman—function sacramentally. In other words, as Hans Boersma argues, "a sacrament (sacramentum) shares or participates in the reality (res) to which it points. According to this understanding, symbols point to and share in a reality that is much greater than the symbols themselves" (Heavenly Participation, 111–12).

The third sense of sacrament and hence the one in which marriage is a sacrament is that marriage is a means of grace, with divinely instituted signs, being efficacious means of communicating the fruits of our redemption in Christ. So, in response to the question of how the mystery of Christ's relationship with his Church is active and operative in marriage, the Catholic tradition responds by claiming that this occurs sacramentally; sacraments are efficacious signs of grace (signum efficax gratiae), actually accomplishing what they symbolize, conveying the sacred reality itself, in, with, and through the sacramental signs, and this effect is a divine action, a work of Christ.

Yes, the sacramental nature of marriage cannot be directly inferred from the Pauline word mysterion (Man and Woman, 93.2).[14] Still, marriage can be the sacrament of this mystery. Says John Paul, "'Sacrament' is not synonymous with 'mystery'. The mystery remains, in fact, 'hidden'—concealed in God himself—in such a way that even after its proclamation (or revelation) it does not cease to be called 'mystery', and it is also preached as a mystery." He adds, "Still, it is at the same time something more than proclamation of the mystery and the acceptance of the mystery by faith." What is that more? The late pope explains: "The sacrament consists in '*manifesting*' that *mystery in a sign* that serves not only to proclaim the mystery but also *to accomplish it* in man" (ibid., 93.5). In sum, John Paul concludes, a sacrament is

> "a visible sign of an invisible reality" [Augustine], namely, of the spiritual, transcendent, and divine reality. In this sign—and through this sign—God gives himself to man in his transcendent truth and in his love. The sacrament is a sign of grace, and it is *an efficacious sign*. It does not merely *indicate* and express grace in a visible way, in the manner of a sign, but *produces* grace and contributes efficaciously to cause that grace to become part of man and to *realize and fulfill the work of salvation* in him, the work determined ahead of time by God from eternity and fully revealed in Christ. (Ibid., 87.5)

Clearly, in the above passage, John Paul makes clear that the sacrament is not just a sign of an invisible reality, but rather an efficacious sign of God's grace. In other words, as Mauro Gagliardi puts it, "The Sacrament is not only a sign of grace but produces the grace of which it is a sign" (*Truth Is a Synthesis*, 620). This is the teaching of Trent's Decree on the Sacraments (Denzinger, §1606).

I'll return to this question of the sacramentality of marriage and the sense, if any, in which spousal love is a sacramental sign of Christ's "*saving love*, which consists in his gift of self for the Church," that is, "*a spousal love by which he married the Church and makes her his own Body*" (*Man and Woman*, 95.7).[15] My immediate concern now is to lay the basis of the sacramentality of marriage by understanding that "great mystery"—albeit not directly and in the strict sense—as a sacrament.[16]

We are, then, closer to the truth here when understanding the resemblance between Christ's love for the Church and the love of husband and wife certainly not as a mere simile, but rather as a reality-depicting metaphorical predication. Still, this resemblance is more than metaphorical; it is analogical.[17] Here, too, Allison is confused. He understands Paul's metaphor to be analogy but not one that affirms "an essential organic unity between Christ and the Church" (*40 Questions*, 65). Why? If it were just a metaphor, then an earthly reality would merely illuminate the mystery of Christ and the Church, a spiritual, transcendent, and divine reality. Furthermore, if it were just a metaphor that would mean that the "spousal relationship that unites the spouses, husband and wife, [would] … help us to understand the love that unites the Christ with the Church, reciprocal love of Christ and the Church in which the eternal divine plan of man's salvation is realized" (*Man and Woman*, 90.1). But the resemblance is not exhausted here; an analogy is at stake because the *primary analogate* is Christ's love for his Church, a nuptial ecclesiology, with the *secondary analogate* being the married love of husband and wife, which is both the sign and the reality of the nuptials between Christ and the Church. But the sacrament of marriage is an efficacious sign of grace. John Paul II rightly argues:

> While the analogy used in Ephesians clarifies the mystery of the relationship between the Christ and the Church, at the same time *it reveals the essential truth about marriage*, namely, that marriage corresponds to the vocation of Christian only when it mirrors the love that Christ, the Bridegroom, gives to the Church, his Bride, and which the Church (in likeness to the wife who is 'subject', and thus completely given) seeks to give back to Christ in return. This is the redeeming, saving love, the love with which man has been loved by God from eternity in Christ. … Marriage corresponds to the vocation of Christians as spouses only when precisely that love is mirrored and realized in it. This will become clear if we attempt to *reread the* Pauline *analogy in the opposite direction*, that is, beginning with the relationship of Christ with the Church and turning next to the relationship between husband and wife in marriage. … As one can see, this analogy works in two directions. While it allows us, one the one hand, to understand better the relationship of Christ with the Church, it permits us, on the other hand, to penetrate more deeply into the essence of the marriage to which Christians are called. It shows in some sense the way in which this marriage, in its deepest essence, *emerges from the mystery* of God's eternal love for man and humanity: from the salvific mystery that Christ's spousal love fulfills in time for the Church. (Ibid., 90.2.3.4)

How, then, is it possible to see the basis of the sacramentality of marriage in the fact that marriage is included in the reality of the realization of salvation in Jesus Christ, in the relationship of Christ with the Church? The latter is the fullness of sacramentality, the primary analogate, of which the sacrament of marriage participates through analogy, the secondary analogate (*Truth Is a Synthesis*, 624). In other words, how are we to understand the claim that the self-giving love of husband and wife in marriage is a visible and efficacious sign of grace, and hence a sacrament? Walter Kasper summarizes a number of presuppositions supporting the sacramentality of marriage. These are:

> [1] The total self-giving of the person that takes place in marriage implies a relationship with God as the ground and the aim of this self-giving; [2] that Christ included marriage in the Christian order [of creation and redemption]; [3] that the relationship involved in marriage is different from other relationships between human beings; [4] that wherever fundamental signs that are intimately connected with the life of Christians and the Church exist and these point to the reality of grace, such signs cannot, within the new covenant, be empty and meaningless; [5] that every community of Christians in Christ includes a making present of Christ and therefore of the Church (see Matt. 18:20), with the result that this can also be said especially of the smallest community in Christ, namely marriage.

Kasper summarily states in light of these suppositions, "It is possible to understand the sacramental nature of marriage and its historical institution on the basis of these presuppositions. Christ instituted the sacrament in light of the New Covenant that he established as an eternal sign of God's victorious grace and consequently by giving that sign [the self-giving love of husband and wife in marriage] a sacramental reality. This sacramental sign represents and expresses the unity of Christ and the Church."[18]

Christians from varying confessional traditions could find general agreement on most of these suppositions except for the concluding thesis suggested by Kasper's summary statement: there is a divinely instituted sign in marriage, and hence marriage is a sacramental sign signifying the mystery of the unity and faithful love of Christ and the Church.

Furthermore, the difference between Reformed and Catholic sacramentology is not over the relationship between the celebration of the sacrament and the proclamation of the Word of God, with the latter always initiating the former (*CCC* §§1122, 1131). In this light, we can appreciate their agreement with the Augustinian teaching concerning the import of the sacramental word: "Let the word be added to the element and it will become a sacrament. For whence comes this great power of water, that in touching the body it should cleanse the heart, unless the word makes it."[19] Allison shows no understanding, in his explanation of the Catholic sacramentology, of the relationship between the sacramental signs, say, of water and bread and wine, and the things signified by those signs. In fact, he has no appreciation of this relationship in the Westminster Confession of Faith and the Second Helvetic Confession.[20]

Indeed, we find a version of this teaching in the Catholic tradition as expressed by John Paul II in his *magnum opus*: "Each of the seven sacraments of the Church is characterized by a definite liturgical action constituted by the word (form) and the specific 'matter'—according to the widespread hylomorphic account that comes down to us from Thomas Aquinas and the whole scholastic tradition" (*Man and Woman*, 98.7). Here we find one of the essential conditions for celebrating the sacrament of marriage: the "matter" and "form" of the sacrament. Thus, in light of the relation between word and element, John Paul describes the structure of the sacramental sign. In a lengthy passage that repays reflection,[21] John Paul II states:

> Marriage as a sacrament is contracted by means of *the word*, which is *a sacramental sign in virtue of its content*, "I take you as my wife/as my husband, and I promise to be faithful to you always, in joy and in sorrow, in sickness and in health, and to love you and honor you all the days of my life." However, this sacramental word is, of itself, only a sign of the coming to be of marriage. And the coming to be of marriage is distinct from its consummation, so much so that without this consummation, marriage is not yet constituted in its full reality. ... In fact, the words themselves, "I take you as my wife/as my husband," do not only refer to a determinate reality, but they can only be fulfilled by the *copula conjugale* (conjugal intercourse). This reality (the *copula conjugale*), moreover, has been defined from the very beginning by institution of the Creator. "A man will leave his fa-

ther and his mother and unite with his wife, and the two will be one flesh" (Gen 2:24). Thus, *from the words* [form] with which the man and the woman express their readiness to become "one flesh" according to the eternal truth established in the mystery of creation, we pass *to the reality* that corresponds to these words.

The unity attained in becoming "two-in-one-flesh" in marriage is grounded in the order of creation (Gen 1:27; 2:24), persists through the regime of sin, and it is affirmed and simultaneously renewed through the redemptive sacrament of marriage. The Catholic tradition affirms that the body is intrinsic to selfhood; the human person *is*, bodily. This affirmation is rooted in the Church's teaching on the soul/body unity of the human person (*CCC*, §§362–68). As John Paul says, "In fact, *body and soul are inseparable*: in the willing agent and in the deliberate act *they stand or fall together*." Therefore, we can easily understand why separating "the moral act from the bodily dimensions of its exercise is contrary to the teaching of Scripture and Tradition" (*Veritatis Splendor*, §49). Elsewhere, John Paul explains that the body is intrinsic to self-identity: "Man is a subject not only by his self-consciousness and by self-determination, but also based on his own body. *The structure of this body is such that it permits him to be the author of genuinely human activity.* In this activity, the body expresses the person" (*Man and Woman*, 7.2). The body is intrinsic to one's own self. Not surprisingly, since the "human body shares in the dignity of the image of God" (*CCC*, §364).[22]

> Both the one and the other element are important *with regard to the structure of the sacramental sign*. ... [In sum] The words of new spouses are part of the integral structure of the sacramental sign, not only *by what* they signify, but also in some sense *with what* they signify and determine.

In other words, male and female shall become one flesh (Gen 2:24), and hence sexual differentiation is a fundamental prerequisite for the two to become one flesh.[23]

> ... Consequently, the [visible] sign of the sacrament of Marriage is constituted by the words [form] of the new spouse inasmuch as the "reality" [matter] that they themselves constitute ['two in one flesh union'] corresponds to them. *Both of them, as man and woman*, being ministers of the sacrament at the moment of contracting marriage, at the same time *constitute the full and real visible sign* of the sacrament

itself. The words [*form*] spoken by them would not of themselves constitute the sacramental sign if the human subjectivity of the engaged man and woman and at the same time the consciousness of the body linked with the masculinity and the femininity of the bride and the bridegroom did not correspond to them [*matter*]. Here one must call to mind again the whole series of analyses of Genesis 1–2 [solitude-unity-nakedness] carried out earlier. The structure of the sacramental sign remains, in fact, in its essence the same as "in the beginning." What determines it is *in some sense "the language of the body,"* inasmuch as the man and the woman, who are to become one flesh by marriage, express in this sign the reciprocal gift of masculinity and femininity as the foundation of the conjugal union of the persons. The sign of the sacrament of Marriage is constituted by the fact that the words spoken by the new spouses take up again the same "language of the body" as at the "beginning" and, at any rate, give it a concrete and unrepeatable expression. ... In this way the perennial and ever new "language of the body" *is not only the "substratum,"* but *in some sense also the constitutive content of the communion of persons.* The persons—the man and the woman—become a reciprocal gift for each other. They become this gift in their masculinity and femininity while they discover the spousal meaning of the body and refer it reciprocally to themselves in an irreversible way... This is the visible and efficacious sign [of God's grace] of the covenant with God in Christ, that is, of *grace.* (*Man and Woman*, 103.3.4.5)[24]

John Paul II develops the sacramental importance of the sexually differentiated bodily-sexual act as intrinsic to a one-flesh union. The *reality* that corresponds to these words and which the sacramental sign signifies and produces specifies the content of this sacramental grace: "The spouses participate in it as spouses, together, as a couple, so that the first and immediate effect of marriage (*res et sacramentum*) is not supernatural grace itself, but the Christian conjugal bond, a typically Christian communion of two persons because it represents the mystery of Christ's incarnation and the mystery of His covenant" (*Familiaris Consortio*, §1). Jesus calls us back to the law of creation (Mark 10:6–7) that grounds an inextricable nexus of permanence, twoness, and sexual differentiation for marriage. In particular, marriage is such that it requires sexual difference, the bodily-sexual act, as a foundational prerequisite, indeed, as *intrinsic* to a one-flesh union of man and woman: "So then they are no longer two but one flesh" (Mark 10:8).[25]

Indeed, there is much that Reformed and Catholic theologies have in common when it comes to the doctrine of the sacraments.[26] They agree that the sacraments are means of grace, rather than merely outward and empty signs. In short, they agree that God really does impart his grace by sacramental means. They also agree, as Bavinck states, that God alone is the author, initiator, and efficient cause of the sacraments (*Gereformeerde Dogmatiek*, IV, 451 [474]).[27] On this question, according to Kuyper, "The Reformed stand with Rome, Luther, and Calvin against Zwingli in their adherence to a divine working of grace in the sacraments" (*SAC*, 101–2 [84]). Where, then, do they differ?

They do not differ on the dipolar structure of the sacrament, for they both hold that sacraments are "each and always composed of a visible and invisible element" (Gagliardi, *Truth Is a Synthesis*, 630). They do not differ on the fact that sacraments are composed of "matter" and "form," of sign and thing signified, by divine institution. They do not differ on the "primary affirmation ... that only God is the Author of grace," that grace is caused only by God, but they do differ on the "secondary affirmation ... that grace is caused by the Sacraments" (ibid. 636). Regarding the secondary affirmation, the difference here is between *sacramental* causality—the sacraments do something as the instrumental efficient cause within the order of grace—and *occasional* causality. The latter means that it is only God who directly causes the grace, with the sacrament being an antecedent condition, or occasion, of God's action. On the view of occasionalism, the grace of God is communicated only with but not through the sign because "there is nothing in the sacrament itself which causes the grace."[28] On this view, says Bavinck, the sacraments are not understood to be "causes and instruments of grace, but as conditions or opportunities by which God communicates his grace." Both Bavinck and Jesuit theologian Bernard Leeming note that before the Council of Trent there were Catholic theologians, such as Bonaventure and Scotus, who seemed to be occasionalists in their sacramentology. Says Bavinck in his study on sacramental theology, "However, after Trent there is no longer any room in the Roman system for this sentiment" (*Saved by Grace*, 484). Elsewhere in this study, Bavinck writes: "After the Council of Trent until the present day [1903], some Roman Catholic theologians have continued to sense the weight of these objections [to sacramental causality, *ex opere operato*] so deeply that they proposed a view of the operation of the means of grace somewhat similar to the Reformed view. It appears, however, that after Trent there is no longer any room in the Roman Catholic Church for such a modified view" (ibid., 137). Less definitively than Bavinck, Leeming puts the point about occasionalism this way: "There has been a general reluctance among theologians since the Council of Trent to propound and defend this view, at least in the definite words 'occasional causality', or 'the sacraments are infallible conditions of God causing grace.' This indicates that there has been a growing conviction in the Church that sacraments are in some sense true causes of grace" (Leeming, 295). Still, according to Berkouwer and Bavinck, the difference between Reformed and Catholic sacramentology is not at all over the real, objective efficacy of the sacraments, wherein the visible sign is not only expressive but also effective in communicating grace. But rather it is over, says Berkouwer, "a totally different understanding of what efficacy is. (*SAC*, 74 [62])" In other words, as Bavinck puts it, "The difference in the doctrine of the sacraments, however, does not concern the question whether God really imparts his grace but in what way he does this" (*Gereformeerde Dogmatiek*, IV, 461 [483]). This is an important starting point for ecumenical discussion that is missing in Allison.

Allison recognizes this difference between himself as an Evangelical that tilts in the direction of Zwinglianism and "one large segment of Protestant theology" (*RCTP*, 243), but he appears uninterested in taking up the convergence between Rome and the Reformed tradition as an opportunity for ecumenical dialogue and for a new perspective in the Rome/Reformation controversy regarding the sacraments.

For example, consider briefly the standard Evangelical misunderstanding of the notion of *ex opere operato* ("by the work performed" or "by force of the action itself") found in Allison's discussion of Catholic sacramentology. Allison emphasizes that, according to Catholic sacramental theology, the sacramental efficacy of grace, in fact, "the ground of its validity ... of the sacraments" is *ex opere operato*, which literally means "by the very fact of the action's being performed" (*RCTP*, 244). He adds that "[t]heir validity is completely attached to their sign, which is virtuous or powerful in and of itself." Rather, he affirms baptism and the Lord's Supper as ordinances rather than sacraments. "The ordinances symbolize the faith and obedience of the people of God. Rather than transmitting grace or serving as means of grace, the ordinances are opportunities for their recipients to express their allegiance to Christ."[29] In short, Allison holds that the sacraments are not means of grace. He stands in the Baptist or "free church tradition" (*40 Questions*, 51).

Although Allison refuses to speak of the sacraments as means of grace, he insists, in a personal email to me of December 4, 2015, that "Just as the ground of salvation is the work of Christ and the means of appropriation of such salvation is faith, so the ground of the efficacy of baptism and the Lord's supper is the work of Christ and the appropriation of such grace is faith. Faith does not make the sacraments effective; I never said it [faith] did. Faith appropriates the benefits of the sacraments." He adds: "I have no problem using that phrase [means of grace] to refer to the sacraments. That I do not use it in my book [*RCTP*] is for a specific reason: when a fundamental disagreement between Catholic theology and Protestant theology [actually some versions of Protestant theology, ones that tilt in a Zwinglian direction, EJE] is over the notion of grace being infused or imputed, the use of 'means of grace' to refer to the sacraments is either ambiguous or confusing, and certainly not helpful." Respectfully, Allison is here not being intellectually straightforward. In fact, ordinances—he does not speak of sacraments—are not "means by which grace is transmitted" (*40 Questions*, 155). Still, if Allison rejects Zwingli, as he insists, here is my follow-up question, which I posed to him but to which he never responded. Is he saying—in the words of Aidan Nichols—that "a sacrament is not merely a declarative sign, but is an efficacious one, efficacious in communicating the fruits of our redemption?" (*Epiphany*, 120). In other words, do the sacraments have soteriological importance such that they are means of salvation? Sacraments by their very nature according to *both* the Reformed and Catholic tradition, *do something*, objectively, in a realist sense, and essentially, with God communicating his grace. How, then, do the sacraments as such objectively accomplish what they are said to accomplish instrumentally and efficaciously as visible means of grace? In short, how do they exercise their efficacy? Do they confer the grace that they signify?

Allison emphasizes that, according to Catholic sacramental theology, the sacramental efficacy of grace, in fact, "the ground of its validity ... of the sacraments" is "*ex opere operato*" (*RCTP*, 244), which literally means "by the very fact of the action's being performed." "Their validity is completely attached to their sign, which is virtuous or powerful in and of itself" (*RCTP*, 244). Allison, for one, misinterprets *ex opere operato* as leading to a view of the sacraments "as being mechanical, impersonal, and effective apart from faith and obedience" (*RCTP*, 245). He seems to take a Catholic sacramentology to be a deistic conception of efficacy, and hence of *ex opere operato*. This deistic interpretation contradicts the Christological foundation of *ex opere operato* or sacramental efficacy. The sacraments are "efficacious because in them Christ himself is at work. ... [T]he sacraments act *ex opere operato* ... by virtue of the saving work of Christ, accomplished once for all" (*CCC*, §§1127-28). His definition of *ex opere operato* seems to confuse the crucial difference between principal cause, who is Christ, and the instrumental cause, which are the sacraments, with God as the ultimate cause of grace, such that in themselves and apart from God they would not communicate grace. Furthermore, he is confused here because he is operating under the presupposition that Christology is reduced to ecclesiology. Thus, significantly, Allison explains, "the reference to 'Christ' cannot be divorced from the 'the Church' because of the Christ-Church interconnection" (*40 Questions*, 153). Hence, it is the Church that is the ground of sacramental efficacy. So, he doesn't take seriously its Christological foundation. No wonder he gives a deistic rendering of *ex opere operato*.

Moreover, Allison's definition of *ex opere operato* separates "the power working in the sacraments from their primary fountain, and looks upon them as working of themselves." He then concludes that "Reformed theology of the sacraments dissents from their validity being *ex opere operato*." He also argues that Reformed theology is against not only "Catholic sacramental theology but even some Protestant views of the sacraments." The latter are strongly suspicious of taking the sacraments to be means of grace because it seems to lead to their being "mechanical, impersonal, and effective apart from faith and obedience." He concludes that both these views "are aligned against the notion that the sacraments... are means of grace that is effective *ex opere operato*, as Catholic theology of the sacraments maintains" (*RCTP*, 245).

Given Allison's quasi-Zwinglian sacramental theology—more accurately, ordinance—he rejects the Reformed, Lutheran, and Catholic teaching that sacraments efficaciously confer divine grace, but also holds "the question of their validity *ex opere operato* [to be] a moot one" (*RCTP*, 245). Allison is wrong in this instance on several counts regarding the dissimilarity between the Reformed theology of the sacraments and Catholic sacramental theology (*RCTP*, 244–45).

In a brief exchange I had with Allison, he rejected my objection that he divorces the notion of *ex opere operato* from its Christological foundation. He started our brief discussion by distinguishing two issues, namely, "the sacraments as means of grace, and the grounds of their validity or effectiveness" (*RCTP*, 243). I said he argued that Catholic sacramentology holds that the sacraments are efficacious means of grace such that they actually accomplish what they symbolize. I added that he claimed the Protestant Reformation rejected this view. Berkouwer disagrees. In his Dogmatic Studies on *The Sacraments*, Berkouwer writes: "We now touch upon a central point of the Roman Catholic analysis of '*ex opere operato*,' for it is undeniable that the Reformation has also placed great emphasis on [sacramental] objectivity" (See *SAC* 75 [63]). So, too, Herman Bavinck, "With this objective view of the sacrament, Calvin stands decidedly on the side of Rome and the Lutherans. … [Calvin] can hardly find words strong enough to express his conviction concerning the real, essential, genuine presence of Christ's own flesh and of his own blood in the Lord's Supper. He declares explicitly that the issue between him and his Roman Catholic and Lutheran opponents involves only the *manner* of that presence."[30] Still, according to Allison, within Protestant theology there were two views, namely, those who continued to hold on the sacraments as means of grace (Reformed and Lutheran tradition), and those, like Zwingli, I would say, who rejected the notion that the sacraments were means of grace and took them to be empty and outward signs in and of themselves, and in which the benefits of the sacraments were delivered only in faith. Here follows an account of our exchange.

He distinguishes the first view from the Catholic view that according to him differ with respect to the "ground of the validity or effectiveness of the sacraments." He defines "*ex opere operato*" as the ground of validity of the sacraments that is "completely attached to their sign, which is virtuous or powerful in and of itself" (*RCTP*, 244). That seems to be a *deistic* conception of the sacramental efficacy and hence of *ex opere operato*. Surely Allison can see here why I thought that he divorced *ex opere operato* from its Christological foundation. His definition of *ex opere operato* seems to confuse the crucial difference between principal cause of grace, who is Christ, and the instrumental cause, which are the sacraments, with God as the ultimate cause of grace, such *that in themselves and apart from God they would not communicate grace*. His definition separates "the power working in the sacraments from their primary fountain, and looked upon them as working of themselves" (Möhler, *Symbolism*, 218n2). He then concludes that "Reformed theology of the sacraments dissents from their validity being *ex opere operato*." He then goes on to discuss the second view. In sum, he states that this position was against not only "Catholic sacramental theology but even some Protestant views of the sacraments." For example, the latter refers to the Westminster Confession of Faith and the Second Helvetic Confession. This second view is strongly suspicious of taking the sacraments to be means of grace because it seems to lead to their being "mechanical, impersonal, and effective apart from faith and obedience." He concludes that both these views "are aligned against the notion that the sacraments … are means of grace that is effective *ex opere operato*, as the Catholic theology of the sacraments maintain" (*RCTP*, 245).

In response to Allison's rejection of my objection, I carefully re-read *RCTP*, 243–45. I still maintain that Allison has a deistic interpretation of *ex opere operato*. This view is mistaken and, indeed, *qua* deistic, it does divorce the objectivity of sacramental efficacy from its Christological foundation. According to the Catholic theology of the sacraments Christ's primary role in the sacraments is foundational. "They [sacraments] are *efficacious* because in them Christ himself is at work: it is he who baptizes, he who acts in his sacraments in order to communicate the grace that each sacrament signifies. … This is the meaning of the Church's affirmation that the sacraments act *ex opere operato* … by virtue of the saving work of Christ, accomplished once for all" (§§1127–28). It seems to me that Allison's understanding of *ex opere operato* misses the Christological foundation. It is worth repeating here why? He is operating under the presupposition that Christology is *reduced* to ecclesiology. Thus, Allison explains, "the reference to 'Christ' cannot be divorced from the 'the Church' because of the Christ-Church interconnection" (*40 Questions*, 153). He cites *CCC* §1127, but fails to see its meaning for properly understanding *ex opere operato*. Otherwise, Allison would not have rejected both Protestant and Catholic views that understand the sacraments as objectively efficacious means of grace that are Christologically grounded.

No wonder, then, that readings, such as Allison's, lead to the charge that Catholic sacramentology suffers from sacramental automaton, ritualism, juridicism, cheap grace, a deistic view of *"ex opere opera-to,"*[31] such that the sacraments are divorced from their Christological foundation, that is, "from their proper and sole source, namely from Christ, the true and only giver of grace, and gives them an independent status" (Adam, 27). In this light, we can understand why Schillebeeckx rejects the very view that Allison rejects as "the headless corpse of sacramentalism" (*Christ the Sacrament*, 88n60),[32] meaning thereby that the sacraments have been severed from the "Christological foundation of the *ex opere operato* efficacy" (ibid., 85).

Berkouwer, for one, took up this ecumenical challenge in his extraordinary 1954 work, *The Sacraments*, as have the last half-century of bilateral ecumenical dialogues between the Pontifical Council for the Promotion of Christian Unity and the various confessional traditions of Methodists, Lutherans, Anglicans, and Reformed. Given the complex nature of sacramental theology, I can only highlight a couple of the most significant aspects of the fruits of this ecumenical dialogue that Allison would have benefited from in his Evangelical assessment of Catholic theology. Furthermore, Berkouwer advances the ecumenical dialogue on sacramentology, particularly, the fundamental matter of Eucharistic presence because he understands that the crux of the matter between Catholic and Reformed sacramentology "is not a difference between *praesentia realis* or not, but a difference regarding the *mode* of this presence. (*SAC*, 299–300, 302 [223, 225, 236])" Explains Berkouwer: "Was there a religious difference or only a difference in the theological formulation of a common motif, namely, that of the comforting [real] presence of Christ? (*SAC*, 299 [223])" Allison overlooks this matter, especially because he and De Chirico assume that there is a religious/theological difference rather than a difference in theological formulations.

I turn now briefly to Berkouwer's interpretation of the Reformed objection to *ex opere operato*. First, Berkouwer argues that the Reformed objection to Roman Catholic thought should not be posed in term of sacramental efficacy.[33] According to Berkouwer, the question is not whether the sacraments are objectively efficacious, but rather how they exercise their efficacy. What, then, is the way in which God imparts sacramental grace?[34] Briefly, Berkouwer insists that there is a "conjunction between the sign and the signified" that is grounded "in the acts of God." He adds, "This is to reject the automatic conjunction which depersonalizes the sacrament, but also to reject the notion of mere sign in itself, for through the Spirit because of its institution by God the sign is full of efficacy with respect to faith. That is why the *per sacramentum* and the *cum sacramento* can be accepted simultaneously without involving a contradiction" (*SAC*, 105-6 [89]). On the one hand, the automatic conjunction view is a deistic rendering of the sacrament such that it is depersonalized having been disconnected from its Christological foundation. On the other hand, Berkouwer also rejects the view that the sacrament is an empty and outward sign. Berkouwer supports *per sacramentum* and the *cum sacramento* in Reformed sacramentology.

Second, grace is efficacious by virtue of the sacramental signs and with those signs. Still, regarding sacramental causality, Berkouwer sides with Bavinck. The latter says, the sacraments are not understood to be "causes and instruments of grace, but as conditions or opportunities by which God communicates his grace" (*Gereformeerde Dogmatiek*, IV, 462n1 [483n58]). Still, according to Berkouwer and Bavinck, and, arguably, the view of Calvin and Luther, the difference between Reformed and Catholic sacramentology is *not* at all over the real, objective efficacy of the sacraments, wherein the visible sacramental sign is not only expressive but also effective in communicating grace. But rather it is over, says Berkouwer, "a totally different understanding of what efficacy is" (*SAC*, 74 [62]).

Third, returning now to the teleology of the Incarnation in the sacramental actions of the Church and the bearing of the Ascension, in particular, upon the Eucharist, the Catholic teaching is that this teleology is "completed in the Eucharistic continuation of the presence of Christ in the world. The Eucharist is the *sacramental* extension of the Incarnation" (Sokolowski, "Phenomenology," 72 [emphasis added]).[35] Let's be clear that the Ascension represents the definitive end of Christ's salvific work—as I argued earlier contra Allison and De Chirico. But it is another matter to hold that the "Eucharist extends the Incarnation in a *sacramental* way. Controversy about the Eucharist is thus related to controversy about the Incarnation" (ibid., 75 [emphasis added]). I will return to develop this claim below.

Eucharistic Presence is the Catholic teaching that Christ is "truly, really, and substantially present" (as Trent stated) in the Eucharist. "To begin with, the holy council teaches and openly and straight-forwardly professes that in the Blessed Sacrament of the Holy Eu-charist, after the consecration of the bread and wine, our Lord Jesus Christ, true God and man, is truly, really, and substantially contained under the appearances of those perceptible realities" (Denzinger, §1636). In the Eucharist, then, Jesus is present bodily. This means that Eu-charistic presence is not merely "by virtue of the sign and the power of the sacrament but in his proper nature and true substance" (ibid., §1651). This is rejected by Allison because it is "grounded on the axiom of the Christ-Church interconnection," and this axiom presupposes "a defective view of the ascension" (RCTP, 317).

I refuted this objection earlier. Roman Catholic thought holds the Ascension to be the definitive end of Christ's saving work. Further-more, asks Allison, if Christ is ascended into heaven, how could it be meaningfully said that he is present "body and blood, soul and divinity" under the species of bread and wine in the Eucharist? "If he is *not* here, how can he be here in his body and blood?" (40 Questions, 66). He cannot really be present, according to Allison, except symboli-cally and spiritually. The brief answer here to this question must be that the bodily presence of Jesus in the Eucharist is not a "physical presence."[36] Reformed theologian Peter Leithart explains, "The Eu-charistic body of Christ is not apparent to the eyes but only to the intellect, something that hardly can be said of a physical substance." Remarking on Aquinas's understanding of Jesus's bodily presence, he adds, "Thomas's distinction between a presence *in loco* and a pres-ence *per modum substantiae* likewise indicates that the presence of the body and blood is not a physical presence. After the consecration, indeed, *no* physical substance remains locally where the accidents of bread and wine appear" (Leithart, 301). Furthermore, the Catholic tradi-tion does not say that the bodily presence of Jesus in the Eucharist is not a sign of his body in heaven. Rather, Eucharistic presence is a sacramental sign of the passion, death, and resurrection of Christ. Leeming concludes: "The real body in its sacramental presence sig-nifies the sacrifice of Christ and its effects" (Principles, 254). Berkouwer agrees, "[Eucharistic] communion is not a communion with Christ's glorified 'body' and 'blood' as a substantial isolated reality, but a com-munion with him in his offering and in his true body and blood, with him, 'who has become flesh and was crucified in history and whose flesh is now in heaven'" (*SAC*, 315 [235]).

Reformed theologian Berkouwer contests views like those of Allison. There is, according to Berkouwer, a contrast here between "symbolism" and "realism." He explains: "Realism was then the interpretation of the Supper in which somehow there is concern for the real Christ in the Supper, while symbolism [which devalues the realism of Jesus's bodily presence] stands for mere illustration, an image, a symbol of the *suffering* and dying of Christ which reminds us of the historical actuality of his death and of its significance" (*SAC*, 289 [215]). This results in the "interpretation of the Lord's Supper as a *nudum signum*, bereft of all reality, except the reality of the sign and the psychological reality of the remembrance" (*SAC*, 289-90 [215-16]). It fails to consider that the sacramental signs of bread and wine come from the hand of Christ, and hence "the signs can no longer be detached from Christ, for he instituted the signs and gave them to his Church as signs of his reconciliation and peace" (*SAC*, 290 [216]). Thus, the sacramental signs of bread and wine are not man-made signs, but "the institution of Christ and to his power in and over the signs. These signs can no longer be detached from him who instituted the Lord's Supper" (ibid.). This institution has divine authority, and hence is not a human ecclesial convention adopted by the agreement of believers (Sokolowski, "Transubstantiation," 105). Otherwise, we land in symbolism and spiritualism. Concludes Berkouwer, "There is then no longer a contrast between symbol and reality for him who knows that through these signs communion is experienced and salvation is represented and given" (*SAC*, 291 [217]).

Fourth, missing in Allison's account of the sacraments, in particular, the Eucharist, is a reference to the conjunction between the sacramental sign and the thing signified. His view is not the view of Reformed Confessions, such as the Second Helvetic Confession (1566).

> And as formerly the sacraments consisted of the word, the sign, and the thing signified; so even now they are composed, as it were, of the same parts. For the Word of God makes them sacraments, which before they were not. ... For they are consecrated by the Word, and shown to be sanctified by him who instituted them. To sanctify or consecrate anything to God is to dedicate it to holy uses; that is, to take it from the common and ordinary use, and to appoint it to a holy

use. For the signs in the sacraments are drawn from common use, things external and visible. For in baptism the *sign* is the element of water, and that visible washing which is done by the minister; but the *thing signified* is regeneration and the cleansing from sins. Likewise, in the Lord's Supper, the *outward sign* is bread and wine, taken from things commonly used for meat and drink; but the *thing signified* is the body of Christ which was given, and his blood which was shed for us, or the communion of the body and blood of the Lord.

Do the sacramental signs of water and of bread and wine simply acquire a new signification—regeneration and cleansing from sins, and body and blood of Christ—but still remain what they are?

> ... And as we learn out of the Word of God that these signs were instituted for another purpose than the usual use, therefore we teach that they now, in their holy use, take upon them the names of things signified, and are no longer called mere water, bread or wine, but also regeneration or the washing of water, and the body and blood of the Lord or symbols and sacraments of the Lord's body and blood. Not that the symbols are changed into the things signified, or cease to be what they are in their own nature. For otherwise they would not be sacraments. If they were only the thing signified, they would not be signs.
> (Beeke and Ferguson, eds. *Reformed Confessions Harmonized*, 213–14)

Yes, there is a rejection in the Second Helvetic Confession of *substantial* presence: bread and wine are not changed into the body and blood of Christ. But the sacramental signs of bread and wine are constitutive of the conjunction between the signs and the thing signified. Says Berkouwer,

> [F]or in the Lord's Supper the crux of the matter is indeed a sign, a symbol, an indication which is given to us for our salvation. But in that case it must be made clear that this sign is not an arbitrary human illustration, but a sign which is given to us by Christ and which therefore can never be detached from Christ. It is a repast, but in the bread and wine we come into contact with those signs which Christ himself uses with a very specific purpose: the strengthening and assurance of our faith. "The certainty that with the bread we also eat and drink the body of Christ lies not in the eating and drinking as such, nor in faith, but in

the receiving of these qualified signs *from the hand of Christ.*" This implies that the signs can no longer be detached from Christ, for he instituted the signs and gave them to his Church as signs of his reconciliation and peace. Therein lies the basis for the Lord's Supper and also the inviolable comfort for faith. There is then no longer a contrast between *symbol* and *reality* for him who knows that through these signs communion is experienced and salvation is represented and given. (*SAC* 290–91 [216–17])[37]

This account focuses on personal communion with Christ, not merely on the benefits. Most importantly, it is about the real presence of Christ in Eucharistic communion, as well as his presence in the sacramental signs of bread and wine. The gift of Jesus Christ himself is the gift par excellence, says John Paul II, "of his person in his sacred humanity, as well as the gift of his saving work" (*Ecclesia de Eucharistia*, §11). Christ himself is really present in his flesh and blood. Berkouwer cites the *Heidelberg Catechism* (Q. & A. 75): "with His crucified body and shed blood He himself feeds and nourishes my soul for eternal life." Q. & A. 79: "so too His crucified body and shed blood are the true food and drink of our souls unto eternal life," and we are "really partakers of His true body and blood, through the working of the Holy Spirit" (*SAC* 303–4 [226]).[38]

Significantly, indeed, crucial to Berkouwer's account of Christ's "real presence" is his criticism of substantial presence, meaning thereby "an abstract interest in the 'body' and 'blood' as substances" (*SAC* 308 [230]). His criticism is particularly directed against the "'depersonalization' [of the real presence of Christ in the Lord's Supper] which is undeniably present both in transubstantiation and in the [Lutheran] doctrine of consubstantiation." "'Body' and 'blood' are here placed by themselves as 'substances' that form the point of departure of true communion." In other words, Berkouwer rejects all substantializing and depersonalizing of Christ's real presence in the Lord's Supper, and hence it is about "the presence of Christ and ... our communion with his true body and blood." That is, "the 'body' and 'blood' are to be understood in terms of Christ's act of reconciliation, not [abstractly as isolated substances] in themselves" (*SAC* 304 [228]). In sum:

Christ's surrender of his body and blood is not an event that can be detached from his person, but it is his act, and in the reality and power of that act Christ

> himself is in the full sense present in the Lord's Supper. In the Lord's Supper, the believer has communion with the glorified Christ because he has communion with his body and blood. This communion is not a communion with Christ's glorified "body" and "blood" as a substantial, isolated reality, but a communion with him in his offering and in his true body and blood, with him "who has become flesh and was crucified in history and whose flesh is now in heaven."
> (*SAC* 314 [235])

Fifth, arguably, Berkouwer's sacramentology of the Eucharist is consistent with Catholic thought. Still, if Christ's real presence is *his* personal presence in his body and blood, and that presence is not man's handiwork, then, as Schillebeeckx stated, "metaphysical realism is essential to the Christian faith" (*Christus Tegenwoordigheid*, 121 [150]). As it stands, however, Berkouwer's thinking reminds me of notions like "transignification" (change in meaning) and "transfinalization" (change in purpose). There is a change of meaning and purpose, but not the substance; substance here refers to "the bread and wine insofar as they exist in themselves, as it were, 'in their own right.' At the moment of transubstantiation, the bread and wine no longer exist in themselves but begin to exist as the effective signs of Christ's Body and Blood" (Kereszty, "On the Eucharistic Presence," at 351).[39] These notions fail to capture the ontological dimension, namely, the "metaphysical density," of Eucharistic presence, and hence the ontological transformation of reality. This point is made by Pope Paul VI with respect to Eucharistic Presence of the sacrifice of the Mass. The voice of the Church, says Paul:

> The voice [of the Church] assures us that the way in which Christ becomes present in this Sacrament is through the change of the whole substance of the bread into His body and of the whole substance of the wine into His blood, which change, truly marvelous and unique, the Catholic Church suitably and properly calls transubstantiation. As a result of transubstantiation, the appearances [Latin *species*] of bread and wine undoubtedly take on a new signification [transignification] and a new finality [transfinalization], for they are no longer ordinary bread and wine but instead a sign of a sacred reality and a sign of spiritual food; but they take on this new signification, this new finality, precisely because they a contain a new "reality," which we can rightly call ontological.

> For what now lies beneath the aforementioned ap-
> pearances [*species*] is not what was there before, but
> something completely different; and not just in the
> estimation of Church belief but rather in reality, since
> once the substance or nature of the bread and wine
> has been changed into the body and blood of Christ,
> nothing remains of the bread and the wine expect the
> appearances [*species*]—beneath which Christ is pres-
> ent whole and entire in His physical "reality," bodily
> [Latin *corporaliter*] present, although not in the man-
> ner in which bodies are present in place. (*Mysterium Fidei*,
> §46)

Did the replacement of "transubstantiation" with "transignification" and "transfinalization" change the content of the teachings of
the faith regarding Eucharistic Presence? Berkouwer argues against
that interpretation. He writes:

> The pope's [Paul VI] intention is to maintain the
> "ontology" of actual presence against every form of
> symbolism that allows this reality to recede. Now, one
> can pose the question of whether this definition of
> the problem, whether the pope's dilemma (ontologi-
> cal versus "only symbolical") truly coincides with the
> new understanding in Roman Catholic theology con-
> cerning the Eucharist today, one in which the words
> "trans-signification" and "transfinalization" play such
> an important role. That question has already been an-
> swered in the negative more than once, since the in-
> tention was never to juxtapose "symbol" and "reality"
> over against one another. Rather, it was the desire to
> transcend this dilemma by means of a deeper insight
> into symbol characterized especially by emphasizing
> that "symbol" has nothing whatsoever to do with lack
> of reality, vagueness or flight. (*Nabetrachting*, 63–68)

I interpret Berkouwer here to suggest that the dualism between
symbol and reality may be overcome by thinking that the sacramental
signs of bread and wine are constitutive of the conjunction between
the signs and the thing signified. As Berkouwer said above: "There
is then no longer a contrast between *symbol* and *reality* for him who
knows that through these signs communion is experienced and salvation is represented and given" (*SAC* 291 [217]). Why? Berkouwer does
not answer this question, but Kereszty does, "The Body and Blood of
Christ appear as bread and wine because the phenomenon of bread
and wine in conjunction with the words and gestures of the Eu-

charistic Prayer expresses most fittingly its new ontological reality: the crucified and risen Christ *as our spiritual food and drink*" (Kereszty, "Eucharistic Presence," 349). In short, "The change is so radical that the bread and wine become truly identical with the reality they express" (ibid., 351). Accordingly, these two conceptual categories—a change in meaning or purpose—can successfully explicate the content of revelation only to the extent that they can deepen our understanding of transubstantiation and thus of the meaning of Real Presence as an ontological reality. In other words, a change in meaning or purpose is necessarily dependent on a change in the Eucharistic substance. This change is metaphysical and Trent called it "transubstantiation."

For now, I argue briefly that transubstantiation is irreplaceable because the "logic of the Incarnation leads on to Transubstantiation," according to Sokolowski ("Transubstantiation," 108). That does not make transignification and transfinalization unessential. But, as he explains, "the bodily aspect of the Incarnation makes Transubstantiation necessary; because the body and blood of Christ become present, the substance of bread and wine cannot remain. While the material character of the Incarnation makes Transubstantiation necessary, it is the divine aspect of the Incarnation, the presence of the divine nature in the Incarnation, that makes Transubstantiation possible (and the possibility is prior to the necessity). Only because the divine substance becomes present in the Eucharist, as the ultimate source of the action being reenacted there, can Transubstantiation occur" (ibid., 109).

In sum: "If the Eucharist is truly the action of God, the bread and wine cannot remain in their substance." This means to exclude the idea that "the Eucharist is primarily the action of the community ... [with] the bread and wine [being] symbols of the gifts the people offer." Only then would "the bread and wine ... remain what they are [and] Transubstantiation would not occur." Finally, Sokolowski concludes "in such an interpretation, it would not be Christ who speaks the words of consecration but the community." Thus, "transubstantiation depends on whose action the Eucharist represents" (ibid., 110).

Sixth, furthermore, Berkouwer argues against views like those of Allison that the eschatological expectation of the return of Christ is *not* obscured by this presence already realized. Real presence is "consistent with the full, eschatological reality of the resurrection, ascension, and Pentecost."[40] What, then, is the relationship between the real presence of Christ and the Ascended Christ?[41] The Protestant Reformers did not accept the antithesis between that expectation and the reality of Christ's presence. They did not minimize his presence but only intended to indicate its nature. Berkouwer cites the then German Lutheran theologian Helmut Gollwitzer (1908–1993): "The 'already' of the promised present and the 'not yet' of the future still to come should not outbalance each other, but should come together and together render the true and full comfort of faith" (*SAC* 315 [236]). Berkouwer explains,

> It is no exaggeration to say that the controversy about the real presence of Christ in the Lord's Supper ultimately comes down to a different insight into the significance of the return of Christ and the significance of the eschatological orientation of faith. This does not mean that speaking of the presence of Christ in the Lord's Supper automatically implies a danger to eschatological expectation, to the "not yet." If that were the case, Roman Catholics, Lutherans, and Reformed would agree on this point, for they all speak of a presence of Christ in the Lord's Supper. Hence everything depends on the manner of Christ's presence in the Supper. (ibid.)

Pace Allison, there is no inconsistency as such between the eschatological expectation of the "not yet" and the "already." What this means is that the Eucharistic mode of Christ's sacramental presence is itself eschatological, the "already" of the promised presence in absence, which is the "not yet" of the future still to come. Furthermore, as Berkouwer suggests the danger to eschatological expectation depends entirely on the mode of Christ's presence in the Eucharist, the Lord's Supper.

Although Christ's real presence has been affirmed through the ages when the Church spoke of a real or substantial change of the bread and wine in connection with the Eucharist, this does not preclude a certain dogmatic development of Eucharistic doctrine between the Patristics and the Medievals, such as Aquinas, on the nature of real presence. This development includes the concept of transubstantiation that entered the dogmatic discussion with the Fourth Lateran Council in 1215, an account of the mode of Christ's Eucharistic presence that was later fully developed by Aquinas's *Summa Theologiae* III, written in 1272, and then affirmed by the Council of Trent (Denzinger, §1652).

I cannot enter here into a critique of Allison's claims concerning the concept of transubstantiation (*RCTP*, 316–19) except to say that just as the development of Trinitarian dogma's introduction of the concept of *homoousios* ("of the same substance") was controversial when used by the Council of Nicaea to define the oneness of being of the Son with the Father, so too the concept of transubstantiation has generated conflict in the attempt to safeguard the Church's faith in the Eucharistic presence. As Bavinck puts this point, "Theology, we know, employs many terms that do not occur in Scripture and that have acquired technical meaning in their own sphere. If theology had to refrain from using such terms, it would have to cease all scientific labor and all preaching and exegesis of God's Word, and indeed even the translation of Scripture, would be impermissible" (*Gereformeerde Dogmatiek*, IV, 473 [472]). Thus, in the development of Eucharistic doctrine, Eucharistic presence means that Christ is truly, really, and substantially present. In the sacramental giving of himself, Christ *identifies* himself, his person, with his body and blood, such that the change the Church calls transubstantiation, is about changing the signs of bread and wine into Christ's body and blood, rather than taking the former to be mere tokens of his sacrificial death. As Sokolowski puts it,

> This fact [of identification] is brought out by a remarkable comment of St. Thomas, who observes that in the Eucharistic Prayer Christ is quoted not as saying, "*This bread* is my body," but "*This* is my body." If Christ had said "this bread" was his body, then the thing referred to would still be bread, but the simple demonstrative pronoun "this" without a noun implies that it is not bread any longer. ("Transubstantiation," 105–6)

Denying this substantial change entails the denial of the bodily presence of the glorified Christ and hence of Christ's sacramental presence. Furthermore, *pace* Allison, rightly understood, transubstantiation is an eschatological concept—a sacramental *parousia* because the fallen creation "already *shares* the eschatological situation of the glorified corporeality [of the body and blood of Christ]." In other words, it is mistaken to see Eucharistic presence as a substitute for the absent ascended Christ, but rather it is a proleptic anticipation of what the Ascension means, namely, as Kelly puts it, "Christ fills all things and the risen and ascended One draws all creation to its fullness in him; this is the context in which 'transubstantiation' is to be understood" ("The Ascension," 338). "Thus, Eucharistic faith is a form of cosmic awareness" (ibid., 346). No one more than John Paul II understood this point. He wrote:

> The Eucharist is always in some way celebrated on the altar of the world. It unites heaven and earth. It embraces and permeates all creation. The Son of God became man in order to restore all [fallen] creation, in one supreme act of praise, to the One who made it from nothing. He, the Eternal High Priest who by the blood of his Cross entered the eternal sanctuary, thus gives back to the Creator and Father all [fallen] creation [now] redeemed. He does so through the priestly ministry of the Church, to the glory of the Most Holy Trinity. Truly this is the *mysterium fidei* which is accomplished in the Eucharist: the world which came forth from the hands of God the Creator now returns to him redeemed by Christ. (*Ecclesia De Eucharistia*, §8)

Of course, there is an eschatological tension here between the "already" and the "not yet," but the "new creation" in Christ already begins with the transformation of the bread and wine into the Body and Blood of the Lord. Schillebeeckx explains:

> But we are still in the "already now" and "not yet" that characterizes the period of salvation between the resurrection and the *parousia*, and the consecrated bread and wine therefore still belong, in their new meaning as "new creation" of the order of salvation, to "this old world" also. For this reason, transubstantiation contains two dimensions—a *change of being* of the bread and wine (in which Christ's glorified body is really offered through the Holy Spirit), but *within the terrestrial, but now* (through this change of being) *sacramental form* of bread and wine, which remain subject, in this secular world, to the terrestrial laws of corporeality. Transubstantiation thus has two dimensions of one and the same undivided reality. This is the essential meaning of the dogma. (*Christus Tegenwoordigheid*, 120 [83])

> The Eucharist is, of its very nature, an event of the period between the resurrection and the Parousia, a period during which earthly realities become historical manifestations of the gift of grace here and now and—in the sacramental liturgy, within the mystery of the Church's community of grace led by its office;

that is, especially in the Eucharist—are withdrawn from their secular independence, their "being themselves," to the extent of becoming the sacramental form in which the heavenly bodiliness of Christ himself—that is, of his real presence for me—appears. ... It is, of course, a *sacramental* earthly presence, due to Christ's real act of making himself present in the gift of holy bread placed at the disposal of all who wish to approach this sacrament in faith. For this reason, the true reality in the Eucharist is no longer bread, but simply the body and blood of Christ in a sacramental form. (Ibid., 120 [84–85])

In conclusion, aside from Schillebeeckx's attempt to deflect the criticism that the dogma of transubstantiation presupposes a defective view of the Ascension, we also get a glimpse here into the argument that transubstantiation presupposes the concept of grace transforming and fulfilling nature, with Christ's real presence being a foretaste of the new creation. What then is essential to the dogma of Eucharistic presence is an ontological depth or density in which the substantial conversion of bread and wine into the body and blood of Christ "introduces within creation the principle of a radical change," according to Benedict XVI, "a sort of 'nuclear fission', to use an image familiar to us today, which penetrates to the heart of all being, a change meant to set off a process which transforms reality, a process leading ultimately to the transfiguration of the entire world, to the point where God will be all in all" (*Sacramentum Caritatis*, §11).[42]

This chapter and the previous chapter 4 have refuted the "Evangelical Hermeneutics of Roman Catholicism" as espoused by Allison and De Chirico. The two axioms of "nature and grace" and the "Christ-Church interconnection" have no grounds as an interpretation of Roman Catholicism.

Where do we go from here in our ecumenical conversation? In a final chapter, I will briefly answer this question.

NOTES

1. Hans Urs von Balthasar, *Parole et mystère chez Origène*, 51, as cited by Marc Cardinal Ouellet, *Mystery and Sacrament of Love*, 27.

2. George Eldon Ladd, *The Presence of the Future: The Eschatology of Biblical Realism*, revised and updated version of *Jesus and the Kingdom*, 331, 333.

3. Yves Congar, OP, *Jesus Christ*, trans. Luke O'Neill, 176, but see also the entire chapter, "The Lordship of Christ over the Church and the World," 167–219.

4. *Lumen Gentium*, §31, but see also §36. For a fuller development of the Church's teaching on the mission of the Laity, see *Apostolicam Actuositatem*. See also, the insightful 1881 essay of Herman Bavinck on the all-encompassing character of the Kingdom of God, "Het Rijk Gods, Het Hoogste Goed," in *Bavinck: Kennis en Leven*, 28–56.

5. *Lumen Gentium*, §8: "Sicut enim natura assumpta Verbo divino ut vivum organum salutis, Ei indissolubiliter unitum, inservit, non dissimili modo socialis compago Ecclesiae Spiritui Christi, eam vivificanti, ad augmentum corporis inservit (cf. Eph 4,16)."

6. Vanhoozer is drawing here on De Chirico, "The Blurring of Time Distinctions in Roman Catholicism." Terms, such as assimilation, reduction, yields, absorbed, violation, yes, even destroyed, are used by De Chirico to describe the relationship in such a way that it suggests the removal of the boundaries between the unique and definitive nature of Christ's Incarnation and the ongoing mission of the Church is indefensible. As De Chirico says, "Roman Catholicism is not intentionally driven by the desire to confuse the time periods of God. It would be uncharitable and prejudiced to think so" (46). Why does De Chirico nevertheless think so? "All the same, the unfolding of its powerful dialectical capacities which introduce subtle distinctions leading to the amplification of the synthesis . . . [reflects] the Catholic genius of 'complexio oppositorum' (convergence of opposites), and epistemological art which is at the same time both fascinating and disconcerting" (46). The Lérinian legacy of Vatican II, as I have presented it above in Chapter One, is a refutation of this charge of dialectical thinking against Catholicism.

7. The next couple of paragraphs are adapted from Eduardo Echeverria; "The One Church, the Many Churches: A Catholic Approach to Ecclesial Unity and Diversity—with Special Attention to Abraham Kuyper's Ecclesiastical Epistemology," 252–53.

8. On this, see Karol Wojtyla, *Love and Responsibility*, 308n1.

9. *Figures of Speech Used in the Bible*, 2nd ed., 727, 735.

10. Kasper, *Zur Theologie der Christlichen Ehe*, 36. Translated by David Smith as *Theology of Christian Marriage*, 39 [30]. More recently, Walter Cardinal Kasper, *The Gospel of the Family*.

11. See also, *Man and Woman* 489n88: "In the great letters of St. Paul, ['*mystērion*'] returns seven times, with the high point in Romans: 'according to my gospel and the proclamation of Jesus Christ, according to the revelation of the *mystery* that was kept secret for long ages but is now disclosed (Rom 16:25–26). In the latter letters, the '*mystērion*' is identified with the Gospel (see Eph 6:19) and even with Jesus Christ himself (see Col 2:2; 4:3; Eph 3:4), which is a turning point in the understanding of the term: '*mystērion*' is no longer merely God's eternal plan, but *the realization* of this plan on earth, revealed in Jesus Christ."

12. So, St. Paul does not merely "illustrate the union between Christ and the

Church from the nature of matrimony." Rather, adds Scheeben, "He wishes to derive the nature and duties of Christian marriage from the union of Christ with the Church as the ideal and root of Christian marriage." So, the great mystery of Christ and the Church "vibrantly lives, operates, and manifests itself in [marriage itself]." Otherwise, as John Paul adds, "this whole analogy would hang in a void" (*Man and Woman He Created Them*, 90.3). See also, Karl Rahner, *The Church and the Sacraments*, 108: "The will of God is operative in the reality itself, in marriage, and gives it a definite intrinsic characteristic which fits it for the function of symbol."

13. Dooyeweerd, too, rejects the "Roman Catholic distinction," as he puts it, "between marriage as a 'natural union' and as a 'sacrament of grace' which is unacceptable from the Reformational Christian standpoint." Given this standpoint, marriage is neither ordained by Christ nor is it an outward sign uniquely conveying an inward and spiritual grace. Nonetheless, he "gratefully acknowledges" that Catholic thinkers, such as Dietrich von Hildebrand, affirm "the Biblical Christian conception of the conjugal bond as a typical and incomparable institutional love-union between husband and wife, as the expression of the eternal love of Christ towards the Church as His Bride" (*A New Critique*, Vol. III, *The Structures of Individuality of Temporal Reality*, 320.

14. Rudolph Schnackenburg, *Ephesians: A Commentary*, "If the 'great mystery' has to do with the connection of Christ and Church, a direct sacramental interpretation of marriage is prohibited. But how can we judge Christian marriage if it is analogous to the relationship between Christ and the Church, when it has been taken up into the merciful activity of Christ through the membership of the spouses in the Body of Christ (cf. v. 30)? Roman Catholic authors conclude that marriage is thereby given a dignity and holiness which might be called 'sacrament'" (256). Wolfhart Pannenberg develops the biblical basis for the sacramentality of marriage in his *Systematic Theology*, Vol. 3, trans. G.W. Bromily, 391-98.

15. According to John Paul, at the basis of the analogy of spousal love "stands the explicit *conviction* [of the prophets, Isaiah, Hosea, and Ezekiel] that the love of Yahweh for the Chosen People can and must be compared to the love that unites bride and bridegroom, the love that should unite spouses. . . . In this way, *the analogy of bridegroom and bride*, which allowed the author of Ephesians to define the relationship of Christ with the Church, has *a rich tradition* in the books of the Old Covenant" (ibid.; see also 87.4, 95).

16. Scheeben acknowledges that "although the text [of Eph 5:25–32] does not formally state that matrimony has the power to produce grace, the reasons why it possesses and must possess such power are there assigned as pertaining to it mysterious character. Thus, the theological exegesis of the passage yields a proof, *ex visceribus causae*, that matrimony has the power to produce grace, a proof that should satisfy us even more than if a demonstration were forthcoming that the Apostle [Paul] used the term *sacramentum* ... in our current sense" (*The Mysteries of Christianity*, 606n10). Germain Grisez writes, "Neither Florence [1439; DS: 1327] nor Trent [1563; DS; 1797–1816] claims that Eph 5:32 by itself *asserts* the sacramentality of marriage. The Church's doctrine that

marriage is a sacrament follows from Eph 5:32 when it considered *together with* other data: Jesus' teaching about the indissolubility of marriage in the beginning, the real efficacy of God's redemptive work in him, Scripture's witness to the sacredness of marriage even under the old covenant, Jesus' use of the marriage and wedding feast analogy to describe the new covenant, and his participation in the wedding feast of Cana" (*The Way of the Lord Jesus*, Vol. 2, *Living a Christian Life*, 599n99). On the matter of theological exegesis, but now regarding infant baptism, both Bavinck and Berkouwer acknowledge (in Berkouwer's words) that "the New Testament did not give an explicit order to baptize children." "Nevertheless," he adds, "it was … felt that the baptism of children was fully legitimate in the light of the confession of God's Covenant" (Berkouwer, *De Sacramenten*, 210 [161]). Bavinck concurs: "We need to overcome our astonishment over the fact that the New Testament nowhere explicitly mentions infant baptism. … The validity of infant baptism does not lapse on that account. … For also that which can be deduced from Scripture by legitimate inference is as binding as that which is expressly stated in it. This is how the church acts every minute of the day in the ministry of the Word, in the practice of life, in the *development of doctrine*. It never stops with the letter but under the guidance of the Holy Spirit deduces from the data of Scripture the inferences and applications that make possible and foster its life and development" (*Gereformeerde Dogmatiek*, IV, 502 [526]).

17. John Paul adds, "It is obvious that the analogy of earthly human love, of the husband for his wife, of human spousal love, cannot offer an adequate and complete understanding of that absolutely transcendent Reality, the divine mystery, both as hidden from ages in God and in its 'historical' realization in time when 'Christ loved the Church and gave himself for her' (Eph 5:25). The *mystery* remains *transcendent with respect to this analogy* as with respect to any other analogy with which we try to express it in human language. At the same time, however, this analogy offers the possibility of a certain cognitive 'penetration' into the very essence of the mystery" (*Man and Woman He Created Them*, 95b.1; see also 97.5). See also, Rahner, *The Church and the Sacraments*, 107.

18. Kasper, *Zur Theologie der Christlichen Ehe*, 40–41 [31]. He is citing H. Volk, "Ehe," *LThK*, vol. III, 681. I slightly altered this summary statement because the English translation failed to capture the nuances from the German.

19. Cited in Calvin, *Institutes*, IV, XIV, 4.

20. On the Reformed Confessions' sacramentology, see *Reformed Confessions Harmonized*, ed. Joel R. Beeke and Sinclair B. Ferguson, 208–15.

21. My comments on this lengthy passage from John Paul II are adapted from my column in *The Catholic Thing*, "One-Flesh Sacramental Union."

22. Gregg Allison develops this thesis in Chapter 1, "The Created Body," of his book, *Embodied: Living as Whole People in a Fractured World*, 21–38.

23. Allison develops this thesis in Chapter 2, "The Gendered Body," of *Embodied*, 39–58.

24. This, too, is the view of Herman Dooyeweerd: *A New Critique of Theoretical*

Thought, Vol. III, 89. Idem, *Reformation and Scholasticism in Philosophy*, Vol. III, *Philosophy of Nature and Philosophical Anthropology*, trans. Magnus Verbrugge and D. F. M. Strauss, "[T]he human spirit cannot carry out any real acts outside its temporal corporal individuality-structure. For that reason, we said: it is the *individual human being* in the integral unity of 'body' and 'soul' who accomplishes the acts. The full person as a totality is the subject of the act. ... In the acts, the 'soul' is actually operative in the entire enkaptic structure of the body, and only in the body does the soul have the capacity to do so, insofar as the acts are included in the temporal order of the body. In other words, we can take the 'acts' neither to be purely 'corporal' nor purely 'spiritual'. They are *both* inseparably connected and precisely for that reason they bear a *typically human* character. Only the act-structure in *its fundamental dependence upon the spirit* stamps the body as human" (162–63).

25. Herman Dooyeweerd's social ontology of marriage attempts to get at the nature of marriage, and he argues that essential to marriage as such is sexual differentiation. The internal structural principle of marriage has an invariant transcendental character. Therefore, Dooyeweerd holds that "marriage is ... intrinsically qualified as a moral community of love for the duration of the common life-span of two persons of different sex." The moral aspect of this love relationship (its qualifying or leading function), shows an individuality type that "refers back to ... the organic life-aspect of the conjugal relation, namely, the lasting sexual biotic bond between husband and wife." Strictly speaking, "The moral individuality-type of the conjugal love-community is *typically* [emphasis added] founded in the sexual-biotic function of marriage" (Dooyeweerd, "Sociology of Law and Its Philosophical Foundations," 83). As he argues elsewhere: the internal structural principle of the marital love-communion, the ethical aspect of this love-community being its qualifying function, may not be detached from, in Dooyeweerd's words, "its biotic foundation in the organic difference between the sexes" (Dooyeweerd, *A New Critique*, III, 320). Again, he says, "According to its two radical functions (the moral and biotic functions) the marriage community can be described as a community of moral life-long love between husband and wife based on a relatively durable organic sexual bond" (Dooyeweerd, *A Christian Theory of Social Institutions*, trans. Magnus Verbrugge, 87).

26. See the magisterial work of Berkouwer, *De Sacramenten*. See also, Kasper, *Harvesting the Fruits*, Chapter 4, "The Sacraments of Baptism and Eucharist," 158–95, which reflects on the fruits of ecumenical dialogue, as evident in the documents produced, between the Pontifical Council for Promoting Christian Unity, on the one hand, and the Methodist, Reformed, Lutheran, and Anglican traditions on the other.

27. God is the principal efficient cause and the sacraments are examples of instrumental efficient causality. On this distinction and its sacramental import, see Aquinas, *Summa Theologiae* III, q. 62, a. 1, ad 1, ad 2; and q. 62, a. 5.

28. Bernard Leeming, SJ, *Principles of Sacramental Theology*, 2nd ed., 290. For Aquinas's critique of occasionalism, see *Summa Theologiae* III, q. 62, a. 4. See also, Gagliardi, *Truth Is a Synthesis*, 636–37.

29. Gregg Allison, "The Ordinances of the Church," *The Gospel Coalition*. See also, Allison, *Sojourners and Strangers: The Doctrine of the Church*, 322–23.

30. "Calvin's Doctrine of the Lord's Supper," *Mid-America Journal of Theology* 19 (2008 [1887]), at 132.

31. Warfield, *The Plan of Salvation*, also charges the Church's view of the sacramental economy with deism (57–59).

32. This note, indeed, the whole appendix, "St. Thomas' Christological Interpretation of Sacramental Ex Opere Operato Causality" (82–89), is not present in the original Dutch edition.

33. For Berkouwer's defense of sacramental efficacy, but not ex opere operato, cf. Berkouwer, *De Sacramenten*, 11–28, 66–107 [13–26, 56–89]. See also G. C. Berkouwer, "*Ex Opere Operato*," Part I, *Gereformeerd Theologisch Tijdschrift* 53, no. 3 (1953): 78–88; idem., "*Ex Opere Operato*," Part II, *Gereformeerd Theologisch Tijdschrift* 53, no. 4 (1953): 93–103.

34. Sacramental causality means "the grace conferred by a sacrament is identically a real relation of dependence on the sacrament as sign, such a real relation being the necessary and sufficient condition for the truth of the traditional affirmation, *sacramenta causant significando*" (Philip McShane, SJ, "On the Causality of the Sacraments," at 424–25). See also, Romanus Cessario, OP, "Sacramental Causality: *Da capo!*" 307–16.

35. Hans Urs von Balthasar echoes this Catholic point: "Only the Eucharist really completes the Incarnation" (*Theo-Drama*, Vol. IV, at 348).

36. On this, see Peter J. Leithart, "What's Wrong with Transubstantiation? An Evaluation of Theological Models," at 301. I have learned much from Leithart's article about the matter of "real presence" in Luther and Calvin.

37. The quote within the quote is from Reformed theologian Herman Ridderbos.

38. Similar claims are found in the Belgic Confession of Faith, art. 35.

39. On this, see Germain Grisez, "An Alternative Theology of Jesus's Substantial Presence in the Eucharist."

40. Leithart, "What's Wrong with Transubstantiation," 320, arguing that this was Calvin's position.

41. On this question, see the instructive article by Anthony J. Kelly, CSsR, "The Ascension and the Eucharist," at 344–46.

42. See also, Joseph Cardinal Ratzinger, *The Spirit of the Liturgy*, trans. John Saward, 173: "The elements of the earth are transubstantiated, pulled, so to speak, from their creaturely anchorage, grasped at the deepest ground of their being, and changed into the Body and Blood of the Lord."

AFTERWORD

BEYOND ANTI-CATHOLICISM AND ESSENTIAL PROTESTANTISM

Anti-Catholicism is a slippery phenomenon, hardly sus-
ceptible of definition, but it does have this characteristic,
that it is unreceptive to any corrections in the caricature
that it fights because it fears that correcting the carica-
ture will mean a weakening of its own negative position.
Anti-Catholicism, with all its apparent emotional force,
is powerless to make a contribution to the controversy
between Rome and the Reformation. ... The emotional
anti-Catholic feels uncomfortable in a new situation in
which by means of new confrontations and new inves-
tigations into exegesis and dogmatics the controversy is
stripped of its simplistic forms. Many Protestants suspect
that by taking these confrontations seriously, we may
water down the differences and lose some of the old con-
victions of the struggle. (VCNT, 27–28 [29])

There can be no ecumenism worthy of the name without a change of heart. ... *The [Second Vatican] Coun-*
cil calls for personal conversion as well as for communal
conversion. The desire of every Christian Community for
unity goes hand in hand with its fidelity to the Gospel. In
the case of individuals who live their Christian vocation,
the Council speaks of interior conversion, of a renewal of
mind. (UR §15)

In Chapter 2, I laid out the Catholic vision of ecumenism. Thus,
in this Afterword I will not repeat that vision here. Taking my
lead from the epigraph above where Berkouwer describes the
"emotional anti-Catholic" and his characteristics, I will suggest a
perspective for moving beyond "anti-Catholicism."

The main title of my book raises the question of whether Roman
Catholics and Protestants—Reformed and Evangelicals—are together. Yes, we are. By virtue of our baptism, we are all incorporated
into Christ, enjoying a unity as brethren in Christ, and hence with

the Church, however imperfect. Catholics may legitimately engage in an ecumenical and apologetical stance toward Evangelical Protestants, as I have in this book. But prior to that engagement should be a recognition that Catholics and Evangelicals, in short, Christ's faithful, are united in the Spirit because they are in communion with the Son and, in him, share in his communion with the Father. "Our *fellowship* is with the Father and with his Son Jesus Christ" (1 John 1:3).

Throughout this book I have argued that we are together having a common cause in the Gospel and in the truth of theological commitments regarding the normative sources of the Christian faith. In the Introduction to this book, I stated that honest answers deserve honest questions. I answered the honest questions raised—even from a faulty set of presuppositions, which I then identified—by Allison and De Chirico in their assessment of Roman Catholicism. Doctrinal differences matter because truth matters, and "authentic ecumenism is a gift at the service of truth" (*UUS* §39).

I argued in Chapter 1, that their acceptance of meaning holism, and the consequent incommensurability that they posit between Roman Catholicism and Protestantism, explains their anti-ecumenical stance. I examined their view of "Scripture, Tradition, and the Church," and found their assessment flawed. I refuted the "Evangelical Hermeneutics of Roman Catholicism" as espoused by them. The two axioms of "nature and grace" and the "Christ-Church interconnection" have no grounds as an interpretation of Roman Catholicism.

Do the writings of Allison and De Chirico contribute to resolving the controversy between Rome and the Reformation? Unfortunately, they do not because of their anti-Catholicism, and this stance stands in a mere protest relationship with Catholicism. As Berkouwer correctly stated, "Every kind of Protestantism that stands merely in a protest-relationship [with Catholicism] is stricken with unfruitfulness. That is why the name *Reformation* signifies far more than Protestantism" (*Recent Developments*, 10). In my view, this is the basic weakness of Allison and De Chirico's approach to Catholicism, and hence their work makes no "contribution to the controversy between Rome and the Reformation." A protest whose mere purpose is to refute Catholicism is unfruitful because divisions within the Church of Christ are no longer experienced as distressing, scandalous, let alone sinful.

Furthermore, "Anti-Catholics therefore are *a priori* skeptical of any talk of attempts at renewal of the Catholic Church" (*VCNT*, 28 [30]). Allison and De Chirico have not moved away from a primarily apologetical and antithetical stance. They are not prepared to ask how we can be open to the truth present in serious ecumenical theological dialogue, and hence they are not receptive ecumenists. Their stance towards Catholicism is primarily apologetical and antithetical. Thus, they have not moved from "antagonism and conflict to a situation where each party recognizes the other as an [ecumenical] *partner*" (*UUS*, §41).

In sum, says Berkouwer, "When our mindset is neither dominated by an anxiety regarding the weakening of one's own positions nor closed to possibly necessary corrections, then all sorts of questions, which early on were raised solely from an apologetical perspective, can now be raised on their own merits, with an honesty and open-mindedness, which is decisively necessary for all theoretical reflection" (*Nieuwe Perspectieven*, 11–12 [my translation]). "Responsible encounter is not a sign of weakness; it is rather recognition of the seriousness of the division of the Church" (*VCNT*, 28–29 [30]).

Moreover, since they do not examine Roman Catholicism with a desire for reconciliation, for unity in truth, their stance is one of mutual opposition between Roman Catholics and Evangelical Protestants. Indeed, their acceptance of the incommensurability thesis only further entrenches this opposition, and hence their anti-Catholicism.

"Anti-Catholicism and the pope as Anti-Christ are," according to Catholic theologian Reinhard Hütter, "identity-markers of essential Protestantism." Hütter explains, "Essential Protestantism requires for its identity Catholicism as the 'other.'"

Allison and De Chirico are essential Protestants. Hütter elaborates:

> Much of essential Protestantism assumes that at the time of the Reformation the true Gospel—lost or at least significantly distorted shortly after the apostle Paul—was rediscovered and the Church in the true sense reconstituted. Virtually everything in-between, the few exceptions only affirming the rule, pertains to the aberration of Roman Catholicism. Essential Protestantism, therefore, in a large measure needs Roman Catholicism and especially the papacy to know itself, to have a hold of its identity as Protestantism.

In contrast to essential Protestantism, there is *accidental* Protestantism. This sort of Protestantism "sees itself as the result of a particular, specific protestation," in short, it "has seen itself to a large degree as a reform movement in the Church catholic."

> For accidental Protestants there tends to be one fundamental difference—and it can be the Petrine office itself—that prevents them from being Catholic. This difference cannot be just any, but must be one without which the truth of the Gospel is decisively distorted or even abandoned. Being Protestant in this vein amounts to an emergency position necessary for the sake of the Gospel's truth and the Church's faithfulness; in short, accidental Protestantism does not understand itself as ecclesial normalcy.[1]

Allison and De Chirico understand their protest against Catholicism as ecclesial normalcy.

Moving beyond anti-Catholicism and hence essential Protestantism requires adopting the following perspective stated by John Paul II in *Ut Unum Sint* (§2) in order to have a change of heart, an interior conversion, as the epigraph above states:

> [1] Christians cannot underestimate the burden of *long-standing misgivings* inherited from the past, and of mutual *misunderstandings* and *prejudices. Complacency, indifference* and *insufficient knowledge of one another* often make this situation worse.
>
> [2] Consequently, the commitment to ecumenism must be based upon the conversion of hearts and upon prayer, which will also lead to the *necessary purification of past memories*. With the grace of the Holy Spirit, the Lord's disciples, inspired by love, by the power of the truth and by a sincere desire for mutual forgiveness and reconciliation, are called to *re-examine together their painful past* and the hurt which that past regrettably continues to provoke even today. All together, they are invited by the ever-fresh power of the Gospel to acknowledge with sincere and total objectivity the mistakes made and the contingent factors at work at the origins of their deplorable divisions.
>
> [3] *What is needed is a calm, clear-sighted and truthful vision of things*, a vision enlivened by divine mercy and capable of freeing people's minds and of inspiring in everyone a renewed willingness, precisely with a view

to proclaiming the Gospel to the men and women of every people and nation.

Heeding this perspective seems best in pursuing ecumenical action that is to get Evangelical Protestants, who share the views of Allison and De Chirico, beyond anti-Catholicism.

NOTES

1. Hütter, "Why Does the Pope Matter to Protestants?," 676–78.

BIBLIOGRAPHY

Abbot, Walter M., ed. *The Documents of Vatican II*. London: Chapman, 1966.

Adam, Karl, *The Spirit of Catholicism*. Translated by Dom Justin McCann, OSB. Steubenville, OH: Franciscan University Press, 1996 [1929], 210.

Allen, Michael and Scott Swain. *Reformed Catholicity: The Promise of Retrieval Theology and Biblical Interpretation*. Grand Rapids, MI: Baker Academic, 2015.

Allen, Prudence, RSM. "Man-Woman Complementarity: The Catholic Inspiration." *Logos* 9, no. 3 (Summer 2006): 87–108. http://www.laici.va/content/dam/laici/documenti/donna/filosofia/english/man-woman-complementary-the-catholic-inspiration.pdf.

Allison, Gregg. *Embodied: Living as Whole People in a Fractured World*. Grand Rapids, MI: Baker Books, 2021.

———. *40 Questions About Roman Catholicism*. Grand Rapids, MI: Kregel Academic, 2021.

———. "The Ordinances of the Church." *The Gospel Coalition* (website). https://www.thegospelcoalition.org/essay/the- ordinances-of-the-church/.

———. *Roman Catholic Theology & Practice: An Evangelical Assessment*. Wheaton, IL: Crossway, 2014.

———. *Sojourners and Strangers: The Doctrine of the Church*. Wheaton, IL: Crossway Books, 2012.

Allison, Gregg and Chris Castaldo. *The Unfinished Reformation*. Grand Rapids, MI: Zondervan, 2016.

Angeles, Peter A. "Cognitive Meaning." In *The Harper Collins Dictionary of Philosophy*, 2nd edition, p. 179. New York: HarperPerennial, 1992.

———. "Factual Meaning." In *The Harper Collins Dictionary of Philosophy*, 2nd edition, p. 180. New York: HarperPerennial, 1992.

Anglican-Roman Catholic International Commission. "The Gift of Authority." September 3, 1998. https://iarccum.org/doc/?d=15.

Augustine. *City of God*. Translated by Marcus Dods, *Nicene and Post-Nicene Fathers* 1/2, edited by Philip Schaff. Buffalo, NY: Christian Literature Publishing Co., 1887. Text from https://www.newadvent.org/fathers/120114.htm, edited by Kevin Knight.

Balthasar, Hans Urs von. *Parole et mystère chez Origène*. Paris: Cerf, 1957.

———. *Theo-Drama*, Vol. IV. Translated by Graham Harrison. San Francisco: Ignatius Press, 1994 [1980].

———. *Theo-Logic: Theological Logical Theory*, Vol. I, *Truth of the World*. Translated by Adrian J. Walker. San Francisco: Ignatius Press, 2000.

———. "On the Task of Catholic Philosophy in Our Time." *Communio* 20, no. 1 (Spring 1993 [first published 1946]): 147–87.

Barth, Karl. *Church Dogmatics* I/I, 2nd edition. Translated by G. W. Bromiley. Edited by G. W. Bromiley and T. F. Torrance. Edinburgh: T&T Clark, 1975.

Bavinck, Herman. "Calvin's Doctrine of the Lord's Supper." *Mid-America Journal of Theology* 19 (2008 [1887]): 127–42.

———. "The Catholicity of Christianity and the Church." *Calvin Theological Journal* 27 (1992): 220–51.

———. *Gereformeerde Dogmatiek*, Vol. I. Kampen: J. H. Kok, 1895. English translation: *Reformed Dogmatics*, Vol. 1, *Prolegomena*. Translated by John Vriend. Edited by John Bolt. Grand Rapids, MI: Baker Academic, 2003.

———. *Gereformeerde Dogmatiek*, Vol. IV. Kampen: J. H. Kok, 1901. English translation: *Reformed Dogmatics*, Vol. 4, *Holy Spirit, Church, and New Creation*. Translated by John Vriend. Edited by John Bolt. Grand Rapids, MI: Baker Academic, 2008.

———. *Het Christelijke Huisgezin*. 2nd revised edition. Kampen: J. H. Kok, 1912 [first edition 1908]. English translation: *The Christian Family*, translated by Nelson D. Kloosterman, with an introduction by James Eglinton. Grand Rapids, MI: Christian's Library Press, 2012.

———. "Het Rijk Gods, Het Hoogste Goed." In *Bavinck: Kennis en Leven*, 28–56. Kampen: J. H. Kok, 1922.

———. *Saved by Grace*. Translated by Nelson D. Kloosterman. Grand Rapids, MI: Reformation Heritage Books, 2008.

Beeke, Joel R. and Sinclair B. Ferguson, eds. *Reformed Confessions Harmonized, With an Annotated Bibliography of Reformed Doctrinal Works*. Grand Rapids, MI: Baker Books, 2006.

Benedict XVI, Pope. "Lecture at the University of Regensburg." September 12, 2006. https://www.vatican.va/content/benedict-xvi/en/speeches/2006/september/documents/hf_ben-xvi_spe_20060912_university-regensburg.html.

———. *Sacramentum Caritatis*, Post-Synodal Apostolic Exhortation. February 22, 2007. https://www.vatican.va/content/benedict-xvi/en/apost_exhortations/documents/hf_ben-xvi_exh_20070222_sacramentum-caritatis.html.

———. *Verbum Domini*. Post-Synodal Apostolic Exhortation. September 30, 2010. https://www.vatican.va/content/benedict-xvi/en/apost_exhortations/documents/hf_ben-xvi_exh_20100930_verbum-domini.html.

Berkouwer, G. C. *Conflict met Rome*. Tweede Druk. Kampen: J. H. Kok, 1949. English translation: *The Conflict with Rome*, translated by David Freeman. Grand Rapids, MI: Baker Book House, 1958.

———. "Ex Opere Operato," Part I. *Gereformeerd Theologisch Tijdschrift* 53, no. 3 (1953): 78–88.

———. "Ex Opere Operato," Part II. *Gereformeerd Theologisch Tijdschrift* 53, no. 4 (1953): 93–103.

———. *De Heilige Schrift*, Vols. I–II. Kampen: J. H. Kok, 1966–1967. English translation: *Holy Scripture*, translated and edited by Jack B. Rogers. Grand Rapids, MI: Eerdmans, 1975.

————. *De Kerk*, Vol. I, *Eenheid en Katholiciteit*. Kampen: J. H. Kok, 1970. English translation: *The Church*. Translated by James E. Davidson. Grand Rapids, MI: Eerdmans, 1976.

————. *Geloof en Openbaring in de Nieuwere Duitsche Theologie*. Utrecht: Kemink en Zoon, 1932.

————. *Geloof en Rechtvaardiging*. Kampen: J. H. Kok, 1949. English translation: *Faith and Justification*, translated by Lewis B. Smedes. Grand Rapids, MI: Eerdmans, 1954.

————. *Nabetrachting op het Concilie*. Kampen: J. H. Kok, 1968.

————. *Nieuwe Perspectieven in De Controvers: Rome-Reformatie*, Mededelingen der Koninklijke Nederlandse Akademie van Wetenschappen, Afd. Letterkunde, Nieuwe Reeks 20, no. 1. Amsterdam: N.V. Noord-Hollandsche UitgeversMaatschappij, 1957.

————. *Recent Developments in Roman Catholic Thought*. Grand Rapids, MI: Eerdmans, 1958.

————. *De Sacramenten* (Kampen: J. H. Kok, 1954). English translation: *The Sacraments*. Translated by Hugo Bekker. Grand Rapids, MI: Eerdmans, 1969).

————. *Vatikaans Concilie en Nieuwe Theologie* (Kampen: J. H. Kok, 1964). English translation: *The Second Vatican Council and the New Catholicism*. Translated by Lewis Smedes. Grand Rapids, MI: Eerdmans, 1965.

————. "Vragen Rondom de Belijdenis." *Gereformeerd Theologisch Tijdschrift* 63 (1963): 1–41.

————. *Wederkomst van Christus*, Vol. I. Kampen: J. H. Kok, 1961. English translation: *The Return of Christ*, translated by James van Oosterom. Grand Rapids, MI: Eerdmans, 1972.

————. *De Mens Het Beeld Gods*. Kampen: J.H. Kok, 1957. English translation: *Man: The Image of God*, translated by Dirk W. Jellema. Grand Rapids, MI: Eerdmans, 1962.

Boersma, Hans. *Heavenly Participation: The Weaving of a Sacramental Tapestry*. Grand Rapids, MI/Cambridge, UK: Eerdmans, 2011.

Braaten, Carl. *Mother Church: Ecclesiology and Ecumenism*. Minneapolis, MN: Fortress Press, 1998.

Brownson, James V. *Bible, Gender, Sexuality*. Grand Rapids, MI: Eerdmans, 2013.

Bullinger, E. W. *Figures of Speech Used in the Bible*. 2nd edition. Grand Rapids, MI: Baker Book House, 1968 [reprint of 1898 edition].

Calvin, John. *Institutes of the Christian Religion*. Translated by Henry Beveridge. Peabody, MA: Hendrickson Publishers, revised edition, 2008.

Catechism of the Catholic Church. Vatican City: Libreria Editrice Vaticana, 2003. https://www.vatican.va/archive/eng0015/_index.htm.

Cessario, Romanus, OP. *Christian Faith and the Theological Life*. Washington, DC: The Catholic University of America Press, 1996.

————. "Sacramental Causality: Da capo!" *Nova et Vetera* 11, no. 2 (2013): 307–16.

Code of Canon Law. Latin-English Edition. Washington, DC: Canon Law Society of America, 1983.

Congar, Yves, OP. *Diversity and Communion*. Translated by John Bowden. London: SCM Press Ltd., 1984.

————. *Jesus Christ*. Trans. Luke O'Neill. New York: Herder and Herder, 1966.

———. *The Meaning of Tradition*. Translated by A. N. Woodrow. San Francisco: Ignatius Press, 2004.

———. *Tradition and Traditions*. Translated by Michael Naseby and Thomas Rainborough. New York: Macmillan Company, 1966.

———. *True and False Reform in the Church*. Translated by Paul Philbert, OP. Collegeville, MN: Liturgical Press, 2011 [1968].

Congregation for the Doctrine of the Faith. "Doctrinal Note on Some Aspects of Evangelization." October 6, 2007. http://www.vatican.va/roman_curia/congregations/cfaith/documents/rc_con_cfaith_doc_20071203_nota-evangelizzazione_en.html.

———. *Donum Veritatis*, Instruction on the Ecclesial Vocation of the Theologian. May 14, 1990. https://www.vatican.va/roman_curia/congregations/cfaith/documents/rc_con_cfaith_doc_19900524_theologian-vocation_en.html.

———. *Mysterium Ecclesiae*. June 24, 1973. http://www.vatican.va/roman_curia/congregations/cfaith/documents/rc_con_cfaith_doc_19730705_mysterium-ecclesiae_en.html.

Craig, William Lane. "God Is Not Dead Yet: How Current Philosophers Argue for His Existence." *Christianity Today* (website). July 3, 2008. https://www.christianitytoday.com/ct/2008/july/13.22.html.

Crump, David M. Review of *Bible, Gender, Sexuality*, by James V. Brownson (Grand Rapids, MI: Eerdmans, 2013). *Calvin Theological Journal* 48, no. 2 (2013): 290–94.

Cullmann, Oscar. "Comments on the Decree on Ecumenism." *The Ecumenical Review* 17 (April 1965): 93–96.

De Chirico, Leonardo. "The Blurring of Time Distinctions in Roman Catholicism." *Themelios* 29, no. 2 (2004): 40–46.

———. "A Biography of Thomas Aquinas' *Summa Theologiae*: Is It Also a Radiography of Roman Catholicism?" *Vatican Files* (website). June 1, 2021. https://vaticanfiles.org/it/2021/06/189/.

———. *A Christian's Pocket Guide to the Papacy: Its Origin and Role in the 21st Century*. Fearn, Ross-shire, Scotland: Christian Focus Publications, 2015.

———. "Cooperating with the Catholic Church? A Lesson from Francis A. Schaeffer (1912–1984)." *Vatican Files* (website). April 1, 2016. https://vaticanfiles.org/en/2016/04/122-cooperating-with-the-roman-catholic-church-a-lesson-from-francis-schaeffer-1912-1984/.

———. *Evangelical Theological Perspectives on Post-Vatican II Roman Catholicism*. Religions and Discourse 19. Bern: Peter Lang, 2003.

———. "*Fides et Ratio* (1998): Three Theses on the Roman Catholic Synthesis between Faith and Reason." *Vatican Files* (website), March 2, 2021. https://vaticanfiles.org/ro/2021/03/vf185/.

———. "Roman Catholicism as 'Temptation' for Evangelical Theology." *Vatican Files* (website). January 1, 2022. https://vaticanfiles.org/es/2022/01/196/.

———. *Same Words, Different Worlds: Do Roman Catholics and Evangelicals Believe the Same Gospel?* London: Inter-Varsity, 2021.

De Ridder, Jeroen and Rene Van Woudenberg. "Referring to, Believing in, and Worshipping the Same God." *Faith and Philosophy* 31, no. 1 (January 2014): 46–67.

Dennison, James T., Jr., ed. *Reformed Confessions of the 16th and 17th Centuries in English Translation*, Vol. 4, *1600–1693*. Grand Rapids, MI: Reformation Heritage Books, 2014.

Denzinger, Heinrich, ed. A *Compendium of Creeds, Definitions on Matters of Faith and Morals*. 43rd edition. Edited by Peter Hünermann. Translated by Robert Fastiggi and Anne Englund Nash. San Francisco: Ignatius Press, 2012).

Devitt, Michael. *Realism and Truth*. 2nd edition. Princeton, NJ: Princeton University Press, 1991 [1984].

Doorly, Moyra and Aidan Nichols, OP. *The Council in Question: A Dialogue with Catholic Traditionalism*. Herefordshire: Gracewing, 2011.

Dooyeweerd, Herman. *A Christian Theory of Social Institutions*. Translated by Magnus Verbrugge. Edited with an Introduction by John Witte, Jr. La Jolla, CA: The Herman Dooyeweerd Foundation, 1986.

———. *Reformation and Scholasticism in Philosophy*, Vol. III, *Philosophy of Nature and Philosophical Anthropology*. Translated by Magnus Verbrugge and D. F. M. Strauss. Edited by D. F. M. Strauss. Ancaster, ON: Paideia Press, 2011.

———. "Sociology of Law and Its Philosophical Foundations." In *Essays in Legal, Social, and Political Philosophy*, 73–89. Lewiston, NY: Edwin Mellen, 1996.

———. *In the Twilight of Western Thought*. Nutley, NJ: Craig Press, 1968.

———. *De Wijsbegeerte der Wetsidee*, Vols. I–III (Amsterdam: H. J. Paris, 1935–1936). Translated and revised in English by D. H. Freeman, W. S. Young, and H. De Jongste as *A New Critique of Theoretical Thought*, Vols. I–IV. Philadelphia: Presbyterian and Reformed Publishing Company, 1953–1969.

———. "Van Peursen's critische vragen bij 'A New Critique of Theoretical Thought'," in *Philosophia Reformata* 25 (1960): 97-150.

Dulles, Avery, SJ. *The Catholicity of the Church*. Oxford: Clarendon Press, 1985.

———. *Magisterium: Teacher and Guardian of the Faith*. Naples, FL: Sapientia Press, 2007.

———. "Moderate Infallibilism." In *Teaching Authority & Infallibility in the Church*, edited by Paul C. Empie, T. Austin Murphy, Joseph A. Gros, and Jeffrey Burgess, 81–100. Minneapolis: Augsburg Publishing House, 1978.

———. "The Theology of Worship: Saint Thomas." In *Rediscovering Aquinas and the Sacraments*, edited by Matthew Levering et al, 1–13. Chicago: Hillenbrand Books, 2009.

———. "Vatican II on the Interpretation of Scripture." *Letter & Spirit* 2 (2006): 17–26.

Dünzl, Franz. *A Brief History of the Doctrine of the Trinity in the Early Church*. Translated by John Bowden. London/New York: T&T Clark, 2007.

Echeverria, Eduardo. "The Accidental Protestant." *First Things* (Feb.2014): 41–45.

———. *Berkouwer and Catholicism: Disputed Questions*. Studies in Reformed Theology 24. Boston/Leiden: Brill, 2013.

———. "A Catholic Assessment of Gregg Allison's Critique of the 'Hermeneutics of Catholicism'." *Called to Communion* (website). August 17, 2015. https://www.calledtocommunion.com/2015/08/a-catholic-assessment-of-gregg-allisons-critique-of-the-hermeneutics-of-catholicism/.

———. "A Catholic Perspective on Marriage and the Gift of Children—With Special Attention to Herman Dooyeweerd's Social Ontology of Marriage."

Pro Rege 46, no. 4 (June 2018): 1–14.

———. *Dialogue of Love: Confessions of an Evangelical Catholic Ecumenist*. Eugene, OR: Wipf & Stock, 2010.

———. *Divine Election: A Catholic Orientation in Dogmatic and Ecumenical Perspective*. Eugene, OR: Pickwick Publications, 2016.

———. "Do You Have to Be a Calvinist in Order to Be a Kuyperian?" *Pro Rege* 49, no. 3 (March 2021): 1–18.

———. "Hierarchy of Truths Revisited." *Acta Theologica* 35, no. 2 (2015): 11–35.

———. *"In the Beginning…": A Theology of the Body*. Eugene, OR: Pickwick Publications, 2011.

———. "The New Man: Nature, Sin, and Grace in St. Paul." In *St. Paul, the Natural Law, and Contemporary Legal Theory*, edited by Jane Adolphe Robert Fastiggi, and Michael Vacca, 89–111. Lanham, MD: Lexington Books, 2012.

———. "The One Church, the Many Churches: A Catholic Approach to Ecclesial Unity and Diversity—with Special Attention to Abraham Kuyper's Ecclesiastical Epistemology." *Journal of Biblical and Theological Studies* 5, no. 2 (2020): 239–64.

———. "One-Flesh Sacramental Union." *The Catholic Thing* (website). June 22, 2017. https://www.thecatholicthing.org/2017/06/22/a-one-flesh-sacramental-union/.

———. "Original Sin, Preterition, and Its Implications for Evangelization." *Perichoresis* 18, no. 6 (2020): 73–101.

———. *Pope Francis: The Legacy of Vatican II*. Revised and expanded 2nd edition. Hobe Sound, FL: Lectio Publishing, 2019.

———. "Realism, Truth, and Justification: The Contribution of Michael Polanyi." *Josephinum Journal of Theology* 26, nos. 1 & 2 (2019): 199–227.

———. *Revelation, History, and Truth: A Hermeneutics of Dogma*. New York: Peter Lang, 2017.

———. "Review Essay: Bavinck on the Family and Integral Human Development." *Journal of Markets and Morality* 16, no. 1 (Spring 2013): 219–37.

———. "The Salvation of Non-Christians? Reflections on Vatican II's *Gaudium et Spes* 22, *Lumen Gentium* 16, Gerald O'Collins, SJ, and St. John Paul II." *Angelicum* 94 (2017): 93–142.

———. "The Splendor of Truth in *Fides et Ratio*." *Quaestiones Disputatae* 9, no. 1 (Fall 2018): 49–78.

———. "Vincent of Lérins and the Development of Christian Doctrine." In *"Faith Once for All Delivered": Tradition and Doctrinal Authority in the Catholic Church*. San Francisco: Ignatius Press, forthcoming in 2022.

Farrow, Douglas. *Ascension Theology*. London/New York: T&T Clark, 2011.

Francis, Pope. *Evangelii Gaudium*, Apostolic Exhortation. November 24, 2013. https://www.vatican.va/content/francesco/en/apost_exhortations/documents/papa-francesco_esortazione-ap_20131124_evangelii-gaudium.html.

———. *Lumen Fidei*, Encyclical Letter. June 29, 2013. https://www.vatican.va/content/francesco/en/encyclicals/documents/papa-francesco_20130629_enciclica-lumen-fidei.html.

Gagliardi, Mauro. *Truth Is a Synthesis: Catholic Dogmatic Theology*. Introduction by Cardinal Gerhard L. Müller. Steubenville, OH: Emmaus Academic, 2020.

Gagnon, Robert A. J. *The Bible and Homosexual Practice: Texts and Hermeneutics.* Nashville, TN: Abingdon Press, 2001.

———. "Marriage in Scripture." Paper presented at a Meeting of Evangelical and Catholics Together, June 5, 2013.

Geiselmann, J. R. *Die Heilige Schrift und die tradition: Zu den neuren Kontroversen über das Verhältnis der Heligen Schrift zu den nichtgeschriebenen Traditionen.* Quaestiones Disputatae 18. Freiburg: Herder, 1962.

———. *The Meaning of Tradition.* Quaestiones Disputatae 15. Translated by W. J. O'Hara. London/Freiburg: Burns & Oates/Herder, 1966.

———. "Scripture, Tradition, and the Church: An Ecumenical Problem." In *Christianity Divided: Protestant and Roman Catholic Theological Issues,* edited by Daniel J. Callahan, Heiko Oberman, and Daniel J. O'Hanlon, 39–72. New York: Sheed & Ward, 1961.

Gilson, Etienne. *Christianity and Philosophy.* Translated by Ralph MacDonald, CSB. New York: Sheed & Ward, 1939.

———. *The Spirit of Medieval Philosophy.* Gifford Lectures 1931–1932. Translated by A. H. C. Downes. New York: Charles Scribner's Sons, 1940.

Grisez, Germain. "An Alternative Theology of Jesus's Substantial Presence in the Eucharist." *Irish Theological Quarterly* 65 (2000): 111–31.

———. *The Way of the Lord Jesus,* Vol. 2, *Living a Christian Life.* Quincy, IL: Franciscan Press, 1993.

Guarino, Thomas. *Foundations of Systematic Theology.* New York: T&T Clark, 2005.

———. "Nature and Grace: Seeking the Delicate Balance." *Josephinum Journal of Theology* 18, no. 1 (2011): 1–13.

———. *Revelation and Truth: Unity and Plurality in Contemporary Theology.* Scranton, PA: University of Scranton Press, 1993.

Hauke, Manfred. *Introduction to Mariology.* Translated by Richard Chonak. Washington, DC: Catholic University of American Press, 2021.

Helm, Paul. *Faith, Form, and Fashion: Classical Reformed Theology and Its Postmodern Critics.* Eugene, OR: Cascade Books, 2014.

Henn, William, OFM Cap. "The Hierarchy of Truths Twenty Years Later." *Theological Studies* 48 (1987): 439–71.

———. "The Hierarchy of Truths." In *Dictionary of Fundamental Theology,* edited by Rene Latourelle and Rino Fisichella, 425–427. New York: Crossroad, 1994.

Horton, Michael. "Meeting a Stranger: A Covenantal Epistemology." *Westminster Theological Journal* 66 (2004): 337–55.

Hütter, Reinhard. "Why Does the Pope Matter to Protestants?" *Nova et Vetera* 6, no. 3 (2008): 675–80.

International Theological Commission. "On the Interpretation of Dogmas." *Origins* 20 (May 17, 1990): 1–14.

Jackman, Henry. "Meaning Holism." *The Stanford Encyclopedia of Philosophy* (Winter 2020 Edition). Edited by Edward N. Zalta. https://plato.stanford.edu/archives/win2020/entries/meaning-holism/.

Jeffrey, David Lyle. "Houses of the Interpreters, Spiritual Exegesis, and the Retrieval of Authority." *Books & Culture* 8, no. 3 (2002).

John Paul II, Pope. *Centesimus Annus,* Encyclical Letter. May 1, 1991. https://www.vatican.va/content/john-paul-ii/en/encyclicals/documents/hf_jp-ii_

enc_01051991_centesimus-annus.html.

———. *Ecclesia de Eucharistia*, Encyclical Letter. April 17, 2003. https://www.vatican.va/holy_father/special_features/encyclicals/documents/hf_jp-ii_enc_20030417_ecclesia_eucharistia_en.html.

———. *Familiaris Consortio*, Apostolic Exhortation. November 22, 1981. https://www.vatican.va/content/john-paul-ii/en/apost_exhortations/documents/hf_jp-ii_exh_19811122_familiaris-consortio.html.

———. *Fides et Ratio*, Encyclical Letter. September 14, 1998. https://www.vatican.va/content/john-paul-ii/en/encyclicals/documents/hf_jp-ii_enc_14091998_fides-et-ratio.html.

———. *Man and Woman He Created Them: A Theology of the Body*. Translation, Introduction, and Index by Michael Waldstein. Boston: Pauline Books & Media, 2006.

———. *Redemptoris Missio*, Encyclical Letter. December 7, 1990. https://www.vatican.va/content/john-paul-ii/en/encyclicals/documents/hf_jp-ii_enc_07121990_redemptoris-missio.html.

———. *Veritatis Splendor*, Encyclical Letter. August 6, 1993. https://www.vatican.va/content/john-paul-ii/en/encyclicals/documents/hf_jp-ii_enc_06081993_veritatis-splendor.html.

———. *Ut Unum Sint*, Encyclical Letter. May 25, 1995. https://www.vatican.va/content/john-paul-ii/en/encyclicals/documents/hf_jp-ii_enc_25051995_ut-unum-sint.html.

John XXIII, Pope. *Gaudet Mater Ecclesia*, Allocution on the Occasion of the Solemn Inauguration of the Second Ecumenical Council. October 11, 1962. https://www.vatican.va/content/john-xxiii/la/speeches/1962/documents/hf_j-xxiii_spe_19621011_opening-council.html.

Joint Working Group of the Catholic Church and the World Council of Churches, "The Challenge of Proselytism and the Calling to Common Witness," *The Ecumenical Review* 48 (1996): 212–21.

Journet, Charles. *The Primacy of Peter from the Protestant and Catholic Point of View*. Translated by John Chapin. Westminster, MD: The Newman Press, 1954.

———. *Theology of the Church*. Translated by Victor Szczurek, O. Praem. San Francisco: Ignatius Press, 2004 [1958].

Kasper, Walter. *The Gospel of the Family*. Translated by William Madges. New York/Mahwah, NJ: Paulist Press, 2014.

———. *Harvesting the Fruits: Basic Aspects of Christian Faith in Ecumenical Dialogue*. London: Bloomsbury, 2009.

———. *An Introduction to Christian Faith*. New York: Paulist Press, 1980.

———. *Katholische Kirche: Wesen, Wirklichkeit, Sendung* (Freiburg: Herder, 2011). English translation: *The Catholic Church: Nature, Reality and Mission*. Translated by Thomas Hoebel. Edited by R. David Nelson. London: Bloomsbury T&T Clark, 2015.

———. *Zur Theologie der Christlichen Ehe*. Mainz: Matthias-Grünewald-Verlag, 1977. English translation: *Theology of Christian Marriage*, translated by David Smith. New York: Crossroad, 1984.

Kelly, Anthony J., CSsR. "The Ascension and the Eucharist." *Irish Theological Quarterly* 78, no. 4 (2013): 338–50.

Kereszty, Roch. "On the Eucharistic Presence: Response to Germain Grisez." *Irish Theological Quarterly* 65 (2000): 347–52.

Küng, Hans. *Infallible? An Inquiry*. New York: Doubleday, 1971.

Kuyper, Abraham. *Encyclopaedie der Heilige Godgeleerdheid*, Vol. II. Amsterdam: J.A. Wormser, 1894. English translation: *Encyclopedia of Sacred Theology: Its Principles*. Translated by J. Hendrik de Vries, with an Introduction by B. B. Warfield. New York: Charles Scribner's Sons, 1898.

———. *De Gemeene Gratie*, Vol. III. Kampen: J. H. Kok, 1905.

———. *Lectures on Calvinism*. 1898 Princeton Stone Lectures. Grand Rapids, MI: Eerdmans, 1931.

Ladd, George Eldon. *The Presence of the Future: The Eschatology of Biblical Realism*. Revised and updated version of *Jesus and the Kingdom*. Grand Rapids, MI: Eerdmans, 1974 [1964].

Leeming, Bernard, SJ. *Principles of Sacramental Theology*. 2nd edition. London: Longmans, 1956.

Leithart, Peter J. "What's Wrong with Transubstantiation? An Evaluation of Theological Models." *Westminster Theological Journal* 53 (1991): 295–324.

Levering, Matthew. *Biblical Natural Law: A Theocentric and Teleological Approach*. Oxford: Oxford University Press, 2008.

———. *Mary's Bodily Assumption*. Notre Dame, IN: University of Notre Dame Press, 2014.

Livingston, James C., Sarah Coakley, James H. Evans, and Francis Schüssler Fiorenza. *Modern Christian Thought: The Twentieth Century*. Minneapolis: Fortress Press, 2006.

Lonergan, Bernard J. F., SJ. "The Dehellenization of Dogma." In Bernard J. F. Lonergan, *A Second Collection*, edited by William F. J. Ryan, SJ et al., 11–32. Philadelphia: Westminster Press, 1974.

Lubac, Henri de. "Apologetics and Theology." In *Theological Fragments*, translated by Rebecca Howell Balinski, 91–104. San Francisco: Ignatius Press, 1989.

———. *A Brief Catechesis on Nature & Grace*. Translated by Richard Arnandez. San Francisco: Ignatius Press, 1984.

Luther, Martin. *Commentary on Genesis*. In *Luther's Works*, Vol. 1, edited by James Atkinson and Jaroslav Pelikan. Philadelphia: Fortress Press, 1958.

———. "The Estate of Marriage." In *Luther's Works*, Vol. 45, edited by James Atkinson, Walther Immanuel Brandt, Jaroslav Pelikan, and Helmut T. Lehmann. Philadelphia, PA: Muhlenberg Press, 1962. http://pages.uoregon.edu/dluebke/Reformations441/LutherMarriage.htm.

———. *The Large Catechism*. Translated by Robert H. Fischer. Philadelphia: Fortress Press, 1959.

———. "A Sermon on the Estate of Marriage." In *Luther's Works*, Vol. 44, edited by James Atkinson and Helmut T. Lehmann. Philadelphia: Fortress Press, 1966.

Mansini, Guy F. "Dogma." In *Dictionary of Fundamental Theology*, edited by Rene Latourelle and Rino Fisichella, 239–47. New York: Crossroad, 2000.

Maritain, Jacques. *Clairvoyance de Rome*. Paris, 1929.

———. *On the Philosophy of History*. Edited by Joseph W. Evans. New York: Charles Scribner's Sons, 1957.

Martin, Francis. "Some Directions in Catholic Biblical Theology." In *Out of Egypt: Biblical Theology and Biblical Interpretation*, Scripture and Hermeneutics Series 5, edited by Craig Bartholomew, Mary Healy, Karl Möller, and Robin Parry, 65–87. Grand Rapids, MI: Zondervan, 2004.

Mascall, Eric. *The Openness of Being: Natural Theology Today*. Gifford Lectures, 1970–1971. London: Darton, Longman & Todd, 1971.

McShane, Philip, SJ. "On the Causality of the Sacraments." *Theological Studies* 24 (1963): 423–36.

Millare, Roland. "The Nominalist Justification for Luther's Sacramental Theology." *Antiphon* 17, no. 2 (2013): 168–90, at 170.

Möhler, Adam Johann. *Symbolism*. Translated by James Burton Robertson. New York: Crossroad, 1997 [1832].

Morerod, Charles, OP. *The Church and the Human Quest for Truth*. Ave Maria, FL: Sapientia Press, 2008.

Mouw, Richard J. *All That God Cares About: Common Grace and Divine Delight*. Grand Rapids, MI: Brazos Press, 2020).

———. *He Shines in All That's Fair: Culture and Common Grace*. The 2000 Stob Lectures. Grand Rapids, MI: Eerdmans, 2001.

Müller, Gerhard. *The Pope: His Mission and His Task*. Translated by Brian McNeil. Washington, DC: Catholic University of America, 2021.

———. *Priesthood and Diaconate*. Translated by Michael J. Miller. San Francisco: Ignatius Press, 2002.

Nichols, Aidan, OP. *Catholic Thought Since the Enlightenment*. Leominster: Gracewing: 1998.

———. *Epiphany: A Theological Introduction to Catholicism*. Collegeville, MN: Liturgical Press, 1996.

———. *Figuring Out the Church*. San Francisco: Ignatius Press, 2013.

———. *The Holy Eucharist: From the New Testament to Pope John Paul II*. Eugene, OR: Wipf & Stock, 2011 [1991].

———. *The Service of Glory: On Worship, Ethics, Spirituality*. Edinburgh: T&T Clark, 1997.

———. *The Shape of Catholic Theology*. Collegeville, MN: Liturgical Press, 1991.

———. *The Splendour of Doctrine: On Christian Believing*. Edinburgh: T&T Clark, 1995.

Norwood, Donald W. *Reforming Rome: Karl Barth and Vatican II*. Grand Rapids, MI: Eerdmans, 2015.

O'Neill, Colman E., OP. *Sacramental Realism*. Princeton: Scepter, 1998 [1983].

Oberman, Heiko. Review of G. C. Berkouwer, Vatikaans Concilie en Nieuwe Theologie. *Evangelische Theologie* 28 [1968]: 388.

Ouellet, Marc. *Mystery and Sacrament of Love: A Theology of Marriage and the Family for the New Evangelization*. Translated by Michelle K. Borras and Adrian J. Walker. Grand Rapids, MI: Eerdmans, 2015.

Pannenberg, Wolfhart. "A Protestant View of the Doctrine of the Lord's Supper," in *The Church*, trans. Keith Crim. Philadelphia: The Westminster Press, 1983 [1977].

———. *Systematic Theology*, Vol. 3, trans. G.W. Bromily. Grand Rapids, MI: Eerdmans, 2009.

Paul VI, Pope. *Mysterium Fidei*, Encyclical Letter. September 3, 1965. https://www.vatican.va/content/paul-vi/en/encyclicals/documents/hf_p-vi_enc_03091965_mysterium.html.

Pius XI, Pope. *Casti Connubii*, Encyclical Letter. December 31, 1930. https://www.vatican.va/content/pius-xi/en/encyclicals/documents/hf_p-xi_enc_19301231_casti-connubii.html.

———. *Mortalium Animos*, Encyclical Letter. January 6, 1928. https://www.vatican.va/content/pius-xi/en/encyclicals/documents/hf_p-xi_enc_19280106_mortalium-animos.html.

Pius XII, Pope. *Humani Generis*, Encyclical Letter. August 12, 1950. https://www.vatican.va/content/pius-xii/en/encyclicals/documents/hf_p-xii_enc_12081950_humani-generis.html.

Pontifical Council for Justice and Peace. *Compendium of the Social Doctrine of the Church*. Washington, DC: United States Conference of Catholic Bishops, 2007.

Pottmeyer, Hermann. "Tradition." In *Dictionary of Fundamental Theology*, edited by Rene Latourelle and Rino Fisichella, 1119–1126. New York: Crossroad, 2000.

Pruss, Alexander. *One Body: An Essay in Christian Sexual Ethics*. Notre Dame, IN: University of Notre Dame Press, 2013.

Puchinger, George. *Gesprekken over Rome-Reformatie*. Delft: Meinema, 1965.

Rahner, Karl. "A Century of Infallibility." *Theology Digest* 18, no. 3 (Autumn 1970): 216–21.

———. *The Church and the Sacraments*. Translated by W. J. O'Hara. New York: Herder and Herder, 1963.

———. *Foundations of Christian Faith: An Introduction to the Idea of Christianity*. Translated by William V. Dych. London: Darton Longman & Todd, 1978.

———. "A Hierarchy of Truths." *Theological Investigations*, Vol. 21. Translated by Hugh M. Riley. New York: Crossroad, 1988.

Ratzinger, Joseph. "Commentary on Dogmatic Constitution on Divine Revelation." In *Commentary on the Documents of Vatican II*, Vol. 3, 167–198, 262–272. New York: Herder and Herder, 1969.

———. "*Deus Locutus Est Nobis in Filio*: Some Reflections on Subjectivity, Christology, and the Church." In *Proclaiming the Truth of Jesus Christ: Papers from the Vallombrosa Meeting*, 13–29. Washington, DC: United States Catholic Conference, 1997.

———. "Gratia Praesupponit Naturam, Grace Presupposes Nature." In *Dogma and Preaching*, unabridged edition. Translated by Michael J. Miller and Matthew J. O'Connell. Edited by Michael J. Miller. San Francisco: Ignatius Press, 2011 [1973].

———. "Grenzen kirchlicher Vollmacht: Das neue Dokument von Papst Johannes Paul II: zur Frage der Frauenordination." *Internationale katholische Zeitschrift* 23 (1994): 337–45.

———. "Primacy, Episcopacy, and Successio Apostolica." in *God's Word: Scripture—Tradition—Office*, edited by Peter Hünnermann and Thomas Söding, translated by Henry Taylor, 13–39. San Francisco: Ignatius Press, 2008.

———. "Revelation and Tradition." in *Revelation and Tradition*, translated by W. J. O'Hara, 26–66. New York: Herder and Herder, 1966.

———. "Six Texts by Prof. Joseph Ratzinger as Peritus Before and During Vatican Council II." Translated and annotated by Jared Wicks. *Gregorianum* 89, no. 2 (2008): 233–311.

———. *The Spirit of the Liturgy*. Translated by John Saward. San Francisco: Ignatius Press, 2000.

Ridderbos, Herman. *The Coming of the Kingdom*. Translated by H. de Jongste. Edited by Raymond O. Zorn. Philadelphia, PA: Presbyterian and Reformed Publishing Company, 1962 [1950].

Rodger, P. C. and Lukas Vischer, eds. "Scripture, Tradition and Traditions." In *The Fourth World Conference on Faith and Order, Montreal 1963*. New York: Association Press, 1964.

Rusch, William G. and Jeffrey Gros, eds. *Deepening Communion: International Documents with Roman Catholic Participation*. Washington, DC: United States Catholic Conference, 1998.

Schaeffer, Francis A. *The Church at the End of the Twentieth Century*. Downers Grove, IL: Inter-Varsity, 1970.

Scheeben, Matthias Joseph. *The Mysteries of Christianity*. Translated by Cyril Vollert, SJ. London/St. Louis: B. Herder Book Co., 1946 [1865].

Schillebeeckx, Edward, OP. *Christus Sacrament van de Godsontmoeting*. Achtste druk. Bilthoven: H. Nelissen, 1966 [1959]. English translation: *Christ the Sacrament of the Encounter with God*. Translated by Paul Barrett, OP, et al. Oxford/Toronto: Rowman & Littlefield Publishers, Inc., 1963.

———. *Christus Tegenwoordigheid in de Eucharistie*. Bilthoven: H. Nelissen, 1967. English translation: *The Eucharist*, translated by N. D. Smith. London/Sydney: Sheed and Ward, 1968.

———. "Ecclesia Semper Purificanda." In *Ex Auditu Verbi: Theologische Opstellen Aangeboden aan Prof. Dr. G.C. Berkouwer*, 216–32. Kampen: J. H. Kok, 1965.

———. *Het Huwelijk, Aardse Werkelijkheid en Heilsmysterie*, Eerste Deel. Bilthoven: H. Nelissen, 1963. English translation: *Marriage, Human Reality and Saving Mystery*, translated by N. D. Smith. New York: Sheed and Ward, 1965.

———. "De Openbaring en haar 'Overlevering'." In *Schrift en Traditie*, 13–20. Hilversum/Antwerpen: Uitgeverij Paul Brand N.V., 1965. English translation: "Revelation, Scripture, Tradition, and Teaching Authority," in *Revelation and Theology*, Vol. I, 3–24. Trans. N.D. Smith. New York: Sheed & Ward, 1967.

———. "Transubstantiation, Transfinalization, Transignification." *Worship* 40, no. 6 (June–July 1966): 324–38.

Schnackenburg, Rudolph. *Ephesians: A Commentary*. Translated by Helen Heron. Edinburgh: T&T Clark, 1991.

Selderhuis, Herman J., ed. *The Calvin Handbook*. Translated by H. J. Baron, et al. (Grand Rapids, MI/Cambridge, UK: Eerdmans, 2009.

Semmelroth, Otto, SJ. *The Church and Christian Belief*. Translated by Thomas R. Milligan. Glen Rock, NJ: Deus Books, Paulist Press, 1966.

———. *The Preaching Word: On the Theology of Proclamation*. Translated by John Jay Hughes. New York: Herder and Herder, 1965.

Sokolowski, Robert. "The Eucharist and Transubstantiation." In *Christian Faith & Human Understanding*, 95–112. Washington, DC: Catholic University of America Press, 2006.

———. "Phenomenology and the Eucharist." In *Christian Faith & Human Understanding*. Washington, DC: Catholic University of America Press, 2006.

Sosa, Ernest. "Serious Philosophy and Freedom of Spirit." *The Journal of Philosophy* 84, no. 12 (December 1987): 707–26.

Sproul, R. C. *Are We Together? A Protestant Analyzes Roman Catholicism*. Orlando, FL: Reformation Trust Publishing, 2012.

Trigg, Roger. *Reason and Commitment*. Cambridge: Cambridge University Press, 1973.

Vandervelde, George. "*BEM [Baptism, Eucharist, and Ministry]* and the 'Hierarchy of Truths': A Vatican Contribution to the Reception Process." *Journal of Ecumenical Studies* 25, no. 1 (Winter 1988): 74–84.

Vanhoozer, Kevin. *Biblical Authority after Babel*. Grand Rapids, MI: Brazos Press, 2016

———. "A Mere Protestant Response." In *Was the Reformation a Mistake? Why Catholic Doctrine is Not Unbiblical*, edited by Matthew Levering, 191–231. Grand Rapids, MI: Zondervan, 2017.

Veenhof, Jan. "Nature and Grace in Bavinck." *Pro Rege* 34, no. 4 (June 2006): 10–31.

Volk, H. "Ehe." In *Lexikon für Theologie und Kirche*, Vol. III. Freiburg: Herder, 1959.

Vos, Geerhardus. "The Idea of Biblical Theology as a Science and as a Theological Discipline." Inaugural Address as Professor of Biblical Theology, Princeton Theological Seminary, delivered at the First Presbyterian Church, Princeton on May 8, 1894. Reprinted in *Redemptive History and Biblical Interpretation: The Shorter Writings of Geerhardus Vos*, edited by Richard B. Gaffin Jr., 3–24. Phillipsburg, NJ: Presbyterian and Reformed, 1980.

Wainwright, Geoffrey. *Is the Reformation Over?* Milwaukee, WI: Marquette University Press, 2000.

Warfield, Benjamin B. *The Plan of Salvation*. Philadelphia: Presbyterian Board of Publications, 1915.

Wojtyla, Karol. *Love and Responsibility*. Translation, endnotes, and foreword by Grzegorz Ignatik. Boston: Pauline Books & Media, 2013 [1960].

Wolters, Albert. "Dutch Neo-Calvinism: Worldview, Philosophy and Rationality." In *Rationality in the Calvinian Tradition*, edited by Hendrik Hart, Johan van der Hoeven, and Nicholas Wolterstorff, 113–31. Toronto: University Press of America, 1983.

———. "What Is to Be Done? Toward a Neo-Calvinist Agenda." *Comment* 23, no. 2 (December 2005): 36–43.

INDEX

CPSIA information can be obtained
at www.ICGtesting.com
Printed in the USA
JSHW052328260622
27361JS00001B/1

9 781943 901241